GOOD HOUSEKEEPING
BABY
BOOK

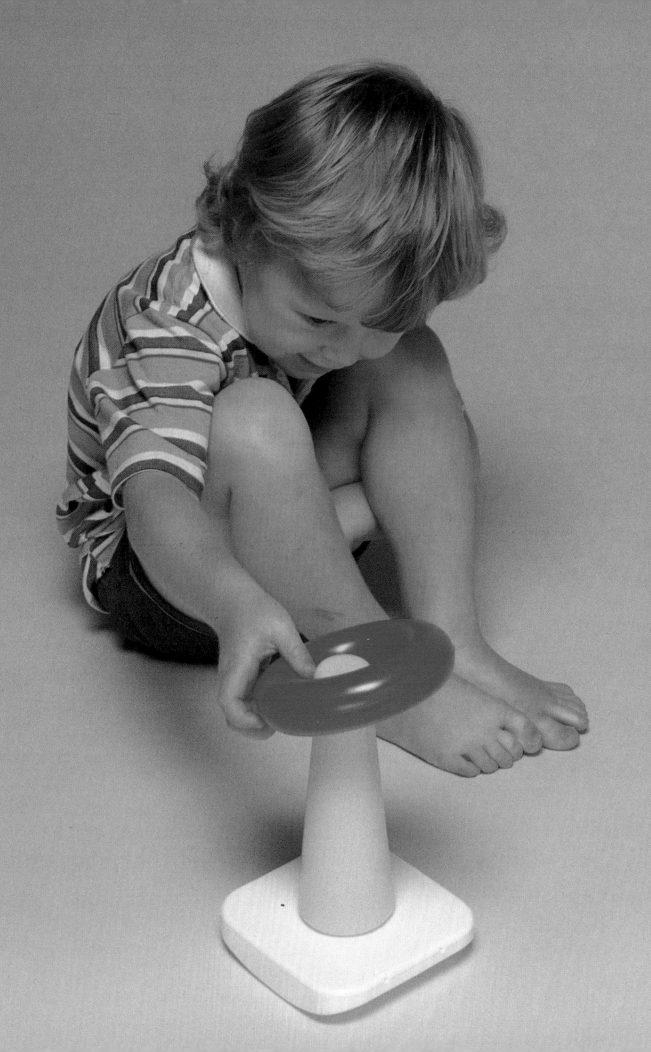

GOOD HOUSEKEEPING
BABY
BOOK

A comprehensive guide
to caring for your
baby and toddler

Consultant editor
Jean Shapiro

Compiled and
edited by
MARGARET CARTER

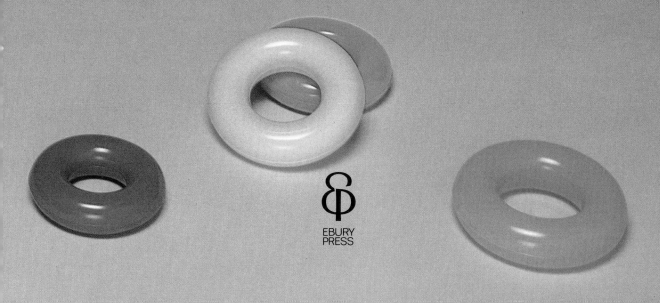

EBURY
PRESS

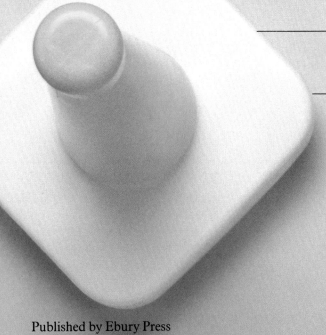

Published by Ebury Press
Division of The National Magazine Company Ltd
Colquhoun House
27–37 Broadwick Street
London W1V 1FR

First impression 1985
Reprinted 1987

ISBN 0 85223 382 5

AN EDDISON · SADD EDITION

Edited, designed and produced by
Eddison/Sadd Editions Limited
2 Kendall Place, London W1H 3AH

Phototypeset by Bookworm Typesetting, Manchester,
England
Origination by Columbia Offset, Singapore
Printed and bound in Yugoslavia

CONTENTS

The editorial team responsible for the
GOOD HOUSEKEEPING BABY BOOK
comprised the following people:

EDITOR-IN-CHIEF
Margaret Carter
former Editor of MOTHER magazine and
currently a writer specializing in baby and
child care topics

CONSULTANT EDITOR
Jean Shapiro
former Editor of Family Centre section,
GOOD HOUSEKEEPING magazine and
currently consultant to Family Matters
section; former editor and author of previous
editions of GOOD HOUSEKEEPING
BABY BOOK

CONSULTANT PAEDIATRICIAN
Donald Garrow BM, FRCP
former Consultant Paediatrician, High
Wycombe and Amersham General Hospitals

FOREWORD

The first Good Housekeeping Baby Book appeared in 1944. Since then there have been many revised, updated and rewritten editions and three generations have relied on it for its common sense and its realistic, practical approach to the joys and problems of parenthood. For this edition, entirely new text and illustrations have been commissioned to provide the most up-to-date and genuinely useful book for new parents available today.

Benefiting from their relationship with readers, Good Housekeeping Family Centre writers and medical advisers have always been closely involved in producing the Baby Book. It is largely their expertise and knowledge of what readers need and want that has made it such a reliable source of help.

Readers will still find everything they need to know about day-to-day baby care here, but today there is a great deal more support and advice offered by health professionals and self-help groups than was available in the past. So we've been able to give extra space to all the fascinating facts about baby and toddler development that recent research has revealed. We have shown too how parents can provide an environment that will encourage the flowering of every child's full potential.

Illustrations and diagrams reinforce the message of the text, and a quick reference A-Z section identifies health problems and gives advice on their treatment.

We hope that this book, like its predecessors, will help to build the confidence of today's parents, so that they too can provide a background of loving care in which the new generation will thrive.

Jean Shapiro
Consultant,
Good Housekeeping Family Centre 1984

BECOMING A PARENT

Having a baby is an everyday occurrence – when it happens to other people. When it happens to you it is unique. Your friends have had babies, your relations have had babies – even your parents, you find to your amazement, have had babies and suddenly admit you to an unsuspected world of knowledge and understanding.

Advice abounds, and usually it falls into one of two camps – the 'paid' and the 'unpaid'. 'Paid' advice is from the experts, the incredible support system which nowadays surrounds the parents-to-be, whether from hospitals, clinics, medical services or the multitude of books, magazines, television and radio programmes dealing with all aspects of child bearing and child rearing.

The 'unpaid' advice is from relatives and friends: some of it falls into the 'I remember when…' category or even the 'Wait until you…' Gloom lies ahead, they seem to imply with a wry sort of relish. Turn a deaf ear in their direction. It's true that a reedy wail at two o'clock on a wintry morning may make your stomach turn over, but how can you express the compensatory delight of a baby's toothless smile of greeting?

But there is a second type of 'unpaid' advice which is often unspoken. It comes from those who seem able to pass on a deep sense of security and love. They may not knit, sew, nor embroider but they are able to exude that comfort and tranquillity without which no sturdy growth is possible. They are lifegivers and if you're lucky enough to have one in your circle, hang on, because they're the salt of the earth. The philosopher, Eric Fromm, says children who have been reared by such people are indefinably different but always recognizable.

Meanwhile, back to reality. Apprehensive, excited, doubtful: setting off on a strange voyage in what at times must seem a pretty frail ship, parenthood is the skill at which you are expected to be expert without having had a trial run. Like water ski-ing, you practise in public.

Becoming a parent is a new beginning. Whether it's your first, second or third child your family pattern is inevitably altered. For most people today parenthood is the deliberate choice and yet, having made the choice, many of the old uncertainties remain. Will you be able to cope? Will you be 'good' parents – whatever that means? Probably for the first time in your life you'll have the responsibility of another life whose welfare must take precedence over your own.

Many of these doubts may be the result of the physical changes taking place in the mother-to-be. Faced with the queasiness many women experience during early pregnancy it is no wonder if she occasionally questions her ability to undertake what lies ahead. And father is pregnant too, inevitably changed by the thought of the coming child. He may feel excluded and unwanted – a woman's thoughts often seem turned inwards at this time; financial commitments may seem overwhelming; he may also feel that now she is becoming a mother he is losing his wife.

Becoming a parent in fact seems to be an experience which holds all possible contradictions. It is learning to grow up and learning to become a child again. It is an imprisonment which sets you free and the flowering of a love which enhances all other loves. It is also not all smiles and gurgles.

Previous generations were usually part of a close-living and large family. There were few only children and often families stayed in one locality for generations. Cousins, aunts, grandparents, parents formed a family support system to be called upon for advice and help. The new parent could always rely on the experience of an older person. Today many families are smaller and more frequently move away from each other. There may well be no comforting relative within reach – perhaps that is why so many baby books abound. Research into childcare and development has been so intensive in recent years that many

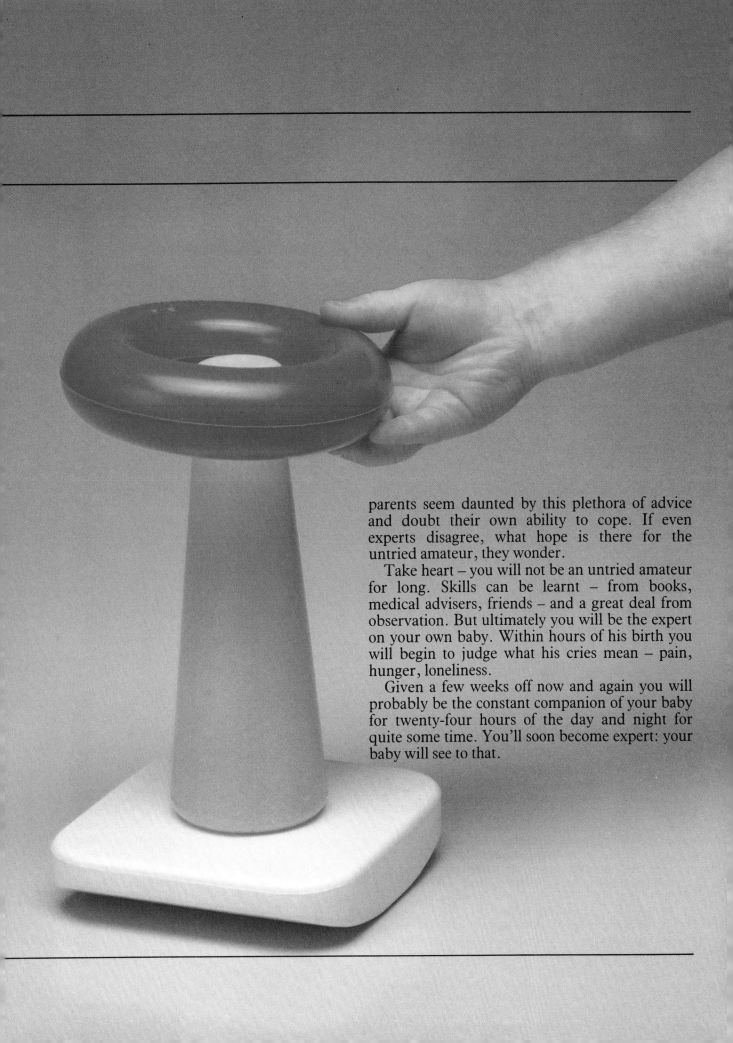

parents seem daunted by this plethora of advice and doubt their own ability to cope. If even experts disagree, what hope is there for the untried amateur, they wonder.

Take heart – you will not be an untried amateur for long. Skills can be learnt – from books, medical advisers, friends – and a great deal from observation. But ultimately you will be the expert on your own baby. Within hours of his birth you will begin to judge what his cries mean – pain, hunger, loneliness.

Given a few weeks off now and again you will probably be the constant companion of your baby for twenty-four hours of the day and night for quite some time. You'll soon become expert: your baby will see to that.

Caring for yourself

You will not be perfect parents: you do not need to be.

All you need to be are 'good enough' parents. That is what the paediatrician D.W. Winnicott wrote and reality confirms that is all that is possible – and desirable. Because what is a 'perfect' parent? What might be perfect for Baby Number One might not suit Baby Number Two at all. The woman who turns into a mother obsessed by having the perfect baby, the perfect home, the perfect marriage usually turns out to be a perfect horror. Likewise father.

No-one sets out deliberately to be a bad parent, so accept without guilt what will be inevitable shortcomings and enjoy being 'good enough'. Obviously the first baby brings the most dramatic changes in his parents' lives and to some extent takes the brunt of being brought up by novices. But it is swings and roundabouts: he also benefits from undivided attention and the sense of novelty which more than compensates for the occasional inexpert handling.

If you are first-time parents, you too will be coping with changes, coming to terms with a new lifestyle startlingly different from your previous pattern, but at least – for most parents – you are in it together: you are both pregnant. No-one has entirely satisfactorily explained that mysterious malady known as 'couvade' which occasionally attacks pregnant fathers – a malady where they show some of the physical symptoms of pregnancy – morning sickness, backache, even an expanding stomach. In certain primitive societies it is still the custom for the pregnant father to take to his bed while the pregnant mother gets on with a normal daily routine.

Today it's made easy for fathers to be pregnant. The whole climate of child-bearing and child-rearing is geared towards the father's involvement. No longer is it his role – as in the best westerns – to pace the floor during labour and obey that mysterious injunction to 'keep the kettle boiling'. In Britain today ninety-five per cent of fathers, informed and participating, are at the birth of their children.

A woman learns very quickly what it's like to be a mother. Even if you intend eventually to return to work outside the home you will before then have had several weeks of day-long physical intimacy with your baby – feeding, cuddling, talking. In today's most usual pattern of employment this is not so certain for father. But an American professor of child development, Alvin Price, has found

Gentle exercise that your body is already used to is beneficial in pregnancy. Swimming is particularly relaxing but you must naturally take care not to become overtired.

a novel way of showing his male students what it is like to be a father.

Using a length of string he ties to the man's wrist a raw egg still in its shell. For a week the student must take the egg everywhere with him: to meals, to bed, to lectures, to the cinema. At the end of the week the professor asks to see an unbroken egg because, 'That,' he says, 'is what it is like to care for a baby.'

So, if you're preparing for the first egg and string to catch up with both of you, it's a help to stand back and look at some of your present life habits: assess what changes will be necessary and begin to prepare for some of them now. Here are a few suggestions for starters:

If the mother is giving up work outside the home, have you both thought about:
living on one income?
making local friends?
taking up another occupation which can be carried on at home?
finding out what support systems like Mother and Toddler clubs are available in the area?

If you share a hobby outside the home at the moment, have you discussed:
whether you will continue to do it together, using baby-sitters?
whether the father will go on his own?
whether the mother will go on her own?
whether each is reconciled to the decision, if you decide to go separately?

If you share domestic jobs at the moment have you thought:
whether you will continue like that?
whether each will take on fresh responsibilities?
whether the system needs reorganizing in view of the extra work which will be involved?

If holidays have featured largely in your life together, have you realized:
back-packing with a baby is not much fun?
one of you might want the same holidays?
How would you feel if one went alone?

Anticipating with realism some of these possible changes will make the transition a great deal easier.

ARE YOU FIT FOR PREGNANCY?

'We'd like a family of course – in a year or two – when we're settled. When we've bought our home.'

Such an attitude today would mostly be applauded as 'sensible' because most parents-to-be prefer to equip their home before they decide to embark on raising a family.

And yet, until quite recently, there has been little emphasis on parents preparing themselves physically for pregnancy by making sure they are in good health *before* they conceive.

The importance of good health before conception and in the first few weeks of pregnancy was highlighted in a study made of the 1944 Dutch 'Hunger Winter' during the Second World War. At that time food in Holland was very scarce and it was found that there were many more deaths and malformations in babies conceived during the months of food shortage than in babies actually born during that time. Lack of proper nutrition was more detrimental to the baby in the very early stages of the pregnancy than in the later.

It's in those early stages of pregnancy that the baby develops most rapidly – and yet mothers-to-be do not as a rule have their pregnancy confirmed by their doctor before they have missed a second period. By that time they could be ten or eleven weeks pregnant and by twelve weeks all the organs and parts of their baby's body will be formed. The balance of nourishment the baby is receiving during those first weeks could be vital to the baby's future health and development.

We are what we eat. Your unborn baby will take from his mother the nourishment he needs. He takes his food from his mother's bloodstream and it comes to him through the umbilical cord which is attached to a fleshy part (called the placenta) of the womb lining. If you're not eating properly – and we'll see soon what 'properly' means – so that your baby is not receiving enough nourishment from your bloodstream, then he'll draw on the stores already in your body. These stores have been built by the food you have previously eaten, but if they are inadequate for both of you then your baby will take what he needs even though he depletes you. He could, for instance, be born with healthy blood yet have left you anaemic because he has drawn from your stores of iron while in the womb.

Food in our western world is plentiful although not cheap, but perhaps surprisingly there are frequent instances of undernutrition. Some of that may be due to the cost of food, or the emphasis on dieting, on rushed and strenuous lives, on the habit of snatching 'junk' food meals of little nutritional value, or the inadequate preparation of the food itself.

Women who are seriously undernourished run the risk of giving birth prematurely, or to low-weight babies or babies prone to infection.

The most dramatic changes in a human fetus occur in early pregnancy. By the end of twelve or thirteen weeks the baby is fully formed. At the end of ten weeks the baby is about 30 mm long (1¼ in) but is clearly human with almost all the major internal organs formed. For the first thirteen weeks of pregnancy the baby is referred to as an embryo: for the last two trimesters (periods of thirteen weeks) he is called a fetus.

By the end of eight weeks almost all the internal organs have formed. Hands, fingers, feet and toes are emerging. The primitive heart has been beating since the twenty-eighth day from fertilization. A rudimentary nervous system is developing and will form the brain and the spinal cord. At five weeks the embryo measures about 2 mm (.08 in): by the sixth week it will have doubled its length. Here it is shown about two-and-a-half times actual size. A face can be discerned with the head large in proportion to the body.

By the end of the twelfth week the fetus is easily recognizable as a human baby. Fingers and toes are still joined by webbing but leg and arm movements are frequent. The heart is now completely formed and pumping blood round the body and to the placenta. The head is still large in proportion to the body. This fetus is one-and-a-half times actual size.

By the end of the fourth week of pregnancy the embryo would be just visible to the naked eye. Here it is shown about seven times actual size. The cells which will form the baby are rapidly developing and the head is clearly visible. This mother-to-be would be about one week past her expected menstrual date.

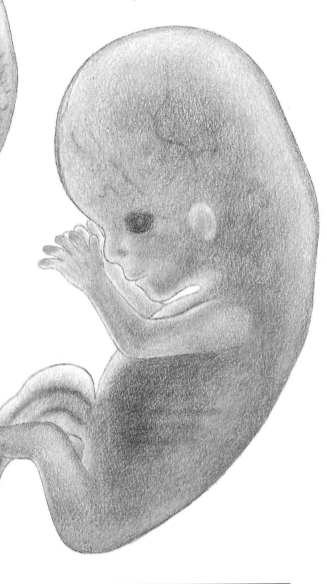

WHAT IS EATING 'PROPERLY?'

The Department of Health and Social Security has a recommended daily intake of the 'right' food for pregnant women and this will be discussed at your antenatal visits. In America the suggested level is higher. In Britain, a study was made by the Maternity Alliance in 1983 of the daily intake of two groups of women – one from a higher income group than the other: not surprisingly it was found that the intake of the lower income group did not meet the daily requirements and their babies were, overall, of a lower birthweight than those of the other group.

All the same, economics need not always be the cause of faulty eating habits. A group of women who had previously given birth to spina bifida babies were given advice about their diets before becoming pregnant again. Among the women who followed the advice there was no recurrence of the same malformation, though this was not so among the

WEIGHT GAIN IN PREGNANCY

During pregnancy your doctor or clinic will advise you to limit your weight gain to 9 – 14 kg (20 – 30 lb). If you are underweight when you become pregnant then you may be advised to put on a little more than the usual recommended amount. If you are overweight before you become pregnant it would be wise to try to lose a little by cutting out biscuits, cakes, sweets etc. **Do not slim while you are pregnant: stop dieting when you stop using contraceptives.** If you are overweight and pregnant then your clinic will suggest ways to cut down a little.

At the end of your pregnancy your weight gain will be spread something like this:

At the beginning and end of pregnancy there will be very little weight gain; most weight is put on as shown opposite.

Breast-feeding helps you to lose weight more rapidly after the birth.

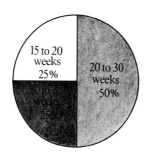

15 to 20 weeks 25%

20 to 30 weeks 50%

Breasts	2kg (4lb)
Blood	2kg (4lb)
Amniotic fluid	1kg (2lb)
Placenta	1kg (2lb)
Baby's weight	3kg (7lb)
Uterus	1kg (2lb)
Mother's body fat	2kg (4lb)

CHART FOR HEALTHY EATING

If during pregnancy you have cravings for unusual food, mention the fact to your doctor. The tendency should not persist for all your pregnancy and you can then return to a normally healthy diet.

'Moderate' helpings would be, for instance, a slice of wholemeal bread with butter or margarine, an apple, 125 – 175 g (4 – 6 oz) of fish or meat, two tablespoonsful of vegetables.

EACH DAY EAT FROM EACH SECTION OF THE FOLLOWING GROUPS:

fresh vegetables and fruit (raw where possible)	dairy produce	bread and cereals	meat, fish, eggs
4 moderate helpings	3 moderate helpings	3 moderate helpings	2 moderate helpings
carrots, parsnips, cauliflower, tomatoes, watercress, sprouts mushrooms, apples, oranges etc.	milk, butter, cream, cheese, yoghurt.	wholemeal bread, wholegrain cereals, muesli, brown rice, etc.	beef, chicken, lamb, pork, eggs, white fish, sardines, etc.

group of women who did not follow the advice.

Eating properly means eating food each day from balanced and varied sources of nourishment. The chart (below left) shows how food should be chosen from each of the sections to provide this nourishment.

All food can be ruined by faulty preparation yet cookery books today even seem to outnumber baby books and it is not difficult to plan and provide a healthy diet.
To begin with:
– wherever possible buy fresh foods
– use them as soon as possible
– do not ruin vegetables by over-cooking in too much water
– eat wholemeal bread, wholegrain cereals
Preparing and serving food can be an expression of affection and the basis of one aspect of family life – it also pays dividends in health and happiness.

THE PREGNANCY 'CLINIC'
Once you suspect you're pregnant you'll have all kinds of questions about your developing baby, and in particular, about the possible effects of smoking, drinking, drugs and illness on your child. In this section you will find the most obvious questions answered:

How do I know I'm pregnant?
Some women seem to know immediately they become pregnant: others remain blissfully unaware for weeks, months and in not a few cases, right up to the delivery room. Usually, however, the first sign is a missed period: breasts may feel full and tingle, the area around the nipple turns brown, there may be a tendency to pass urine more frequently.
How do I make sure? Go to your doctor, use a do-it-yourself pregnancy kit, or ask a chemist to test a urine sample. If you take a sample it must be the first urine passed in the morning having drunk nothing either that morning or during the night. If you go to your doctor he may test the sample himself, send it away for analysis or confirm your pregnancy by an internal examination.
And when? It used to be usual to wait for two missed periods before going to a doctor for confirmation. Nowadays it's considered better to confirm the pregnancy as soon as possible since in these early days important decisions can be taken about drugs, smoking, drinking. The baby is already developing rapidly in the first few weeks after conception.
When is it due? And where? Your doctor will work out the probable date of delivery (280 days from the first day of your last menstrual period). He will discuss where to have your baby – home, National Health or private hospital. In the case of the latter he'll suggest a consultant to care for you throughout pregnancy and to deliver your baby. You may find that your doctor advises against having your baby at home if it's your first pregnancy, if you have a previous or family history of complications, if you're over thirty, or if your home circumstances are unsuitable.

Most doctors consider that hospital births are safer because if medical intervention is necessary then all equipment and help is ready to hand. On the other hand many women do not wish to give birth in the more clinical surroundings of hospital and would rather be at home. You should discuss this fully with your doctor and ask him if the Flying Squad Ambulance service operates in your area and is efficient. This is an ambulance staffed with equipment to deal with emergencies at home or to get you to hospital quickly. To some extent where you live will dictate some of your decisions.

Can I smoke?
Smoking in pregnancy is the most effective way of poisoning your baby's bloodstream.
Why? Whether you inhale or not the nicotine and carbon monoxide pass into your bloodstream and cause the blood vessels in the placenta to constrict. This means less oxygen and nutrients reach your baby. It affects his heartbeat and respiratory system.
Suppose I continue? You may still give birth to a good-sized baby but the overall pattern is that babies born to mothers who smoke weigh less than they might have done. Smoking also reduces your appetite so you may not be eating as well as you should. Smoking in late pregnancy increases the likelihood of premature birth, miscarriage, haemorrhage or abnormality.
How can I stop? Often smoking is associated with another habit – morning coffee, afternoon tea. You could be lucky and go off these, in which case you may be able to break the smoking habit too. Another suggestion is your own 'aversion therapy': if you feel sick, think of a cigarette: the two become associated in your mind and may stop the wish to smoke. Tell everyone you're trying to give up so that they can encourage you.
What about a smoky atmosphere? This will not cause as much damage but it is still unpleasant and unhealthy. If your partner smokes, try to make him give up too. You can support each other's efforts.
I just can't stop – and I'm a guilty, nervous wreck. Life is hard. Now you have two hazards instead of just one. Stress, guilt, tension can all affect your health, send your blood pressure up, increase your heart rate.

Try to assess which is doing you more harm – smoking or stress. Again, try to think of other ways to relieve tension – eating an apple, taking a walk. It is not easy – but here again constructive support from a partner helps enormously. The effects of smoking have been conclusively proved to be potentially dangerous to your baby.

Can I drink?
'There is no doubt that heavy drinking, whether regular or occasional, can harm the fetus and should be avoided during pregnancy or when pregnancy is contemplated'
So said a Department of Health and Social Security directive on the subject in December 1983.
Can I drink at all? Opinion is at present divided on this but there's no doubt that alcohol passes from the bloodstream to the fetus. One study indicated that ten single drinks a week resulted in an increased risk of bearing a low birthweight baby.
Suppose I did not realize I was pregnant? It is considered that an occasional drink will not harm the baby and it is important that mothers-to-be who have had the occasional drink before they knew they were pregnant should not worry unduly that this will affect their baby. Evidence as to what – if any – other damage is caused to the fetus by drinking in pregnancy is inconclusive, but in the present state of research it's wise to limit drinking in pregnancy to an occasional glass of wine and to avoid spirits.

Can I take drugs? No. When you stop using contraceptives, flush all the out-of-date drugs in the house down the lavatory. Take the rest to your doctor and ask him which, if any, are safe for you to take.
I am already on drugs for a medical condition. What should I do? Tell your doctor if you wish to become pregnant or think you are. He'll prescribe alternatives.
What about tranquillizers? Mild tranquillizers don't seem to affect the baby but powerful ones will. Avoid taking sleeping, travel and anti-sickness pills.
Pain-killers? If taken in large quantities, aspirin, codeine and paracetamol can cause difficulties. Ask for advice.
And antibiotics? Penicillin and sulphonamides appear to be harmless but remind your doctor that you're taking them. Tetracycline and streptomycin should not be taken, nor should cannabis and LSD. Drugs or medicaments taken for heart conditions, diabetes, epilepsy may cause difficulties. Discuss with your doctor before becoming pregnant.
I'm running a fever! A very high temperature could harm a baby in the early stages so if you have flu or a feverish cold try to lower your temperature by a tepid sponge, drinking lots of fluids and going to bed. Don't worry overmuch if you did have flu in the early days – the chances of harm are relatively slight.

What about x-rays? Tell your doctor or dentist that you are, or may be, pregnant and ask if x-rays are essential. Avoid them if possible.
Vaccinations? They should be avoided in the first four months.
And rubella? This is a different matter. Rubella (German measles) is dangerous to the fetus and may result in deafness, blindness and brain damage to the baby. Before you become pregnant check that you are immune by means of a simple blood test. If you are not, then you should be vaccinated but do not then conceive for a further three months.
Do not have a rubella vaccination while you are pregnant: if you are not immune but are pregnant then you can be vaccinated after the birth of your baby.
If you think you may have been in contact with rubella and are pregnant then tell your doctor immediately – he may offer you an injection of gamma globulin. If rubella is confirmed by blood tests early in pregnancy you may be offered a termination. Even if you've been vaccinated, check your immunity when planning your pregnancy. (See Immunization on page 66).

The Health Education Council publishes leaflets on all aspects of care in pregnancy. They're available through your doctor or clinic or from the address on page 230.

The possibility of miscarriage
Most pregnant women worry about the possibilty of miscarriage which, if it is to occur at all, happens most commonly in the first three months of pregnancy when it is usually the result of the development of an abnormal fetus. The first sign of threatened miscarriage is usually vaginal bleeding although this may occur without a miscarriage. Medical advice is always necessary and usually your doctor will advise rest at home. If miscarriage occurs, keep the expelled sac for the doctor to make sure that nothing remains in the uterus which would require surgical removal.
Miscarriage during middle pregnancy is much less common and may be due to the premature opening of the cervix. If this is threatened, or has been experienced in a previous pregnancy, then under general anaesthetic a stitch is inserted round the cervix which will keep it closed until labour begins.

What exercises can I do?

These exercises can be continued throughout pregnancy but show them first for approval to your physiotherapist or doctor in case there are special circumstances in your case. Build up gradually the number of times each is done until you have reached the maximum number indicated.

Exercises such as these below help to keep your body flexible as well as strengthening arms, shoulders and torso muscles. Do the sequence once at first, then build up to three times a day.

With legs straight apart and feet flexed up, hold your right foot with your right hand, keeping your torso straight and left arm above your head.

Bend over to your right, keeping your face to the front and your back straight. Now bounce your torso and arm gently up and down.

Repeat the movement to your left, keeping your right shoulder slightly back. As before bounce gently up and down.

For relaxing and breath control, sit cross legged, wrists and hands relaxed on your knees. Drop your head forward, inhaling through your nose to a count of 3 then exhaling to 3. Can be done whenever you are feeling tense.

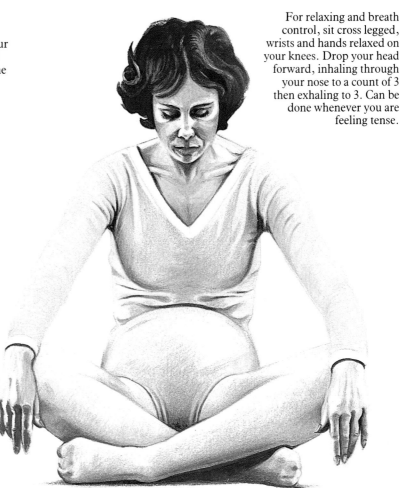

These exercises help to strengthen important pelvic muscles and may be done whenever you can during the nine months of pregnancy.

Breathe in deeply through the nose and let the abdominal wall expand.

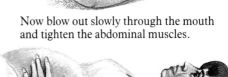

Now blow out slowly through the mouth and tighten the abdominal muscles.

Looking ahead

WHAT TO EXPECT

Home or hospital? And if hospital, which? Midwife, your own doctor, consultant? Natural birth, active birth, analgesics, anaesthetics, drugs, episiotomy, shaving, enema?

Decisions, decisions: was it easier after all in the westerns when mother clutched the bedpost and father put the kettle on? Not a bit. Look at the conquered diseases, the eliminated handicaps, the reduced rate of child and maternal mortality. Here is a brief, basic summary of what to expect to help you plot your course through the sea of alternatives available.

Home birth If you decide on a home birth you will be attended throughout your pregnancy by a community midwife who is attached to your doctor's surgery. The advantage here is that you will get to know her well and she will also deliver your baby. You'll have the reassurance of being in familiar surroundings and if you have other children, of not being separated from them.

Hospital If you choose hospital then your doctor will suggest one or two locally and arrange for your 'booking in' interview at their antenatal clinic. If you want to go to another hospital then think about the distance involved. Visits to the antenatal clinic there may be wearisome in later pregnancy.

Your first visit to the antenatal clinic will be longer than subsequent visits. It will involve urine tests, measuring your blood pressure, taking your weight, an internal examination, taking a sample of blood and many details. You may feel overawed by the busy atmosphere and the line of waiting mothers-to-be but if you have questions to ask and everyone seems too rushed to answer them, ask if you can make an appointment to come back later.

Antenatal clinics After this first visit you'll be asked to attend your local antenatal clinic every four weeks up to the twenty-eighth week of pregnancy. This visit will entail taking your blood pressure, weighing you, testing your urine and feeling the lie of the baby by palpation – that is feeling your stomach when you are lying flat. The midwife or doctor will also listen for the baby's heart. After the twenty-eighth week you'll be asked to go more frequently – probably once a fortnight and, for the last month, once a week.

At one of your antenatal visits, you will probably be given an ultrasound scan. It can be done at any time but most likely will be about the sixteenth week. The scan will show if you are expecting twins, how the baby is lying and how old she is. It is quite painless

A litte self-indulgence in pregnancy does no harm as your body prepares for the birth of your baby. Feelings of apprehension and excitement may alternate.

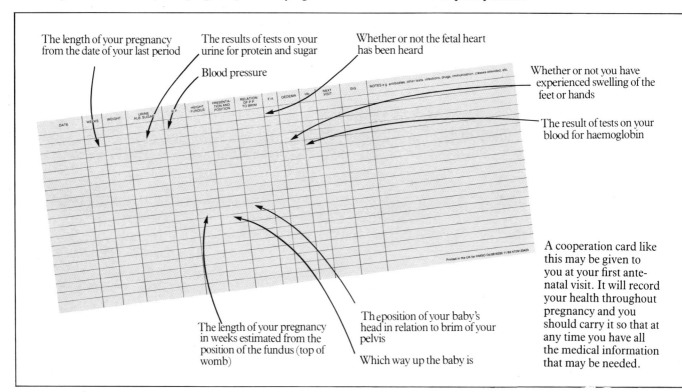

The length of your pregnancy from the date of your last period

The results of tests on your urine for protein and sugar

Whether or not the fetal heart has been heard

Blood pressure

Whether or not you have experienced swelling of the feet or hands

The result of tests on your blood for haemoglobin

The length of your pregnancy in weeks estimated from the position of the fundus (top of womb)

The position of your baby's head in relation to brim of your pelvis

Which way up the baby is

A cooperation card like this may be given to you at your first antenatal visit. It will record your health throughout pregnancy and you should carry it so that at any time you have all the medical information that may be needed.

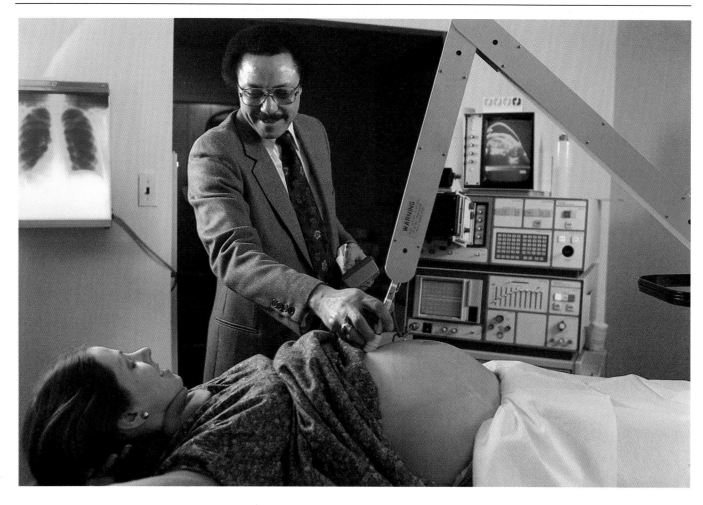

At about sixteen weeks an ultrasound scan may be given to check the baby's position, health and size. The scanner is passed over the abdomen and sound waves are translated into a picture of the fetus on the screen (see below).

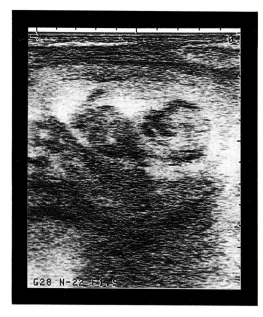

and you will be able to see your baby on a screen. The scan uses sound waves to build up a picture of the baby and it's an exciting moment when you first see your baby, probably moving, in the uterus. You will be asked to lie on your back and your abdomen will be smeared with oil so that the scanner can be passed backwards and forwards over the skin. If you can't distinguish the picture, ask for it to be explained to you.

Among other benefits, antenatal clinics are a first-class chance to get to know other mothers-to-be in your locality. Many a baby-sitting circle or lifelong friendship has begun in the queue. It can be wearisome if the clinic is crowded and there are long waits but such care is vital to the health of your baby and yourself. Women who do not, for whatever reasons, attend these clinics until late in pregnancy are statistically known to give birth to babies of lower birthweight, who are more prone to handicap, infection and to prematurity. You owe it to your baby to attend regularly.

Antenatal classes Antenatal clinics are concerned with your physical well-being and that of the baby, whereas antenatal classes are geared towards the experience of birth

TERMS YOU MAY MEET DURING PREGNANCY

Amniocentesis A test which shows if there is a risk of Down's syndrome, spina bifida, haemophilia or muscular dystrophy in the baby. It is offered to older mothers, when there is an increased risk of Down's syndrome, or to mothers when there is a history of such illnesses in the family. Usually performed from sixteen to eighteen weeks of pregnancy, a needle is inserted through the abdominal wall into the amniotic fluid which surrounds the baby in the womb. A sample of the fluid is drawn off and tested and the result – for spina bifida – is known in a few days, and – for Down's syndrome – in a few weeks. The latter test also tells the baby's sex. If abnormality is detected you may be offered a termination so, if you do not wish to have an abortion whatever the result of the test, you should first consider whether you wish to have the test at all. The test carries a very slight risk of bringing on a miscarriage.

Oedema Swelling of ankles, feet and hands caused by water retention. Resting with feet higher than the heart is helpful.

Stretch marks During pregnancy the skin over your stomach and breasts stretches to make room for your growing baby and for its supplies of milk. After the birth you may find this has caused 'stretch marks' – thin silvery lines over your stomach, the upper part of your legs and under your breasts. Massaging your skin with a good cream will help to keep the skin supple and may make stretch marks less likely.

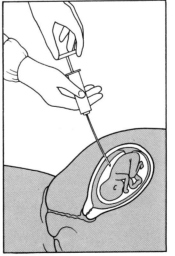

Amniotic fluid is drawn from the womb for an amniocentesis test.

Antenatal classes provide the opportunity to make friends, discuss feelings and attitudes towards birth as well as to learn methods of relaxation and baby care. The atmosphere is informal and there is plenty of time to ask questions.

and caring for the baby. You'll be asked to attend classes in about the fifth or sixth month of pregnancy, and you'll probably find there are one or two in your area from which to choose. They are usually run by a team of three – health visitor, midwife and physiotherapist. You will be asked to bring along the baby's father (or a friend, if you prefer), and some classes will be held in the evening so that it is more convenient for anyone working during the day to attend.

The classes may vary a little in content, depending on the staff running them, but all will discuss methods and positions in which to give birth, the use of drugs and analgesics, feelings during birth, how to feed, bath and change a baby. Breast-feeding is discussed and relaxation exercises taught. There will probably be a film shown of a birth and also a visit to the local hospital where your baby is to be born.

Such visits are a great help in making you familiar with equipment that may surround you at birth.

Classes are also run by the National Childbirth Trust (NCT) and usually there is a charge for these although this is often reduced if you are hard up. They are given in the home of one of the NCT teachers, who will herself be a mother. These classes are again an invaluable way of making friends. If later you should have difficulties with breast-feeding then the teacher will put you in touch with someone who will come along and help. NCT classes (the address should be in your local directory, if not write to the address on page 230) place great emphasis on breathing and relaxation exercises and on preparing yourself for birth.

Methods of care If you are having your baby in hospital, there are still alternative methods of care.

You may be looked after by your own doctor (GP) if he is on the 'obstetric list' – that is, qualified to look after you during your pregnancy and to deliver your baby – and either he or a midwife will deliver you in what is known as a *GP unit* in a hospital. It is usual to have this kind of birth if your doctor foresees no complications. When antenatal care is shared between your doctor and a hospital, it is known as shared care.

Or you may have your baby in a *consultant unit* in your hospital. This is a department under an obstetrician consultant whom you may not see but who has overall charge of the midwives, doctors and general medical team in the unit. If it is a teaching hospital you may also be seen by medical students.

In some hospitals the *domino scheme* operates. Here a community midwife who has looked after you during pregnancy brings you into hospital and delivers you. After a short stay – perhaps a few hours or perhaps a day and a night – the midwife will bring you home and settle you in.

After the birth Once you return home you will be visited daily for ten days by a midwife and after that by a Health Visitor. Health visitors work with your local clinic or doctor. They are all midwives who have taken an extra health visitors' course and they are an invaluable help during pregnancy and after. They will visit you in your home (you may ask to see one before you have the baby) and can deal with all your queries about the health of the family, which forms to fill in, what services are available locally, and so on.

BENEFITS AND ALLOWANCES

The Department of Health and Social Security (DHSS) has issued a leaflet *Babies and Benefits* (1984) which tells you just what allowances and grants are available to mothers-to-be. You can get a copy from your GP or at the antenatal clinic. Benefits include free milk and vitamins in certain circumstances, free spectacles and dental treatment, free National Health Service prescriptions plus these grants and allowances (1984):

Maternity Grant A once-only payment to help with the expense of having a baby. If you have twins you get two grants, and so on. Available to all expectant mothers who have lived in Great Britain for more than twenty-six weeks before the baby's expected birth-date.

Maternity Allowance Payable each week for eighteen weeks – eleven weeks before the expected birth, the week of birth and for six weeks after, though not if you're in paid work at the time. Check your eligibility at your local DHSS office.

Child Benefit Payable each week for each child, including the first. It begins at birth and continues until the child is eighteen, so long as she remains in full-time education. Payable at your Post Office through a weekly order book or by direct transfer into your bank or building society.

Benefits must be claimed at specific times but *Babies and Benefits* gives details of when and how to claim. These details were correct in 1984 but are, of course, liable to change.

Because they visit you at home they are also very much aware of your home circumstances and they can always advise and help in all sorts of ways.

Just what is 'active' birth? So much has been written and spoken about 'active' birth, 'natural' birth, 'birth without pain', and the differing methods of achieving this, that it's no wonder the first-time parent becomes confused.

However, all these terms and possibly slightly differing methods of approach have a common basis – the belief that a woman should be in control of her own labour. The varying classes, books and films on the subject have the common aim of educating parents to that achievement.

Many parents still feel that in pregnancy and labour the woman is 'taken over' by the system, made to feel part of a conveyor belt on which, although she is physically well cared for, her feelings are ignored. She does not *give* birth: birth is something that *happens* to her. Technology has taken over.

Even the position in which most women in the west were obliged to give birth – on their backs with their legs in raised stirrups (the lithotomy position) – was devised by an eighteenth-century obstetrician at the French court. Previously a woman had walked, squatted or used a birthing stool – just as many women today give birth in so-called 'primitive' societies. Nowadays the birthing stool is being re-introduced into some hospitals where it is found that gravity logically assists the birth passage. Although the lithotomy position made the use of forceps easier, their use might not have been necessary at all if the woman had been free to choose her position. Research has now shown that contractions are stronger and more effective if the woman is upright.

Today many of the procedures which were once routine in many hospitals are being questioned. Is episiotomy (page 42) necessary? Or shaving? Or an enema? And if you're coping well with contractions, why should you be given analgesics as a matter of course? Does the baby really need to have a scalp monitor attached? And why shouldn't the father remain with his partner during labour and birth? Is hospital birth *really* safer for both mother and baby – or merely more convenient for the medical staff?

It is because of all this that an increasingly vocal chorus is being raised about such issues and as a result changes are gradually being made in many hospitals.

Mothers-to-be may well seem daunted on occasions by the complicated equipment which may be used to assist birth: on the whole fathers-to-be seem not so intimidated, regarding the technological advances as yet further proof of increased efficiency. Yet both may feel that because so much equipment is available it will be used as a matter of course – even when the baby is not in need of such help. Hospital birth, in fact, has often

A return to older tradition? The medieval print (above) shows a wooden birthing chair then in common use. Below, an advanced example of a modern birthing chair now in use in some hospitals. The sitting position aids gravity and is said to speed delivery.

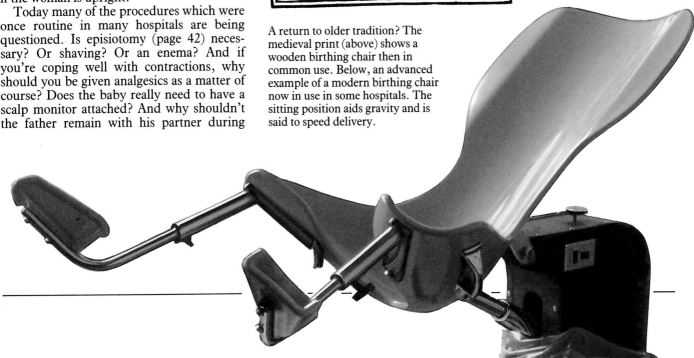

become too impersonal, too clinical and may detract from the intimacy of birth.

Attempts have been made in some hospitals to make hospital rooms comfortable and more like home. 'Birthing rooms' with chairs, carpets and a high bed suitable for delivery have been furnished so that mother and father can stay in the same room for labour and delivery. After the birth medical staff leave parents and baby together to make their own acquaintances in peace. Notice is taken of the parents' wishes regarding birthing procedures and, where possible, the mother is allowed freedom of movement during labour. It is best to discuss all these points with your doctor or at the first visit you make to the antenatal clinic.

'Painless' Birth In Britain the philosophy pioneered by *Dr Grantly Dick Read* has been known and accepted for some years. His argument was that ignorance produces fear, that fear leads to tension and tension produces pain. His aim therefore was to teach relaxation through specific breathing exercises, and to impart proper information about the birth process combined with physical exercises to keep the body supple.

His methods are still being taught today.

Psychoprophylaxis ('prevention by mind') originated in Russia and was then developed in France by *Lamaze* before coming to Britain. The teaching centres more on breathing than relaxation. The emphasis is on treating labour pains as stimuli not as pain. This is one of the systems taught by the National Childbirth Trust.

Sheila Kitzinger, who is Advisor to the NCT, has further developed and expanded some of these methods and added her own experience. Her method is to teach mothers-to-be to respond 'purposefully and creatively' to the process of birth, and to achieve the skill of releasing muscles at will during labour while the mind is clear and able to understand what is happening. She also teaches exercises, thought processes and 'touch relaxation', where the woman's partner is able to recognize and massage tension away and help her relax.

Frederic Leboyer, a French obstetrician, has turned attention to the trauma of birth from the baby's point of view, not the mother's. He has introduced the idea of receiving the baby into this world with

Fetal heart rate is monitored by the machine strapped to the mother's abdomen. Uterine contractions are also recorded.

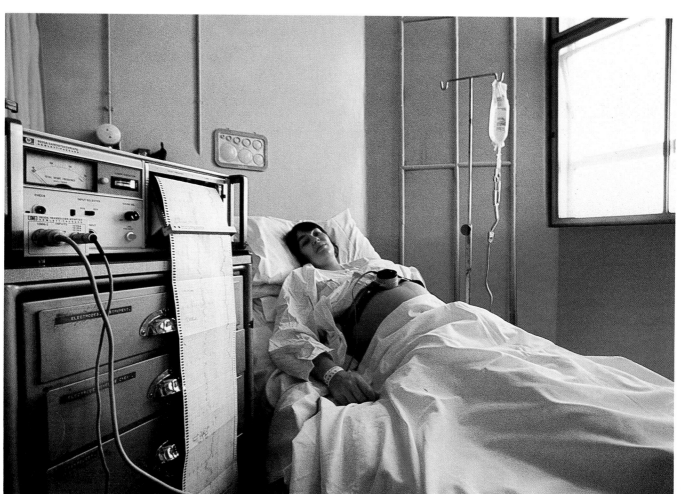

dignity and respect and many hospitals now employ a modified version of his ideas. At the moment of delivery lights are lowered, voices are kept to a minimum and the baby is received in near silence and handed to her mother. Often the father is allowed to cut the umbilical cord and to immerse the baby in her first 'bath' – lukewarm water which reproduces as much as possible the liquid of the womb from which the baby has emerged. Babies received by this method are thought to cry less and appear relaxed and more aware of their surroundings.

Another French obstetrician, *Michel Odent*, at his hospital at Pithiviers in France has created an atmosphere in which birth can take place naturally without drugs or technology. His admiration of midwives and the instinctive way they respond to a mother's needs has made him champion 'non-interference' at birth, even when medical intervention might seem necessary. His mothers on occasion have even given birth under water: such deliveries were not planned but came about because the mothers were so comfortable in water they did not want to move. The water, Dr Odent claims, will not harm the baby who has lived in fluid for nine months and who will not breathe until she comes into air. (*Birth reborn*, a film made at Pithiviers, has been shown on television).

Janet Balaskas teaches an attitude of mind and body to 'active birth' and has devised a programme of preparation for birth where the woman is in control of her own body.

Now that you have a better idea of some of the things that will happen to you during your pregnancy, it's time to consider more practical aspects of your baby's impending arrival – preparing your home.

Birthing rooms – where the mother remains in the same room for labour and delivery – are now becoming usual in many hospitals. There are usually easy chairs and the atmosphere is made as 'homely' as possible. There are facilites for the father to stay with the mother before, during and after delivery.

French obstetrician Frederic Leboyer has pioneered the 'gentle birth' where lights and voices are lowered at the moment of the birth. This mother and baby have just enjoyed a gentle birth and have been left alone.

WHAT YOU WILL NEED

A new baby means new expense but at least the expense decreases with the number of children you have: so much equipment can be passed on. The first baby in the family is usually a great novelty and attracts many presents which help with the budget. A lot of equipment can also be bought secondhand or borrowed from friends and relations (see page 30 on secondhand buys).

It is a temptation to begin buying as soon as you know you are pregnant but it is wiser to wait a while. Many of the larger pieces of equipment – such as cot or high chair – will not be needed for some weeks so you could defer buying them until later. In the meantime you may well have changed your mind as to what would best suit you or you may find that, talking to other mothers, you could buy or borrow from them as well as benefiting from their experiences of what is or is not necessary.

Mail order catalogues are a source of endless information. Get two or three and compare their different offerings and prices, and remember that it's safety not appearance that matters. All goods with the BSI Kite mark will have been manufactured to strict safety regulations; some imported items may not reach these standards so it is vital that you check for yourselves any areas where there might be potential danger. A guide as to what to look out for is given in the lists below.

Although it is sensible not to buy too soon it is also best not to delay so long that you find shopping tiring. About the sixth month is a good time to think seriously about the basic buys listed below, to which you will naturally add your own preferences and tastes. You will find advice on how to use all this equipment in the next section, Daily care (page 46).

For sleeping

Your new baby could sleep happily in a drawer or a laundry basket or anything flat-bottomed and draughtproof. You will probably prefer her not to, however, so you will need:

- a carrycot, Moses basket or crib, any of which will need its own properly fitting mattress (see page 29).
- three or four flannelette or cotton sheets
- a waterproof undersheet
- one or two blankets
- two covers

A pillow is dangerous for a young baby who could suffocate by being unable to turn her head away. A full-size cot is unnecessary at first because it could be draughty for a new baby who will feel more secure within the confines of the smaller carrycot or crib.

Moses baskets are cheap, attractive and lightweight to carry about. You could line one yourself to save expense (make the lining detachable for washing). The basket will not last more than a few months as once the baby gets mobile and wriggles about it becomes unsafe. The disadvantage is that it will not be waterproof and it doesn't have a hood.

A carrycot has advantages in that you can use it for car journeys or for short walks.

Do not buy a carrycot with a non-porous or plastic lining against which the baby could turn her face and become unable to breathe.

A bouncing cradle lets your baby in on the action. She can sit comfortably in it from a few weeks old and see what's going on. There is also on the market a high chair which converts to a swing and reclining chair.

For wearing

- three or four envelope-type vests
- three or four stretch suits or baby gowns
- one or two cardigans
- one or two baby hats
- one or two shawls – or use cot blankets

Bootees and mitts are not necessary if your baby is well wrapped in a shawl or in the pram.

Stretch suits or baby gowns should fasten underneath – otherwise every time you change your baby she will need to be undressed. She can wear the same type of clothes for day or night. You may prefer to use a sleeping bag for nights or you could buy nightgowns with drawstring bottoms to keep toes warm.

A baby should never be put to sleep in a baby 'nest'. They are not meant for this purpose and if so used could be dangerous as babies can suffocate in them. Nor should any gowns have drawstring necks which might tighten and strangle the baby.

Nappies – towelling or disposables? Each has its merits. Terries are usually more comfortable, more absorbent and help to prevent nappy rash. They are one outlay (buy the best you can afford: 'seconds' of a good make have usually only very slight faults) but there is the hidden expense of your labour and the washing. On the other hand they can be passed on to other babies or, if not, they come in useful later as dusters, and general moppers up. You will also need two sterilizing buckets, sterilizing powder, nappy pins and four pairs of plastic pants. The tie-on pants are best to begin with – they are not so leakproof but they let in air which helps to prevent nappy rash.

If you buy disposables then you can at least spread the expense. Buy the best you can afford – those with their own attached plastic covering are most efficient: some

For wearing: here are some of the basics you'll need for your new baby. No doubt they'll be added to later by gifts or your individual preference.

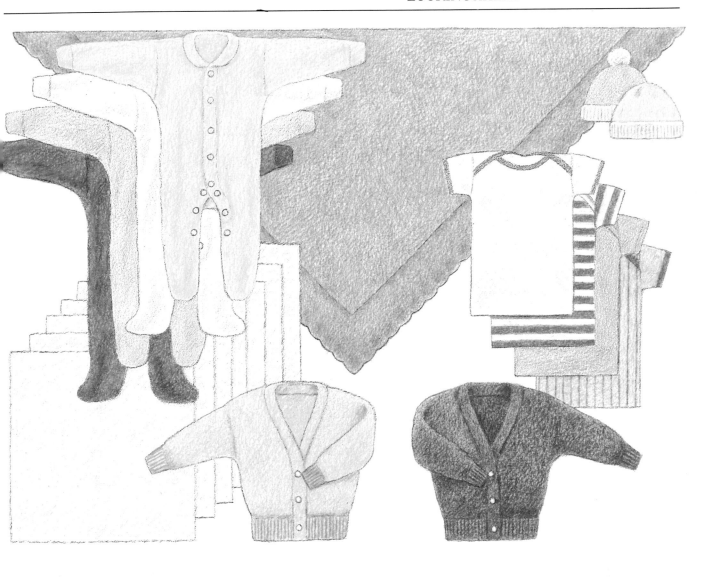

kinds let moisture through but not back to the baby which makes life more comfortable for her. Buy four packs to begin with.

You may find that a mixture of towelling and disposable nappies suits you best – the latter for travelling or going away, the former for everyday wear.

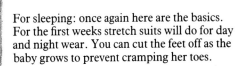

For sleeping: once again here are the basics. For the first weeks stretch suits will do for day and night wear. You can cut the feet off as the baby grows to prevent cramping her toes.

For bathing

- cotton wool
- baby oil or lotion
- zinc and castor oil cream
- round-edged scissors
- a natural sponge
- a brush and comb
- towels
- bath apron for yourself

The bath apron will need to be waterproof-lined or you can wear an ordinary PVC apron with a towelling apron over. (It is easy to make your own by sewing tabs at neck and waist to an ordinary towel.)

You can buy special baby baths, either on stands or for putting on a flat surface. You don't really need them – a large bowl would do, or the handbasin or the kitchen sink (though care must be taken to avoid the baby coming into contact with a hot tap). There is a good inflatable bath on the market which does not take up much room, or a sponge Bath Cushion which, when put in the bath, moulds round the baby and keeps her supported and your hands free.

A changing mat is a good idea: some fold up into carrying bags for nappies, etc. It would not be difficult to make your own – a towelling envelope into which you can slip a plastic foam pad.

For feeding

If breast-feeding you will need two nursing bras – either front-opening or with detachable cups.

If bottle-feeding, you will need:

- ten bottles for a twenty-four-hour supply, either glass or plastic
- ten teats
- ten caps
- two bottle brushes
- sterilizing unit
- sterilizing tablets
- measuring spoon
- measuring jug
- funnel

For travelling and outdoors
- a pram or baby carriage
- safety straps for the back seat of the car (see page 33)
- a cat net for sleeping outdoors
- a baby sling for carrying her: it should have holes for legs to come through and a head support. A young baby can be carried in front but when she can support her own head and is heavier a back sling may suit you better. This should have head rest and leg holes; some have steel frames for extra support and protection.

Baby buggies are not suitable for young babies. They do not have enough back or head support and anyway are too near the ground, traffic fumes, dust and animals.

For buying later
Eventually you will need a cot (there are some on the market which turn into first-size beds), a high chair (some will fold into low chair and play table) or you may prefer a chair which clips on to the back of an ordinary chair for meal times. These are useful when away from home though are not, of course, suitable as car seats.

In the room where your baby sleeps
This may be her own room, your bedroom or that shared with another child. You need:
- a flat changing surface (which might also double as bathing surface)
- storage space for nappies, clothes and so on
- low nursing chair for yourself
- a low table or storage unit for beside the chair on which to put oddments, pins etc.

A wall tidy is useful for oddments and a kitchen roll for mopping up.

Lined curtains make a more restful light and a dimmer switch is useful for checking all is well. Look out for furniture with rounded corners, washable wallpaper, wipeable surfaces. Carpet, cork tiles or non-slip cushion vinyl are warm for flooring; wood can be splintery, little mats are dangerous and slippery both for you and when your baby begins to crawl and stand. (There's more about safety on page 30.) If your baby is sharing your room you may find a properly balanced screen will give you all privacy and shade the light from your baby.

Babies are more susceptible to cold than adults as they cannot shiver. Although they possess 'brown fat' – marvellous body cells that increase their temperature in response to cold – keep the room up to 20°C (68°F) in case bedclothes are kicked off.

A cot or crib mattress must fit properly to the sides of the cot. It would not be difficult for your baby to wedge fingers or toes between the cot and the mattress if this is not properly sized.

Baby carriers make transport easier and there are different models and strengths of carriers available for children of different ages.

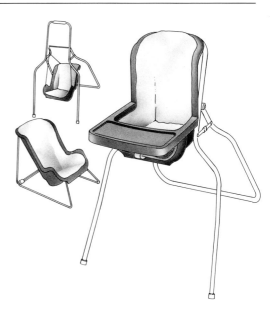

High chairs which convert into low chairs or swings are space saving and economical.

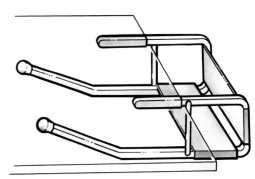

This portable 'clip-on' baby seat grips your table top when the child sits in it. An active child could wriggle free, however, so keep a close eye on its use.

This high chair converts to a play and meal time table. Watch for the width of rungs and stability.

There have been one or two instances of babies suffocating by turning into the waterproof covering of a mattress. Visivent mattresses are flame retardant and have air holes to minimize the risk of suffocation.

What you buy for your baby will largely be determined by your lifestyle and where you live. If you have no room for a pram, then you will need to buy a smaller conveyance. If you are short of room space then you can cut down on equipment such as baby baths. If you live in an upstairs flat you will need collapsible pushchairs or strollers. If you already have a toddler then you will need to buy a pram to take a toddler seat and a shopping tray, or possibly some kind of twin buggy to take both baby and toddler.

If buying secondhand

Although reputable baby equipment is now protected by the safety regulations of the British Standards Institute, this may not apply to equipment manufactured before the regulations became law.

When buying secondhand it is vital to look for inadequate brakes and locks, flaking paint, repainted furniture where toxic paint has been used, flammable materials, sharp edges, or equipment that can tip over.

IS YOUR HOME SAFE?

Unfortunately most houses are far from safe for babies and the best time to take a long, hard look at the world into which your baby is coming is before she arrives. That way you have more time to think about possible danger areas before they turn into accident zones. 'Accidents will happen' is nonsense: it is the parents' job to make the home as safe as possible. Your baby will be unable to protect herself for some years so you have to do it for her, sometimes by removing the hazards, sometimes by example and teaching.

Precautions will vary with every home, every lifestyle, and to a certain extent with the parents' nature. There is a very real case to be made against *over*-protection. It could stifle your baby's natural instinct to explore, curtail her freedom and turn her into a grumpy, over-anxious toddler. Some parents hold that – for instance – stairgates are unnecessary, believing that even a crawling baby can be taught to climb upstairs on her knees and then later taught to crawl backwards down to safety. You would need to spend a lot of time supervising your baby, however.

If you live upstairs, unprotected stairs down would present a real hazard to an unsteady toddler. The picture is different again if your toddler or crawler has a younger brother or sister to distract your attention, or if you live upstairs and need to go down to a washing line or the front door. A stairgate then would be essential for the times when you couldn't tuck the youngster under your arm and take her with you. A stairgate would

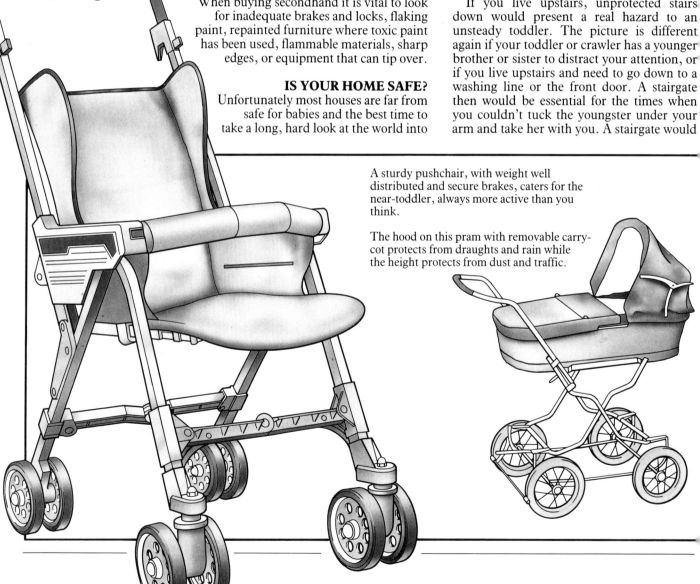

A sturdy pushchair, with weight well distributed and secure brakes, caters for the near-toddler, always more active than you think.

The hood on this pram with removable carrycot protects from draughts and rain while the height protects from dust and traffic.

also be invaluable if you were trying to carry the baby, the washing, the shopping basket and the baby buggy. Occasionally getting out with a baby is worse than moving an army – do you carry the baby downstairs and leave her somewhere where she cannot hurt herself while you go back for your handbag, the keys, the shopping list and the pushchair? Or do you perhaps take all the equipment down first and then rush up for the baby?

In the same way there are times when playpens can be invaluable but not if they are used as long-stay prisons – a baby needs to explore but small children need times for undisturbed play and more than one toddler has found sanctuary inside the pen while the baby crawls around balefully outside.

These are areas where you will make your own decisions, but there are other precautions which no-one can ignore.

The early days are the easiest – at least then your baby is reasonably stationary. Even so, a great deal of your time will be taken up with protecting her. While you are going about the daily routine of feeding, changing, washing, you will find that you are instinctively adopting all sorts of habits which have evolved without conscious thought, but which your baby has provoked by her helplessness and by your recognition of her dependence on you for survival. As you lift her, you support her head because you know that her neck muscles are not yet strong enough to support it. When you put her down you do so gently, not releasing your hold until the mattress has received her weight. When you change her you keep one hand on her to prevent her wriggling away – even though the other hand is obliged to fold a nappy, search for a pin and unscrew a pot of cream all at the same time. You'll take care never to leave her unattended on a bed or chair for instance where she can easily wriggle off.

As your baby grows and becomes more physically adventurous she will become exposed to more dangers. At the same time she will be learning new skills and achieving independence in areas where she previously needed help. At six months, for instance, as she sits on your lap, you won't have to support her head but you will have to watch that she doesn't swipe out at the teapot.

So physical development will govern what scrapes she can get into. But before we detail just some of those hazards, try an experiment. Get down on your hands and knees and crawl round the room. You will be amazed at what you find – from trailing lamp flexes to sharp edged tables, from electric sockets to the cat's supper – treasure trove for a baby but a minefield for her safety.

With a baby it is always later than you think. She will give no warning that she is crossing from one stage to another – you will be the early warning system there. Charts can only give indications, never the entire picture. But for a beginning ...

Strollers are lightweight folding pushchairs. Some have reversible seats so baby can see you or look ahead. A clip-on umbrella or parasol will protect from rain or sun, and a see-through plastic cover will keep baby totally dry.

CHILDPROOFING YOUR HOME

AT ONE MONTH

She has poor head control,
is still learning to coordinate sucking,
breathing, swallowing,
can't turn away from danger,
may wriggle her way across cot if she gets
a purchase with her heels when crying.

POSSIBLE DANGERS AND HOW TO PREVENT THEM

Suffocation, choking and strangling
No pillow: no duvet: no plastic lining to
crib: use fitting mattress: use cat net if
appropriate.
Don't tie pacifier to cot by a long string.
No drawstring round neck of nighties or
matinée jackets.
Don't leave a bottle propped for feed.
Keep small toys out of reach.
Don't tie anything round her neck.

Being trapped
Check cot bars distance as laid down by
BSI.
Avoid lacy shawls which trap fingers.

Falling
Do not leave her when changing etc. (she
could wriggle off a high surface).

Check that cot bars are not too far apart –
there is a regulation width. Make sure also
that the mattress fits snugly to the side of
the cot so that fingers are not trapped.

FROM THREE TO SIX MONTHS

She can lift head,
carry objects to mouth,
reach and grasp small objects,
roll over,
can pull self to sitting position,
sit with minimal support,
first tooth appears.

POSSIBLE DANGERS AND HOW TO PREVENT THEM

To the previous list add:
Poisoning
All paint on furniture etc. should be non
toxic.
Put pills, medicines, cleansers etc. out of
reach.

Swallowing
Everything goes in her mouth: watch for
small toys, buttons, anything sharp or
swallowable.

Is your kitchen as safe as it might be? This is the
room in which the young baby will spend much
of her time, and it is also the most dangerous
area in the house. Take a look at this typical scene
and see if you can pinpoint the hazards.
1. Overhanging handles can tip boiling water on
   to curious faces.
2. Cupboards without childproof locks will swing
   open to reveal inviting containers with lethal
   contents.
3. Mugs and kettles too near the edge of worktops
   will soon be found by grasping hands, and
   hanging flexes and electrical sockets are
   particularly deadly.
4. The knife and fork, matches and heavy ashtray
   on the table are all within reach of the child in
   the high chair, and the handbag is just asking
   to be explored.
5. A child should never be left in a high chair in
   any room without a safety harness.

Keep one hand on her even when attending to her.
Keep cot sides up.

Burning and scalding
Avoid using a hot-water bottle but if you must, it should be covered and not too near baby's body – she might not be able to move away.
Watch hot taps if bathing in sink and test temperature of bath water with your elbow.
Do not handle hot liquids when holding her: a sudden jerk could spill them.
Watch for the sun: it moves round. If baby is sleeping outside, you'll need to move the pram accordingly.
Always buy flame-resistant clothes and equipment.

Journeys and weather
Use properly fitted and BSI standard carrycot restrainer in the back seat of car.
Never hold a baby in your arms, even if you are strapped in with regulation safety belt.
Do not keep objects in the car which could become loose on impact.
Never leave a baby unattended in the car.
Watch high winds: pram hoods can be wind traps. If necessary, pull rather than push the pram.

It is now illegal in Britain for babies to travel in the front seat of cars. BSI approved straps fixed to back seat secure this carrycot firmly.

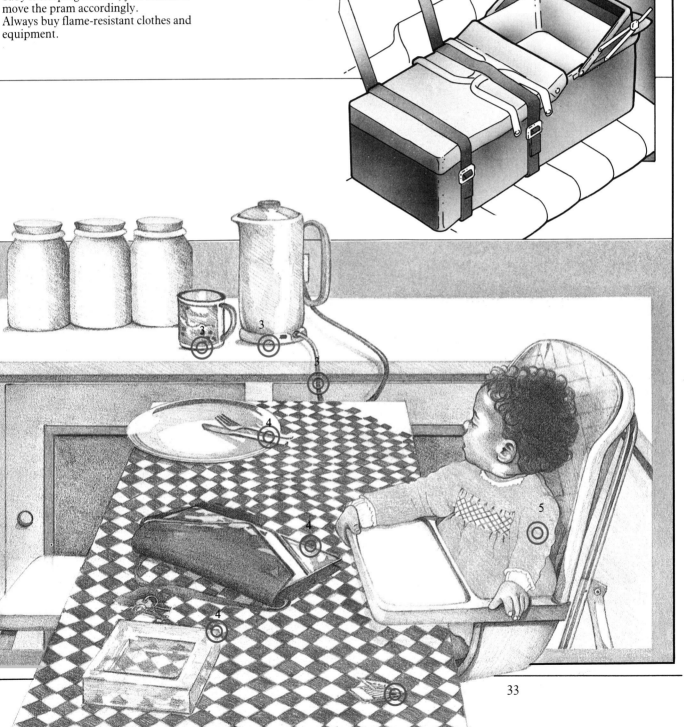

SIX TO TWELVE MONTHS

She can self feed with fingers,
sit well alone,
may be crawling, standing, walking,
can unwrap objects,
knows 'no',
tries to remove barriers,
has several teeth.

POSSIBLE DANGERS AND HOW TO PREVENT THEM

To the previous list add:

Falling

Use stairgates, playpens; buy sturdy high chair: use safety strap in high chair or buggy; do not leave her on elevated surfaces; fit window locks. A footrest on high chair means she will kick out less and reduce likelihood of toppling over.

Burning and scalding

Put guards on cookers and fires: turn pot handles in; put safety caps on electric sockets, get rid of trailing flexes, cords, tablecloths etc. Move anything dangerous out of reach on the table, i.e. hot liquids and foods. Don't leave her alone in a bath, however shallow and

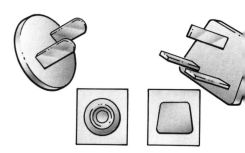

Electric sockets, windows, cupboards, doors – all are beginning to be within reach of your crawling/walking baby. Now is the time to make sure that safety covers and locks are in place. The illustrations here and far right show examples with British Standards approval.

TWELVE MONTHS TO THREE YEARS

She will stand, walk, run, climb,
understand commands and directions,
ask questions,
walk upstairs unaided,
begin to jump,
imitate parents,
explore and test limits.

POSSIBLE DANGERS AND HOW TO PREVENT THEM

To the previous list add:
Don't allow running in the house, if possible.
Don't allow her to carry glasses, glass containers. Keep stairways well lit. Encourage picking up of toys. Always hold hand when crossing street. Continue to use car safety seat appropriate for age and development. Put your own tools etc. away. Supervise all water activities–encourage swimming lessons.

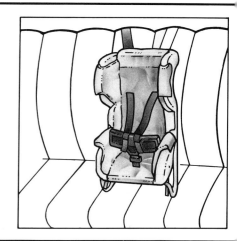

The first aid kit should contain:

telephone numbers of your doctor, the local hospital, ambulance service, health visitor and a poison centre.
- adhesive bandages of assorted sizes
- packet of safety pins
- small scissors
- crepe bandage
- cotton wool
- two triangular bandages
- non adherent dressings
- tweezers
- eye bath
- anti-histamine cream
- antiseptic cream
- thermometer (Some doctors would prefer parents not to have a thermometer as they think it causes unnecessary worry. They argue that it is usually obvious when your baby has a temperature.)

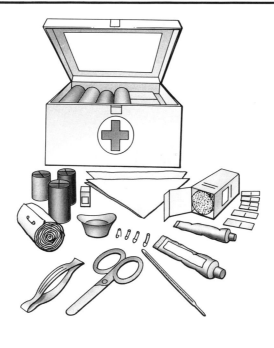

MORE SAFETY MATTERS

Although your own home may be accident proofed as much as possible, this is not always the case with other people's homes. If you visit a house regularly – grandparents' for instance – it is sensible to suggest that they keep a basic first aid kit, and also remove precious ornaments or other possible causes of accidents before you arrive. Garden ponds are a particular hazard (see page 214).

First aid kit This should be kept in a childproof locked box. If your child sees you put the key on top of the box she will be sure to climb up and see if she can open the box for herself.

Road Safety

Your child will not be going out alone under the age of five, and certainly not under the age of three. However, it's still vital to instil good pedestrian habits as soon as possible. Don't run across the road 'taking a chance' – use the zebra crossing. Don't cross behind temperate: she could drown or turn on tap. Do not leave her in bath with another small child who could turn on taps.

In the home
Pad sharp furniture corners: don't leave chairs near windows: remove rickety furniture, toppling lamps: coffee tables are dangerous – they tip and have sharp edges. They also mean that finger food is within reach (peanuts are dangerous as they can be inhaled and damage the lungs). Lower the cot mattress so that she can't climb out. Don't let her run round in socks on slippery surfaces. Check toys for loose bits, flaking paint etc. Keep pills, poisons, plastic bags, out of reach. *Never ever* put poison, gardening weedkillers, acids into a bottle the baby

may associate with a drink – e.g. old lemonade bottles. Open windows at the top not the bottom.

Make sure you
Teach the meaning of words like 'hot', 'no', keep first aid kit in the house (see below left), teach her to chew food properly, provide the freedom to explore. Make a safe area where she can crawl, explore, push, pull and tumble on to padded surfaces. She will learn to cope with danger and learn her own limits.

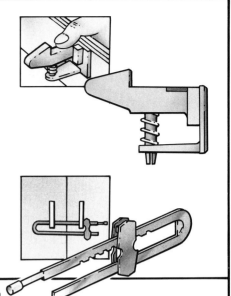

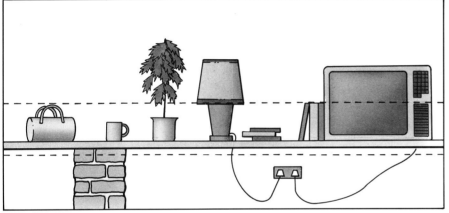

With a safety-approved car seat (far left) the 'back seat driver' is able to see what's going on while protected from sudden jolts and stops.

The physical abilities of the baby dictate the dangers she may meet. You may find it wise to rearrange your possessions further *up* the walls to levels **A** and **B** as her field of activity increases and she is exposed to further hazards.

parked cars: if you're not using a harness or reins, hold her hand (if she's holding your hand she can let go; if you are holding hers, she can't.)

Burning and fires
Children die every week from fires in the home, so this is an area of major concern as regards safety. Here are some guidelines:

DO NOT leave cooking unattended.
DO NOT keep curtains, dishcloths etc. near a flame.
DO NOT keep matches where children can find them.
DO NOT smoke cigarettes and/or leave them about when lit.
DO NOT store inflammable material.
DO NOT put ash or cigarette butts in wastepaper baskets.
DO NOT overload electrical points.
DO NOT use free-standing paraffin heaters which could be pushed over electric fires.

DO put guards round fires. A smoke detector is a safety precaution: it will give the alarm in time to get children out of danger. It should be put on a ceiling or high on a wall where smoke and heat first accumulate, and placed in the middle of a room as smoke reaches corners last. If your house has several storeys, put the detector where it can be heard in bedrooms as well as downstairs, or use more than one.

DO have a fire escape plan ready. Keep a ladder handy if you have a high level flat. Don't install double glazing which can't be broken in an emergency. If fire breaks out, don't open the door without thinking. Feel the air under the door: if it's cold, open the door cautiously, if hot, try to get out by another exit – window etc. Do not get dressed, concentrate on getting out. If the atmosphere is smoky, then crawl. The cleaner air will be closest to the floor.

The birth

Few states can have collected as many folk myths and superstitions as pregnancy and labour. Even the current abundance of articles, books and discussions on the subject can't dispel some of the mystery and the apprehension.

But few women today go into labour with little knowledge of the subject. Already you will have discussed the position in which you would prefer to give birth, attended relaxation classes, understood the reasons for some of the procedures, including episiotomy, Caesarean section, the use of forceps, and so on.

So – when the day at last comes – you will be ready, more or less. But *before* the day comes – if you are going into hospital – get your bag packed. (If you're at home for the birth your midwife will give you a list of what she wants you to have prepared.)

It is a good idea also to pack a case ready for the baby when he comes home: this will include shawl, vest, nappies, nightgown, bonnet. If your partner is absent minded, make him a list of clothes to bring into hospital for you to come home in. It has been known for fathers to forget shoes and tights, or something equally vital.

Think ahead, also, to when you come home again. Hopefully you will have help but shopping may still be difficult so now is the time to stock the larder and freezer with emergency rations.

Make sure you know the answers to these questions. How are you getting to the hospital? Ambulance, taxi (do you have the telephone number?) or car? If you are going by car, has it enough petrol? Do you know the route and the right entrance to the hospital? Do you know the telephone number? Do you have, between you, enough loose change to tell relatives what's happening? Do you have their telephone numbers?

A flask and a packet of sandwiches may do much to keep up father's morale. Labour takes some time – you can't guarantee the canteen will be open. Thus equipped, you can both sit back and wait.

HOW WILL IT START?

Labour is in three stages, although you may not always recognize when you are passing from one to another. The first stage is when the cervix is gradually being drawn up into the uterus and dilating. When the cervix is fully dilated the baby begins his journey down the birth canal and his birth comes at the end of the second stage. The third stage is the delivery of the placenta.

Labour usually begins by iself but on some occasions it is necessary for the baby to be induced – that is, for labour to be started artificially. This will be done if there is any risk to the mother or baby: perhaps of high blood pressure in the mother, or if the baby is late or seems distressed.

Induction is always planned so you will be prepared and will have the chance to talk about it with your midwife before going into hospital. There are three ways of beginning labour – either through a hormone drip in the arm, by breaking the waters (which is

The time of birth – for which the previous nine months have been a preparation – is now nearing.

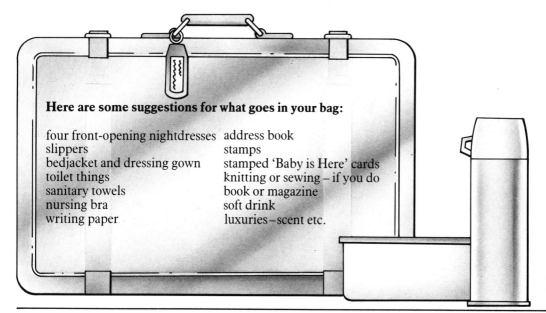

Here are some suggestions for what goes in your bag:

four front-opening nightdresses	address book
slippers	stamps
bedjacket and dressing gown	stamped 'Baby is Here' cards
toilet things	knitting or sewing – if you do
sanitary towels	book or magazine
nursing bra	soft drink
writing paper	luxuries – scent etc.

Keep the case packed – then the journey won't catch you unprepared!

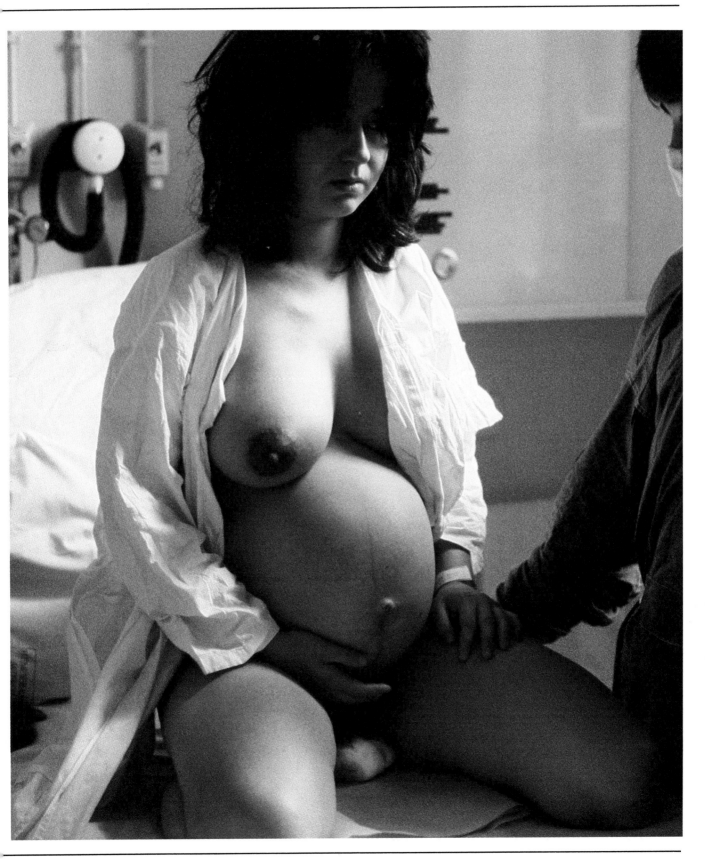

painless), or by the insertion of a pessary in the vagina. When they begin, the contractions will be strong and will not build up as they would do if labour began normally.

The first sign of normal labour may be the release of the mucus plug which has sealed off the uterus from the cervix. Another sign may be the breaking of the bag of waters surrounding the baby. You will probably have been told to ring the hospital or the midwife when this happens. When contractions begin they will feel like a tight belt being drawn round your stomach and into your back, and then being released. You may experience false labour pains (known as Braxton Hicks contractions) for some days before real labour starts, but you can judge if labour is in earnest by timing the contractions and the space between them. They need to come closer and closer together and each to last longer before you can be quite sure. You can stay at home, moving about normally, sitting or adopting any position you find best, until contractions come regularly and more freqently than every five minutes unless you have been advised differently by your hospital and need to set out earlier. Don't let the driver brake abruptly.

When you get to the hospital a midwife will go through some of the routine you are already familiar with from your antenatal clinic: taking your blood pressure, listening to your baby's heartbeat, feeling for his position. If your waters have not broken she may rupture the membranes (this is painless) and, as discussed, in some hospitals it is routine to give enemas and shave the pubic hair. This is not essential and if you do not want this you should ask for it not to be done.

You will be asked to take a shower or bath and put on a hospital gown. Many hospitals allow your partner to stay with you during all this: some do not. You will have asked before what is the procedure so you will know what may happen. Once you are bathed and ready he will stay with you and support you in any of the ways you have practised – rubbing your back, singing, even playing Scrabble!

PAIN RELIEF IN LABOUR

With a first baby, the first stage of labour usually lasts about eight to twelve hours and for most of that time you can be moving around, sitting or lying as you feel suits you best. You may be able to drink but will

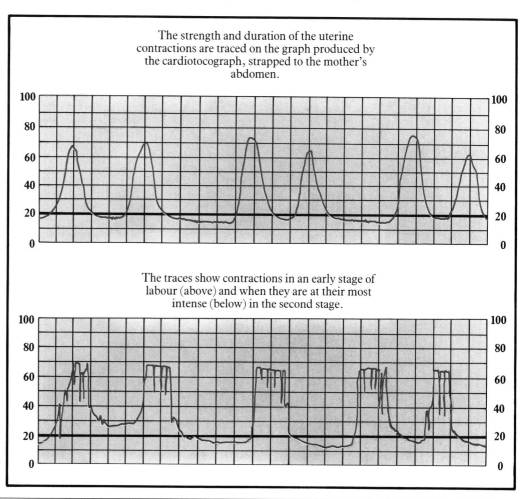

The strength and duration of the uterine contractions are traced on the graph produced by the cardiotocograph, strapped to the mother's abdomen.

The traces show contractions in an early stage of labour (above) and when they are at their most intense (below) in the second stage.

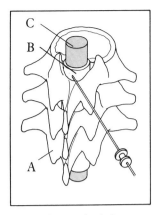

Epidural anaesthetic is injected into the space (B) between the spinal cord (C) and the bone of the vertebrae (A). The nerves carrying pain are blocked of sensation.

A mask held by the mother controls the flow of oxygen and nitrous oxide. She is able to time inhalations to give most relief as contractions reach their peak.

probably not be able to eat anything in case you need an anaesthetic later on.

The contractions gradually get stonger until the cervix is between 7 – 8 cm dilated (2.75 – 3 in). You may feel that you need pain relief as the contractions are building up in strength. Pethidine is the most widely used analgesic and is given by injection. It takes about twenty minutes to work and then the effect lasts for up to four hours. It has the effect of 'distancing' you from pain but not entirely doing away with it. The disadvantage is that it may make you feel sick or sleepy, and if given too near the delivery (within an hour or so) then the baby may be sleepy also.

Entonox is a mixture of oxygen and nitrous oxide and you administer this yourself through a hand-held mask. It takes about fifteen to twenty seconds to work so you time the moment to take it as a contraction begins. You are then able to 'ride over' the peak of the contraction as the gas is at its most effective. It has no side effects. You will probably be able to practise using the mask at antenatal clinics.

Epidural block is a method of numbing the nerves which carry the feeling of pain to the brain although the process is not available in all hospitals. A needle is inserted into a space between the spinal bones and a plastic tube threaded down the needle, which is then withdrawn. The tube remains in place and a local anaesthetic is passed down which usually results in complete pain relief. Because you can no feel contractions you will have to be told when to push and there may be a feeling of heaviness and helplessness in the legs. The anaesthetic takes about twenty minutes to work and it is most commonly used when there has been a long labour, and the mother is becoming weary and increasingly distressed.

THE FINAL STAGES

At the end of the first stage of labour you will be in transition. This is the most exciting and dramatic stage. You may find that your legs shake uncontrollably, you may find fault with the people around you – particularly the father – and even conclude that the whole business has been a mistake and you would like to go home. Contractions are now coming very close together: they may have sharp peaks and there is little pause between them. This is the time when your partner's

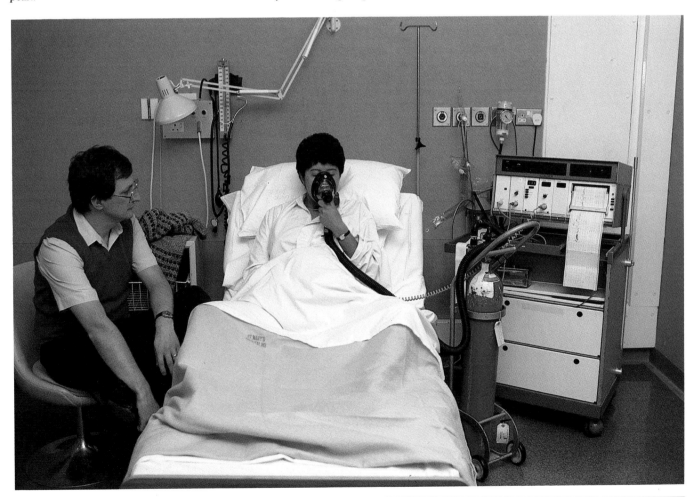

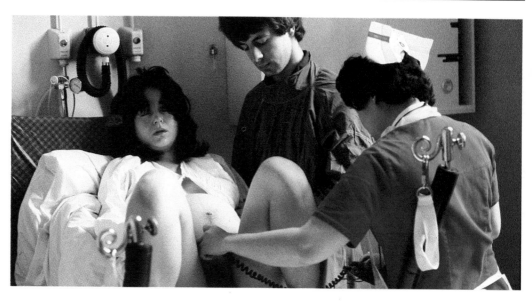

The birth is now imminent and, supported by her partner, the mother-to-be is able to relax between contractions, putting into practice the information learnt at antenatal classes. At the stage of transition her natural urge to push will help the baby on the last stages of his journey.

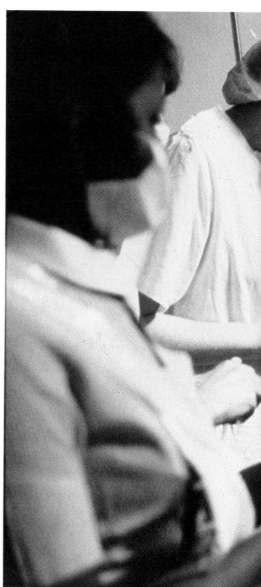

support is most valuable and necessary.

You may feel an almost uncontrollable urge to push, but may also be told to resist this which will mean that the cervix is not yet fully dilated. When you really can't control the pushing you will feel great surges of energy coming with the contractions. As soon as the cervix is 10 cm (4 in) dilated, the uterus and vagina will have become one birth canal. The desire to bear down will come with the contractions: in between you can rest.

With a first baby the second stage of labour may take one or two hours: with subsequent babies it may only last ten or fifteen minutes. The next step will be the appearance of the top of your baby's head in the vagina. It will go back between contractions but eventually the widest part will remain at the opening and you will feel stretched to your utmost. At this time you will probably be told not to push otherwise you might tear the surrounding tissue. It is now that an episiotomy (see page 42) may be performed under local anaesthetic. Your midwife or doctor checks to see that the cord is free of the neck and the baby's head slips out. At this stage you may be able to sit up and watch as the head emerges, the shoulders twist and free themselves, and the baby slithers out.

What will he look like? He may be covered in vernix, a cream-like coating which eases and protects him on his passage, his head may be moulded by his journey down a

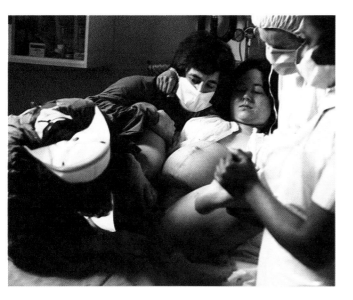
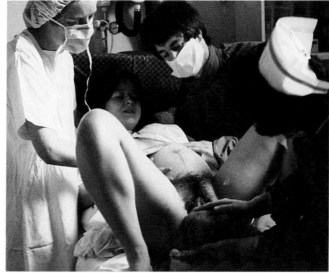

Midwife and assistant brace the mother-to-be's legs (above left) for last-moment efforts before the head is born (above).

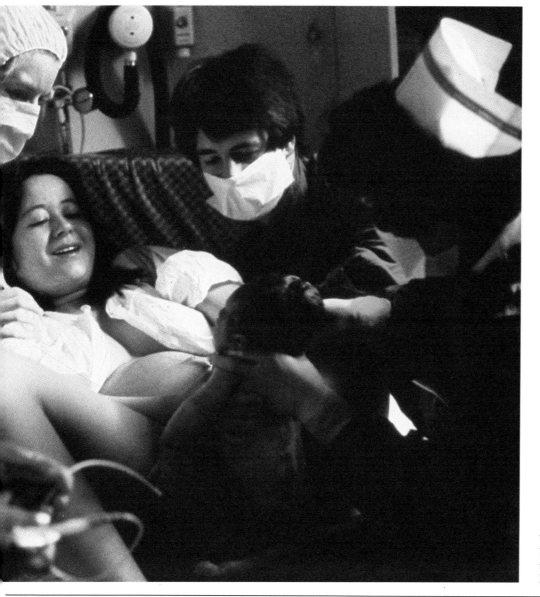

With cord still attached the baby is lifted and placed on the mother's abdomen or to her breast.

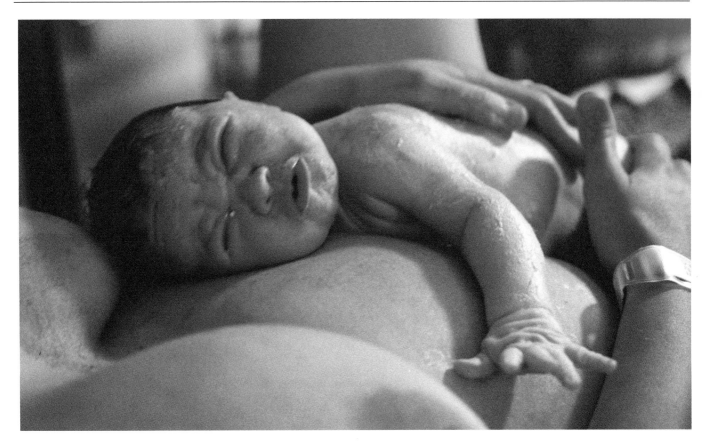

The vernix (which covers the skin of the new baby) will be naturally rubbed off, or if it hardens, may be gently washed off.

Terms you may meet during labour and birth

episiotomy: cutting of the perineum, under local anaesthetic, to make the vaginal opening bigger and to prevent tearing, as the baby is eased through. Stitches are needed afterwards. There is currently much discussion as to whether the operation is needed as often as it is performed. The position of the mother as she gives birth may make it unnecessary. Discuss with your doctor or midwife before the birth.

forceps: instrument to help the baby out of the vagina; shaped like shallow spoons which fit round the baby's head. As you push – under a local anaesthetic – the baby is gently pulled.

breech birth: when the baby arrives bottom first. This may cause no difficulties but may also be a reason for a Caesarean birth.

vacuum extraction: method of aiding delivery, possibly because the baby is becoming distressed or contractions are not strong enough. A metal cap is fixed to the baby's head and he can then be gently pulled.

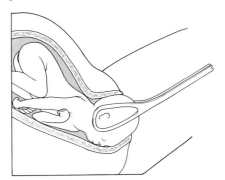

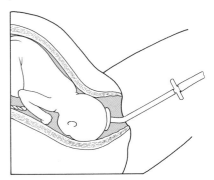

narrow passage (the baby's scalp bones are not yet joined to allow them to contract as he comes), his face will probably be puckered, his nose may be squashed, and he may be a purple colour from bruising or because he has yet to take the first breath of air which will send oxygen into his lungs. Don't be alarmed or distressed if he does not look like the ideal baby of some advertisements: he will improve rapidly!

BIRTH BY CAESAREAN SECTION
If for some reason it is necessary to deliver the baby quickly then a Caesarean section may be performed. A cut is made in the abdomen into the womb and the baby is lifted out. Usually the cut made is horizontal and low down so that it will be hidden as the pubic hair grows. The section can be done under a general anaesthetic, or by an epidural block when you remain conscious all the time but feel no pain, only sensations of pulling and lifting. A screen will be put across the lower part of your body so that you don't see what is happening but the doctor or anaesthetist will tell you what is being done. In some hospitals you'll be asked if you would like to wear headphones and listen to music to take your mind off the proceedings.

The whole operation only takes about ten

---

scalp monitor: electrode inserted through the cervix and clipped to the baby's scalp. Connected to a machine which shows the baby's heartbeat, it is used to check that the baby is getting enough oxygen.

electronic fetal monitoring: methods to check fetal heartbeat and the uterine contractions. A scalp monitor may be used (see above), or a small machine may be strapped to the mother's abdomen which records the fetal heart rate while a second small unit also strapped to the abdomen records uterine contractions.

pain relief: epidural block, pethidine, entonox – see main text. See also next two entries.

hypnosis: the method is not widely available so you may have to find out for yourself where to be taught the technique. Talk it over first with your midwife or doctor. For address for enquiries see page 230.

acupuncture: technique of relieving pain through the insertion of small needles into key points of the body. Not all hospitals or doctors would agree to the method being used in labour but there is increasing interest in the subject and some doctors are qualified acupuncturists. Address for details on page 230.

---

minutes and the advantage of the epidural block is that you can see and hold your baby straight away. Some obstetricians will let the father stay in the room, others won't. After a Caesarean it is necessary to stay in hospital for about ten days and there will be a certain discomfort from the wound.

THE BABY'S FIRST MINUTES
It is now the custom for your baby to be put on your stomach or handed to you to cuddle even while he is still attached by the cord. Tidying up can wait. When the cord has stopped pulsating, it will be cut and tied. The baby may be weighed and he may have needed his respiratory tract sucked free of mucus. He will be rated according to what is called the Apgar scale. His breathing, heart rate, skin colour, muscle tone and reflex response are observed. Five minutes later, these are observed and noted down again. His weight and length are recorded, the size of his head noted, a check made to see that his palate is whole and his legs bent and gently circled to make sure there is no dislocation of the hip. Sometimes these tests are made close to the mother so that she can see what is happening and ask the doctor anything she wants to know.

After the birth, or perhaps just before, you will be given an injection in the thigh to help the womb contract. The placenta shears away from the wall of the womb and is expelled, probably with another push from you, and helped by the midwife pulling gently on the cord.

After these immediate routine tasks are done it is becoming usual for mother, father and baby to be left together to become acquainted. If your baby is born at home, many of the constraints of a hospital delivery will not, of course, apply.

Much emphasis has recently been placed on the 'bonding' process when parents and child first learn to know each other. It is agreed that learning to love your baby – which does not come with an automatic rush – is strengthened and hastened by these early moments of contact. You will probably want to hold your baby immediately after birth – not be taken away to another room or see him banished to a cot. But because this is so obvious and natural a reaction, it could be that parents who for some reason are not able to have this early contact could fear that they will never make such a deep relationship with their baby. It sometimes seems that every positive reaction has a negative converse! The chances are that you will both begin your love affair with your baby when, within seconds of his arrival, he is placed in your arms. If this is delayed, don't worry – much has been written recently about the

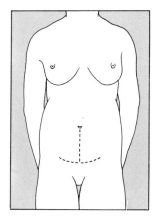

The sites of cuts for Caesarean birth – either transverse, below the pubic hair, or vertical.

importance of bonding, but in fact it is highly unlikely that any delay will brand you both for life! Your affection will surely be strong enough to bridge that gap of waiting? If your baby has for some reason to be kept in an intensive care unit, you will find the staff will be sensitive to your feelings. Many hospitals set up a television screen by the mother's bed, so that she can watch her baby in another room.

One hospital – Wycombe General Hospital, High Wycombe, Buckinghamshire – has facilities for the majority of mothers to be admitted to the Special Care Unit with their sick or premature newborn babies. Parents are increasingly being allowed to take part in the nursing care of their newborn babies.

Getting to know each other. In the first moments after birth, father, mother and baby are left alone to make each other's acquaintance.

Monitored constantly by sophisticated equipment, most premature babies now survive to healthy childhood.

DAILY CARE

For nine months as parents-to-be, you have been objects of interest and even glamour to your relations and friends. The adjective 'glamorous' may seem far from accurate as, wearied and hampered, the mother-to-be enters the last few weeks of pregnancy. Yet a pregnant woman is glamorous, carrying as she does that mysterious quality of giving birth. Daily there are enquiries about her health, her well-being. She arouses interest, concern, and she provokes and receives care.

Then the baby is born. 'It' becomes 'he' or 'she'. Cards, flowers, gifts arrive. Friends come to admire, exclaim, perhaps envy. Heads peer into the pram, there is excitement and affection. She is still at the centre of the universe.

That's mother.

And father? Hopefully he will have been home for the first week or two to share the new responsibilities. Particularly with the first baby it will be a time of happiness and heightened emotions. And then, quite suddenly, the visitors depart, gifts stop arriving and father goes back to work.

And mother is left holding the baby.

And overwhelmingly it may hit her just what she's let herself in for. Even if she intends going back to work outside the home there will be some weeks of maternity leave left. How cosy the outlook had previously seemed – and now in reality it may appear terrifying, boring and endless. Your baby may sleep from one feed to the next, go through the night without waking, and take his feeds like clockwork: you may feel for him that complicated mixture of love, pity and protectiveness that a young baby arouses: you may be coping admirably, recovering your strength and your figure ... and yet, and yet, unaccountably the suspicion may lie almost dormant in your mind: 'Is this *all*?' Feed, wash, push the pram, cook, do your exercises ... overnight you wonder if you've turned from a person into a function.

And father?

Father is back at work. He has bored everyone to death with the photographs, expounded on childbirth as if he were a professor of obstetrics, described in detail how *he* reacted to the birth ... but on the way home, does the jauntiness fade a little? Naturally he hopes to see the baby before he goes to bed – although there is always the late feed to make up for it if he happens to miss him earlier in the evening ... and it would be convenient if he could see the next instalment of the television serial from a static armchair instead of pacing about with his son's decibels interrupting the plot. Of course the baby will be much more interesting when he does more than burp, cry, sleep and leak at both ends ... meanwhile, has his wife turned mysteriously and suddenly into a mother who spends her entire evening looking harrassed while she catches up in the kitchen on all the jobs she has been unable to fit in during the day? Togetherness flew out of the window as the stork flew in.

There are a lot of shifting patterns taking place: changes, anxieties, new preoccupations, uncertainties ...

The chapters in this section are about some of the changes taking place in a family to which a new baby – and the first makes the most difference – has been born. We talk also about practical matters – how teeth grow, how to feed your baby, how to cope with bedtime – but the first pages explain and explore what the new

parents may be feeling. Helpless? Insecure? Somewhat let down and – particularly the mother – lonely and no longer carefree? If you experience some of these emotions you are not alone: the feelings of weariness, bewilderment and, possibly at times, downright unhappiness, of new parent-hood, are almost universal. Acknowledge that you may need outside help. Acknowledge boredom, acknowledge depression and you are more than half way to conquering them. Because conquer them you will.

Meanwhile the cause of all these complicated reactions is lying passive with a smug smile on his face. 'Only wind, dear,' says your mother. 'Young babies don't really smile ...'

Who says they don't?

The first months

EARLY DAYS

Ever felt the whole thing was a mistake? No-one wants to spoil the pleasure of parents-to-be in their coming baby with warnings of gloom to come, but all the same it does help to know in advance some of the realities of having a baby in the home.

It is natural to look on birth as the climax of pregnancy and to forget that it is at the same time the beginning of a new life; for all the family.

For the moment, let's concentrate on the mother. For the first few weeks she will still be recovering physically and emotionally from labour and birth. She may be sore when she sits down and, until the milk flow has regulated itself, she may have the added embarrassment of 'leaking', so that she feels despairingly that she is not even in control of her own functions. Her figure is not yet back to normal, daytime jobs go on into the evening, and even if the baby reacts 'just like the book' to feeds and sleep, he still makes an incredible amount of work.

She sleeps with one ear open. If the baby cries she thinks he must be ill (that is, she must be doing something wrong) and if he doesn't, maybe he's too ill to cry? Standards of housekeeping and cooking have fallen; going out is like moving an army. If she runs out of some household necessity she can't just pop out to the shops. A friend has offered to baby-sit while she and father go out for a candlelit supper, but all the time she knows she would rather have had one long, uninterrupted sleep and she hasn't anything to talk about anyway – except the baby. Tiredness is a way of life. Moreover, the baby down the road looks prettier.

The psychiatrists call it maternal preoccupation. And the good news is that it all gets better.

Some of the intensity will fade as you begin to feel physically better and as the baby settles into a routine. You may not much care for the routine but at least you'll know what to expect. By the time your baby is a few months old life will be quite different: there will still be the work but there will also be the pleasure of a responding, growing baby. And you will have grown more used to your new life. But in the meantime...?

If your seat is sore, always sit on a cushion or rubber ring; putting a handful of salt in your bath also helps. Your milk supply will regulate itself but in the meantime you can wear breast pads or tuck lint inside your bra.

It is natural to look on birth as the climax of pregnancy and forget that it is at the same time the beginning of a new life for all the family.

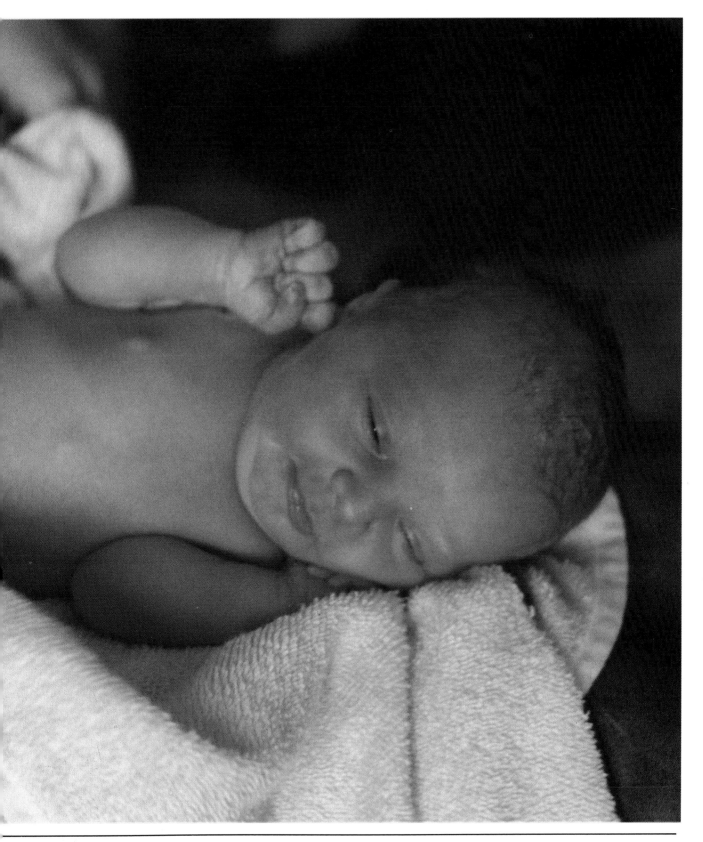

Don't let the pads get soggy or you'll get sore.

Limit your visitors or, if you want their company, make use of them. Forget the pre-baby days when you cooked special meals and generally waited on guests – instead, ask if they will bring in some shopping on the way to you. If a relative or friend comes to stay to help you, make sure she (or he) does just that. Suggest dividing the chores between you: you do the cooking, she does the shopping or vice versa. She takes the baby for a walk while you do something else (like having a sleep) or you go shopping and she looks after the baby.

This is not selfish; it's sensible. The health of the family often depends on the health and attitude of the mother – so look after yourself.

If you are offered help, take it. And if you can afford a home help then employ one.

All this is not to overlook the primary help giver – the father – whose support, encouragement and practical aid will undoubtedly contribute overwhelmingly to the well-being of all the family.

Most homes are run to some sort of routine with a settled order of housework, cooking and shopping. Now's the time to think of the end result you need and, if necessary, plan a different routine, lowering standards if you find them unrealistic.

A comfortable home needs adequate warmth, enjoyable meals, reasonable tidiness, clean clothes to wear and mostly good-tempered inhabitants. Get the first four right and you are well on the way to the fifth: unless you make a martyr of yourself. What the new mother may feel she's doing is conducting some sort of orchestra where all three members only occasionally play together – but when those times come, relax and enjoy the music!

An untidy house can make you feel you are losing control. If possible isolate the baby equipment – nappies, clothes and so on – to one room, so that it does not take over the whole house. Your baby may not have his own room but if you can keep one room in the house – kitchen, living room or wherever – reasonably tidy then you will always know that there is at least one oasis of gracious living around for the unexpected visitor. If you know that your baby is likely to be restless during the morning, and that you will not get around to vacuuming until after mid-day (and this worries you), try doing it last thing at night. You could do it while your partner bottle-feeds or he could while you breast-feed. It need only take a few minutes, need not be turned into a performance, and you will begin the next day feeling on top of things. You could also lay the breakfast table

the night before.

If it sounds like hard work remember that you would be doing these jobs anyway – you are only doing them at different times.

An automatic washing machine is a lovely thing. If you have one, can you trust it enough to put the washing in last thing at night before you go to bed, knowing that you will come down in the morning, not to an indoor swimming pool in the kitchen, but to

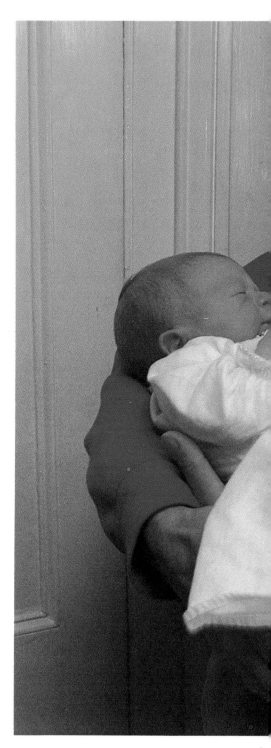

a load of clean washing, some of it ready for ironing (if you really need to iron)? If you haven't a machine can you visit the launderette, say twice a week, to coincide with shopping, meanwhile keeping the baby washing down daily?

For a while you may have to forget the sauces and the soufflés. On the other hand, if you have a nice cooperative baby who always sleeps during the evening, and if you enjoy cooking and the evening meal has always been one of the highlights of your time together, then cook as usual. But don't think you must, just to show you can cope: do it because you both enjoy the product.

Most partners will quite willingly take on some of the evening chores like giving a feed or finishing off the meal, if they know what they are meant to be cooking, and it is there to cook. Be methodical about stores: you

Getting to know each other. A father does not always have the same opportunity to be with his baby as the child's mother – so time together is doubly important.

Should I exercise after baby is born?
Labour has been hard work for your body; muscles have been working intensely and if they are allowed to remain stretched and weak they will take longer to recuperate. By beginning postnatal exercise as soon as twenty-four hours after your baby's birth you will be helping them to regain elasticity and your figure to return to normal. Don't be discouraged if at first you seem to make little progress: practising little and often is the answer. One of the most essential exercises is learning sphincter control. Sphincters are rings of muscles that can be made to contract – this is what happens when you control a bowel movement or stop a urine flow. Practise this latter whenever you have the opportunity – it's particularly encouraging because you know when you're succeeding!

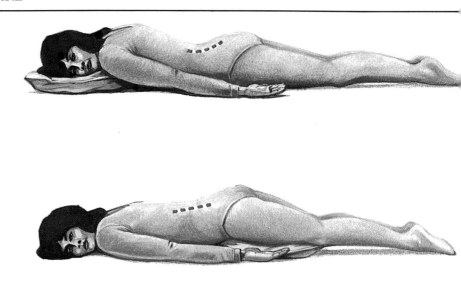

Stretched during delivery, the vaginal outlet will recuperate more quickly if helped by exercise. Pelvic floor control is one of the most essential exercises to learn – and can be practised on many occasions – standing, waiting in queues, squatting for housework, when you're ironing or sitting. To practise, lie on your back with your legs apart and, breathing normally, concentrate on the area surrounding the vagina and urethra; draw up the pelvic floor tightening the sphincter and feeling the inside passage tense. Hold each time for about two seconds and do only two or three at a time to start with. You can gradually work up to fifty a day. If you've had stiches you'll find it more comfortable to do this exercise while lying on your front.

To stengthen your back muscles, kneel with head lowered and back rounded and bring one knee up as close as possible to your head, pulling in the stomach and vaginal muscles. Kick your leg back and up, raising your head and keeping your hips parallel to the floor. Bring the leg back, then change to the other leg, repeating three times and working up to seven or eight times.

Twice a day for half an hour, try to rest on your stomach (left). If you've had stitches you'll find this particularly comfortable. It also helps to relieve back strain, but you'll need a pillow under hips to prevent that 'sagging feeling' which will hollow your back and undo the potential good.

If your breasts are tender (below), put one pillow under your head to support them and two under your hips to keep the pelvic tilt correct. A pillow under your legs will also be comfortable.

Don't do this – it hollows your back and can strain the back ligaments.

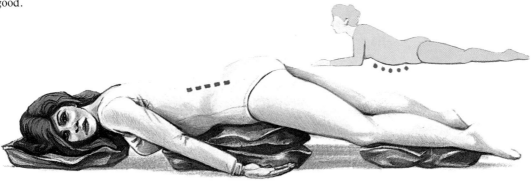

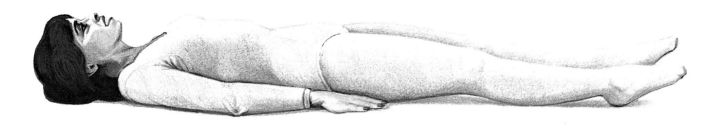

This exercise will help to trim and tone your waist. Begin by doing it once or twice then gradually work up to doing each seven or eight times.

With feet apart and arms stretched and clasped above your head, tighten your stomach muscles, trying not to arch your lower back or bend forward.

Curve to the right, keeping your back straight and stretching from your waist. Bounce gently up to four times.

Repeat the same exercise, bending slowly to the other side. Remember to keep your arms straight and your hands clasped.

Check with your doctor that this is a suitable exercise for your baby and don't begin until he is able to support his head strongly (about six months). His chest should be on your knees and his hands firmly held. Raise your feet slightly as you gently stretch his arms out sideways. Lower your legs and bring his hands in to meet. Stop if he doesn't like it and do not in any case repeat the exercise more than three or four times.

53

may not be able to shop every day (if that has been your custom), so you could shop once a week, or less frequently if funds allow. Deliveries to the door are a godsend, so don't forget the man who probably calls every day: the milkman. You will find he very likely carries any number of essentials you had not previously thought of buying from him.

Make good use of frozen foods and convenience foods and if you have a freezer then cook several batches of food at a time. Stewing steak, for instance, can be a casserole, ingredients for a pie, have wine added, be mixed with various sauces or vegetables – the varieties are as endless as are today's cookery books. There is no need to wait until the evening to prepare food: do it during the day if you have time, then you won't be rushed at the last minute when everything may seem to be happening at once. Slow cooking – either in a special cooker or as stew or casserole in the oven – is one good way of coping: the meal will not get over-cooked if you are delayed by the baby. On the other hand, you could get tired of casseroles and rice pudding ... so ring the changes. Another alternative – more expensive – is to have a grill and salad.

If you can get into the habit of preparing one good, cooked meal a day like this – your pattern might be that you eat mid-day – it will help when your baby begins on solids since appropriate food cooked for adults can also be used for the baby (see page 81).

For the first few weeks your baby will no doubt wake in the night for a feed. If this happens at about two in the morning, and he then wakes again at five or six, you will not be getting long periods of sleep. During the day, take every opportunity you can to rest or have a nap. If the baby settles well during the morning, but is wakeful during the night or evening then there's nothing sinful about having a morning sleep yourself. If you know that the evening meal is under control, the house is reasonably clean and there are nappies in the cupboard, you could sleep the sleep of the just whatever the time on the clock. At least the feed times anchor you to a chair – hopefully with your feet up and the phone off the hook.

Naturally you will want to give your baby your attention at feed times, but as you both become more relaxed about it there is no harm in catching up on your reading at the same time. One young mother fulfilled a

Opposite Here's something to look forward to! At first it may seem as if your baby is taking up every minute of your time and the broad analysis of a typical mother's day shown here confirms this. A glance at the other two charts shows how the pattern changes at six months and two years, creating more time for the mother to enjoy for herself.

Take advantage in the early days of every opportunity to rest. If the baby sleeps, then you sleep too. Enough rest in these early days is invaluable.

New baby

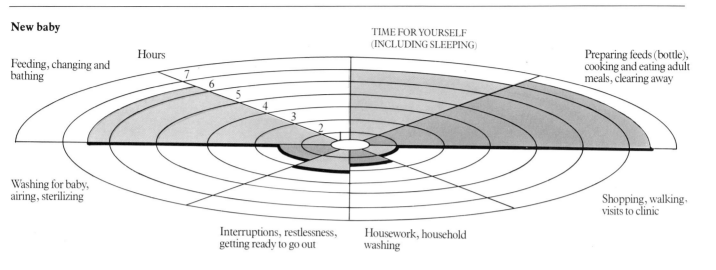

Hours

TIME FOR YOURSELF
(INCLUDING SLEEPING)

Feeding, changing and
bathing

Preparing feeds (bottle),
cooking and eating adult
meals, clearing away

Washing for baby,
airing, sterilizing

Shopping, walking,
visits to clinic

Interruptions, restlessness,
getting ready to go out

Housework, household
washing

At six months

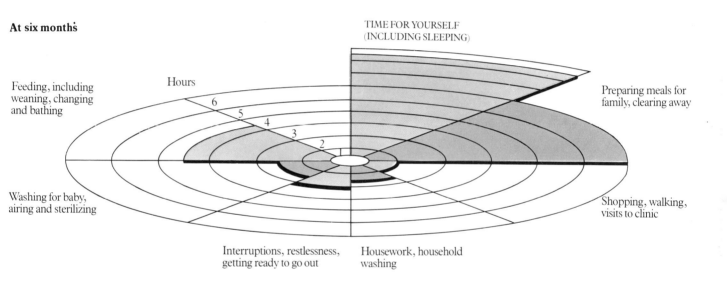

Hours

TIME FOR YOURSELF
(INCLUDING SLEEPING)

Feeding, including
weaning, changing
and bathing

Preparing meals for
family, clearing away

Washing for baby,
airing and sterilizing

Shopping, walking,
visits to clinic

Interruptions, restlessness,
getting ready to go out

Housework, household
washing

At two years

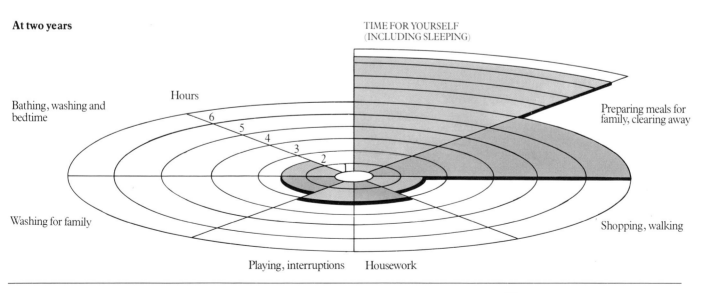

Hours

TIME FOR YOURSELF
(INCLUDING SLEEPING)

Bathing, washing and
bedtime

Preparing meals for
family, clearing away

Washing for family

Shopping, walking

Playing, interruptions

Housework

lifetime ambition while feeding her first baby: she read *War and Peace*. He slept soundly for the whole of the Battle of Austerlitz.

Do not expect your baby to behave like a mechanical doll. He will soon show his own preferences, his own happy times and the times when he is rather more restless. It is possible (see page 93) gradually to help him into a routine which fits in with the family, but this will not happen at once. From two months onwards, when he is beginning to respond more and 'become a person', it will be very much easier to integrate him into your own life. He will enjoy company – especially yours – and be happy to watch you from a bouncing cradle or carrycot, where he can be propped up a little so that he can see what's going on. He will enjoy outings, watch mobiles, begin to reach out for cot toys. For a while the new mother is wise to be content to take life at a slower pace. Once he becomes mobile, she will get all the exercise she needs!

In these early days, your health visitor may well become your lifeline to sanity. She will help with feedings, questions, problems and generally provide invaluable support of encouragement and advice. But another invaluable support will be the relationship between you both as parents. The first few months of a baby's life are when mutual reassurance and praise can make the difference between happiness and depression. The mother needs to be told she is coping – and that she is still desirable and attractive as a woman: she needs to be cared for and looked after. That may sound something of a tall order for father only now getting used to his own new role. However, days spent alone with a baby can seem very long for a woman and, for a while, it may be that her partner's concern for her will be the only reassurance she has that she is valued and interesting, apart from her function as a mother.

SKINCARE

At birth your baby will probably be covered with a greasy white substance called vernix, which is made up of sloughed skin cells and oil from glands in the skin. Usually this is washed off by the midwife, or it will be left to dry out and wear away.

Your baby is pale and slightly bluish in colour because there is only a small amount of blood coming to the skin, and a decreased amount of oxygen in that blood. As your baby breathes, more blood flows to the skin and his colour becomes pinker. After some hours his colour is much improved. Skin textures vary from one baby to another:

Here are some minor imperfections you may notice on your new baby's skin.

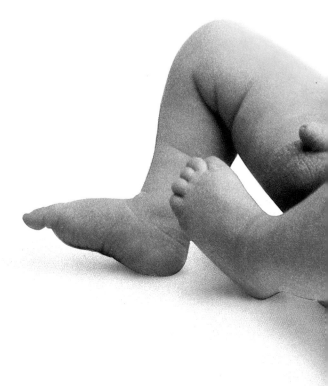

Stork marks
(Hemangiomas) – flat red blotches on the nape of the neck, forehead or bridge of the nose and the majority disappear during the first few months. Some may be soft and raised with a texture like a strawberry, and others may be large, deep red patches called port wine stains. Strawberry marks virtually always disappear spontaneously; port wine stains do not. These too are generally harmless, but your doctor can determine the significance of such marks. Most require no treatment.

Freckles – similar to moles but lighter and always flat. Caused by cells making too much pigment which is activated after exposure to sun. Moles do not change but more freckles may appear with frequent sun exposure.

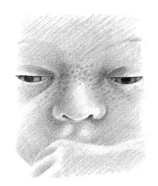

Skin tags – small protrusions of skin usually on the trunk or in the folds of skin. They are the same colour as the surrounding skin, are not painful or harmful, but can be injured because they protrude from the skin. Can be surgically removed with a local anaesthetic at any age.

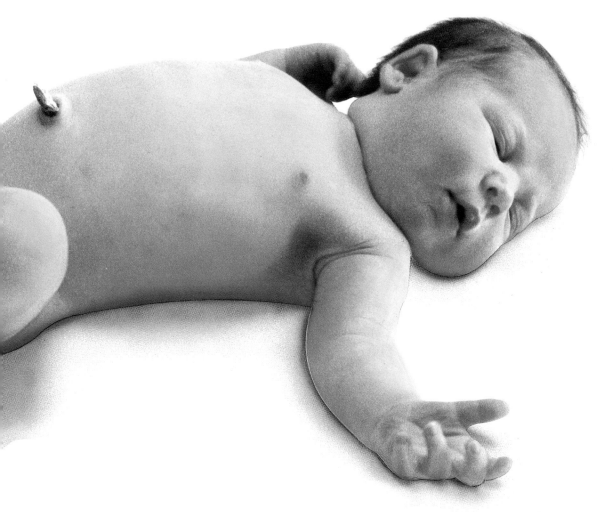

Mongolian spots (no connection with mongolism or Down's Syndrome) – may be mistaken for bruises. They are flat, bluish-grey spots, usually 2 cm (1 in) in diameter and most often appear on the lower back. May occur in groups of three to five and have indistinct borders. Occur most often in dark-skinned races and fade in time.

Moles – dense collections of cells producing a pigment. May be flat or dome shaped, sometimes with hair growing from them. If situated where clothing causes friction they should be removed because they may become malignant. They are also sometimes removed for cosmetic reasons, but otherwise need no treatment in childhood.

The illustration shows the typically wrinkled skin on the soles of the feet of a full-term baby.

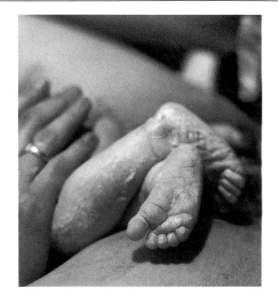

premature babies have a smoother, thinner skin than the full-term babies whose skin is thicker, and who have prominent wrinkles on the palms of their hands and soles of their feet. Late babies may have skin almost like parchment – cracked and peeling – and there may be deeper creases on the soles and palms, while the skin itself is quite dry.

Over the next few days your baby's skin will change dramatically. The outer layer will dry out, flake and peel, and the next layer will come to the surface: this will be the soft skin for which babies are renowned. The skin will stay soft for a year or two, and then gradually thicken as he grows.

You may worry that your baby's head has a peculiar shape – rather more pointed than you had expected (see picture), but this is caused by the tight passage that the baby has passed through. The bones of the skull overlap so that they can slide together to make the passage of his head easier. Pressure against the scalp during delivery sometimes causes tiny blood vessels to burst and bleed in the space between the scalp and skull, resulting in a soft swollen area called a cephalhaematoma. Although this may look alarming it is absolutely harmless and requires no treatment: the bleeding stops by itself and the blood is reabsorbed. The moulded head also corrects itself into a more conventional shape in one or two weeks.

Some babies are born with a full head of hair and others are nearly bald. The hair at birth is not permanent growing hair: it often changes its characteristics quite dramatically as the baby grows older. A normal head of hair usually develops by the age of two.

The hormones in your body during pregnancy can cause enlargement of the breasts in both sexes, and in the genitals of baby girls. Sometimes the breasts secrete a milk and the

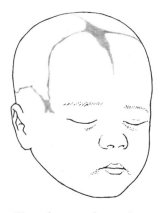

The soft spot or fontanelle on your baby's head allows the bones of the skull to overlap during its tight passage down the birth canal. The baby's head may be moulded to a point by its journey but it will regain a more usual shape in a week or two.

enlargement may persist for several weeks before subsiding as the hormones gradually disappear. No treatment is necessary: do not squeeze or massage the breasts – it will not do any good and it may promote infection. The enlargement of the baby girl's genitals is also temporary although the hormone effect may be so strong as to cause her to menstruate with some blood-tinged discharge.

Fingernails may be neat or so long as to need trimming with blunt-ended manicure scissors. Your baby could accidentally scratch himself if his nails are too long, but wait until he is relaxed – after a feed perhaps – before trimming them, or trim them while he is asleep.

At birth, your baby may have numerous tiny white spots over the nose, chin and forehead. They are called milia and are caused by blocked oil glands. They need no treatment and soon clear up. Other imperfections of the skin which may appear are shown on pages 56-7.

Common disorders
From about two to fifteen months the most common skin problem your child is likely to have is *nappy rash*. Initially a reddened skin in the nappy area, as the rash progresses the skin becomes more intensely red and develops a bumpy texture. Small pustules may develop and the rash become infected.

The major cause is prolonged contact of the skin with a wet nappy, but inadequate rinsing of detergents or washing powders may be responsible. Change the nappy frequently or leave the nappy off, particularly

Always use round-ended scissors to cut your baby's nails. It is safer to do it when the baby is asleep. If the nails are still sharp, mittens will prevent him from scratching himself.

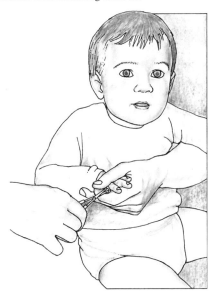

when your baby is in the open air. When you change the nappy, thoroughly clean the baby's bottom with a wet cloth or swab and pat him dry. The use of baby powder is controversial – it is dangerous if inhaled, so keep the tin out of your baby's reach. If you decide to use powder, choose the medicated kind and apply by sprinkling it first on your hand, and then spreading it in a thin film on the affected parts.

As a general rule any rash with a fever is caused by an infection until proved otherwise. The majority of these are mild and of short duration, but you should consult your doctor all the same. Meanwhile sponging down with tepid water will make the child more comfortable, and will not prevent diagnosis of the illness.

Eczema may be due to contact with a substance (laundry detergent remaining in the clothes, metals used in some jewellery, or a specific material such as wool) or an article of diet (see Allergies, page 206).

You will find that for every substance there is at least someone somewhere whose skin will find it irritating: if it can be identified it should be removed but this may be very difficult.

Skin injuries

The most common skin problems occur at a later stage and are those accidentally inflicted on himself by a toddler – cuts, scrapes, bruises and bumps. Treatment is often unnecessary but some rules to help are:

Any knock to the head should be taken seriously, especially if accompanied by headaches, sleepiness or nausea. Consult your doctor for advice.

Abrasions should be cleaned and a sterile protective dressing applied. (See page 206 for further details.)

Cuts should be cleaned and bandage applied to bring the edges of the wound together. If deep, a cut may need stitches – this can usually be recognized if the edges of the cut will not meet unless pressure is exerted to bring them together.

A penetrating wound – such as from a thorn or animal bite may require treatment to prevent tetanus.

With proper attention, most of these problems to your child's skin can be avoided. Cleanliness alone will prevent many of them, and appropriate action will limit others. Your child's skin is really a durable body covering and requires minimal care.

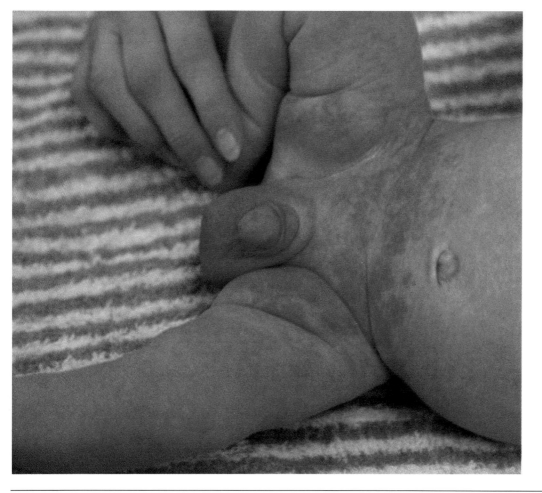

Fresh air and sunlight are the best cures for nappy rash. If the rash is severe antibiotic cream will help.

What about bathing?

It used to be the practice to bath a baby everyday – but towel bathing or topping and tailing is quite adequate. You don't even have to put the baby in the bath.

When towel bathing, hold the baby securely on your lap and remove only the minimum amount of clothing. As you sponge pay particular attention to the skin creases; you can sponge the baby's hair and gently rub dry before you put on the vest.

Topping and tailing is even quicker and is a good way of washing your baby with the minimum of disturbance. In both cases use cream around the nappy area sparingly and only when necessary.

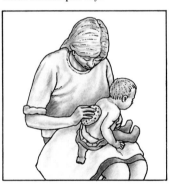
1

TOWEL BATHING	**TOPPING AND TAILING**
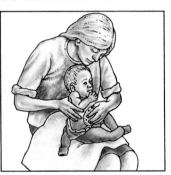	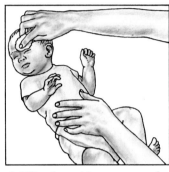
1. Soap the baby's front and then rinse off and pat dry.	1. Wipe face with separate swab of lint for each eye. Dry.
	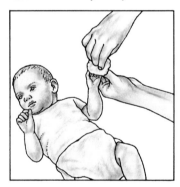
2. Soap the back as you lean your baby forward. Rinse and dry.	2. Wipe hands with fresh swab of lint.
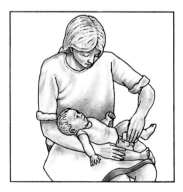	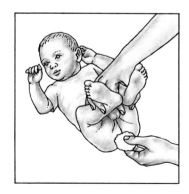
3. Dress in vest and soap bottom and then legs and feet. Rinse and dry.	3. Remove nappy and holding feet securely use cotton wool to clean soiled area.

5

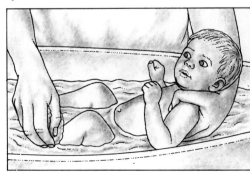

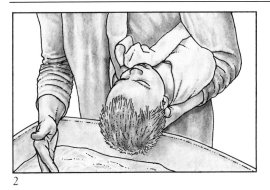

2

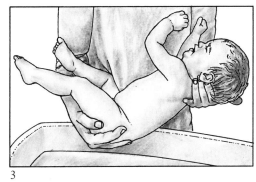

3

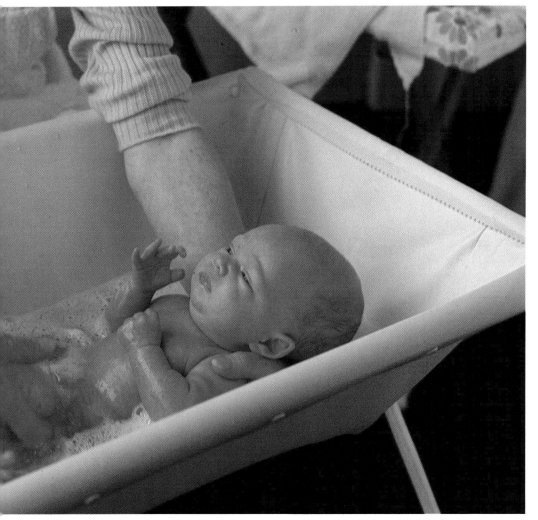

6

7

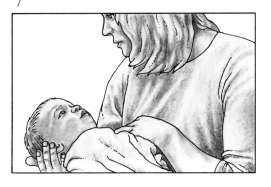

GIVING YOUR BABY A BATH

First, gather everything you'll need. Make sure the room is warm enough – between 24 and 27°C (75 to 80°F). Put cold water first into bath, then warm. Test the temperature with your elbow. The water should feel neither too hot, nor too cold.

1. Wrap your baby in a towel and wipe each eye with a separate piece of lint; then each side of face.

2. Holding your baby along your left arm as shown, wash hair backwards over the bath. Rinse and dry.

3. Unwrap and gently lower the baby into the water taking care to support him as shown.

4. With your arm supporting his head and your hand holding his upper arm, gently wash and rinse his body.

5. Continue washing and rinsing while you smile and talk to your baby to reassure him all is well.

6. Lift him out supporting his head and bottom so he cannot wriggle free. Lay him on a towel.

7. Wrap up and cuddle your baby while he is being dried. Pay particular attention to all the creases.

What about the nappy?

Of the many ways of folding towelling nappies here are four, two for smaller babies and two for larger. Try them all to discover which method suits you best. The stages are numbered and quite easy to follow but in case of doubt here are the instructions for each method shown.

The triangle method – less bulky for a new baby
1. Fold the top half over the lower
2. Fold down the top double thickness
3. Add liner, bring the point up
between the legs and fasten with one pin

The parallel fold – suitable for a larger baby
1. Fold top and bottom points to overlap
2 and 3. Fold in the sides level with the top edge
4. Add liner, bring the lower section up between the legs and pin both sides

The triple absorbent fold – for a young baby
1 and 2. Fold nappy into four and pull out top layer
3. Turn the nappy over from left to right
4 and 5. Fold in twice the two middle layers to make a thick panel in the centre
6. Add liner and fold up between legs and pin

The triangle method

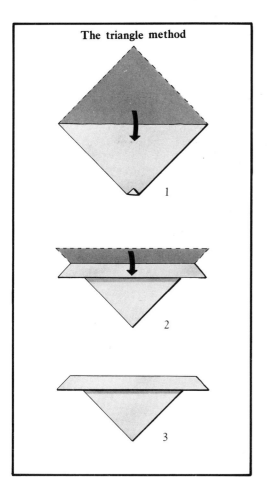

The parallel method

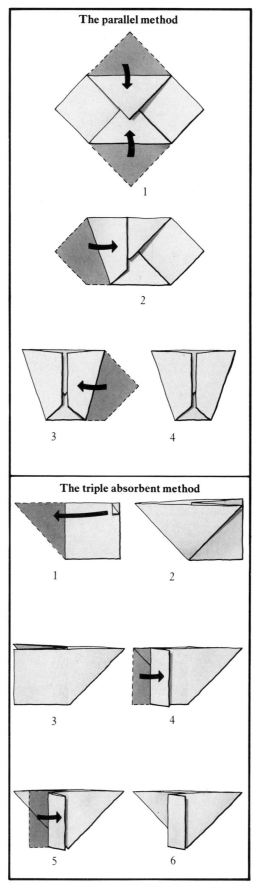

The triple absorbent method

The kite method

The kite method – suitable for a larger baby
1. From a diamond shape fold in the corners in the order shown
2. Fold up the narrowest point, add liner and bring the point up between the legs and pin

What about changing and dressing?

Shown right is a range of nappies and pants available. Towelling nappies can be bought ready-shaped. Protective pants can be one piece to tie at the sides, or to pull on with or without fasteners. Disposable nappies (far right) can be used with pants designed for them, or bought as more expensive 'all-in-ones'. The examples shown are as follows:

1. Muslin nappy
2. Shaped towelling nappy
3. Towelling nappy
4. One-piece tie-on plastic pants
5. Pull-on plastic pants
6. Plastic pants with pop fasteners
7. Disposable with tie-on plastic pants
8. Disposable and pants all-in-one
9. Disposable with popper pants
10. Disposable all-in-one with elasticated legs

Be careful about where you decide to change and dress you child. Even a new baby can wriggle quickly to the edge of a dangerous drop while your back is turned. You need a firm flat surface: a bed or the floor is suitable for dressing, but a padded and waterproof mat is better for changing. A mobile strung above the dressing and changing area will help to divert the baby's attention.

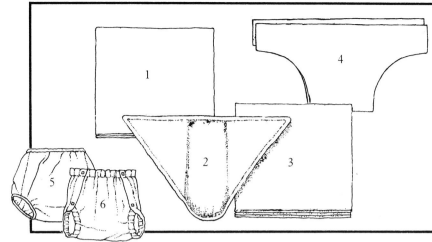

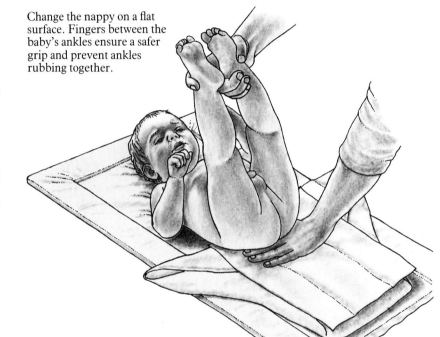

Change the nappy on a flat surface. Fingers between the baby's ankles ensure a safer grip and prevent ankles rubbing together.

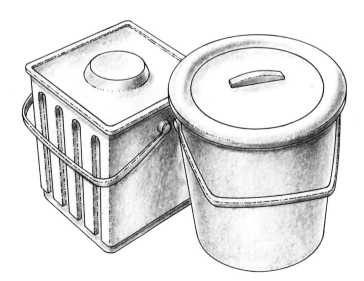

Soiled nappies should be put in a bucket of cold water to which a sterilizing agent has been added – allow to soak for the time stated. Change the water daily. Wash on 'hot' in a washing machine or by hand with hot water detergent. Rinse very well. Wet nappies can be put into a separate bucket of cold water. They need only be well rinsed and then dried.

It can be unnerving for the new parent to face dressing the baby for the first time. Tiny arms and legs look so vulnerable but don't worry – babies are tougher than you think. Here are some pointers to help:

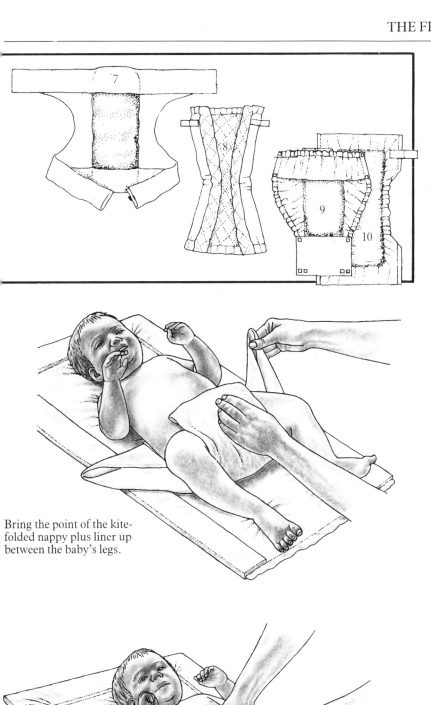

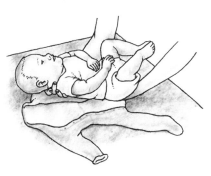

Raise the baby's head slightly and slip the vest over after stretching the neck wide first. Stretch one armhole and gently feed one hand through. Then the other on the other side.

Bring the point of the kite-folded nappy plus liner up between the baby's legs.

Spread the unbuttoned baby suit flat and lower baby into it.

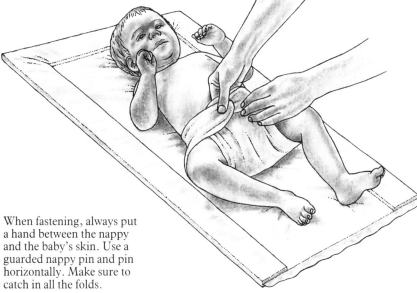

When fastening, always put a hand between the nappy and the baby's skin. Use a guarded nappy pin and pin horizontally. Make sure to catch in all the folds.

Again stretch and concertina the arm-hole and push your hand through to draw back the baby's arm. Repeat with the other arm and legs and button up.

IMMUNIZATION

Did you have measles as a child, or whooping cough or German measles? Probably you did – but your child need not because a revolution in the last twenty years or so has greatly reduced their incidence and severity. Diphtheria, tetanus and polio have been virtually eliminated.

Immunization in Britain is routinely available, free, for whooping cough (pertussis), diphtheria, tetanus, poliomyelitis, measles, German measles and tuberculosis. Smallpox has been eradicated from the entire world, so this vaccination is no longer necessary.

When a disease has become rare why bother to immunize? This is putting the horse before the cart – diseases have become rare because immunization has made them so. If, for instance, a child contracts diphtheria and mixes with children who have not been immunized against that disease then they too will most probably catch the same illness. This is how epidemics begin and this is why immunizations need to continue.

How does immunization work?

When a body is attacked by a germ it manufactures antibodies to fight that germ. If the illness attacks a second time the antibodies already present in the bloodstream prevent the illness taking hold. Immunization stimulates the body to produce antibodies by giving a mild form of the illness. The antibodies thus produced protect the child against an attack of the 'real' illness. If – as happens rarely – the child does catch the illness after immunization, the attack will be mild.

In pregnancy, many, but not all, anti-bodies in your bloodstream pass over to your baby, and for a few months after birth will continue to provide immunity. The colostrum – the first milk produced (see page 74) – also contains protective antibodies but this early protection gradually fades. Your baby cannot be immunized while he still carries the antibodies passed to him by you because the immunization would not 'take': this is why the timing of vaccinations is important – they have to be done when the natural protection has faded but hopefully before he becomes exposed to diseases.

Antibodies to whooping cough cannot cross from the mother to the baby: they are too large to get across the placenta. Immunization against the diseases mentioned is free in Britain and can be arranged through your doctor, health visitor or local clinic. The recommended timing for receiving them is shown below.

You should not have your baby immunized if he is unwell, he is being given medicines, he has had previous side effects from immunizations, he has had fits or convulsions or if anyone in your immediate family has had fits or convulsions. If this is true of you or your baby you must consult your doctor.

Rubella is dangerous if contracted early in pregnancy when there is a twenty per cent chance that the baby will be handicapped: there is also a risk of miscarriage. The most common birth defects caused by rubella are blindness, damage to heart and arteries, deafness and mental retardation. For this reason rubella immunization is offered routinely to all girls from ten upwards.

AGE	DISEASE	DETAILS
From three months	Diphtheria Whooping Cough Tetanus Polio	The first three – the triple vaccine – are given together in one injection. The diphtheria and tetanus can be given together without the whooping cough which can be given on its own. Polio is given orally at the same time.
Five to six months	The same as above	
Nine to eleven months	The same as above	The three injections are necessary for protection
Twelve to twenty-four months	Measles	By injection
If one is missed through illness or absence this can be given later without beginning again.		
About five years	Diphtheria Tetanus Polio	Booster
Girls of ten to fourteen	Rubella (German measles)	By injection
Girls and boys of about thirteen	Tuberculosis	By injection
Fifteen to nineteen on leaving school	Tetanus Polio	

If you are not sure if you are immune a test will determine this, and if negative you should then be immunized before becoming pregnant. An interval of three months should elapse between the injection and trying to become pregnant. A single dose of rubella vaccine will give long-term protection and booster shots are not necessary.

Always keep a record of immunizations – there is a space for this on page 232.

SYMPTOMS OF ILLNESS	DURATION	COMPLICATIONS
Diphtheria: sore throat, fever, hoarseness, cough	Two weeks	Inflammation of the heart, paralysis, death in ten per cent
Whooping cough: cold symptoms, severe coughing spells with characteristic whoop	Weeks to months	Pneumonia, brain damage, convulsions
Tetanus: muscle spasms	Two weeks or more	Death in fifty per cent of patients
Polio: fever, nausea, head and stomach-ache, stiff neck, backache	One week	Paralysis, death
Measles: fever, cough, runny nose, red eyes, rash	Ten days to two weeks	Ear infection, pneumonia, brain inflammation
Rubella (German measles): rash, swollen glands at back of neck, swelling or pain in joints	Three days	Inflammation of the brain, abnormal bleeding

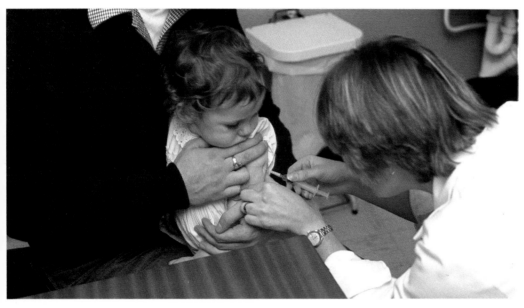

Immunization has virtually eliminated several childhood ailments. Protection depends on following the programme schedule.

What possible side effects may immunization have?

The risk is small and certainly smaller than the risk of suffering from the diseases themselves. Your child may cry a little more than usual, be slightly feverish, and there may be redness or soreness where the injection was given. Very rarely a child may have a convulsion, but will usually recover quickly with no lasting effects.

Once in every few million doses someone who comes into contact with a child who has received the polio vaccine may develop the symptoms.

And what about whooping cough?

About ten years ago a 'whooping cough scare' in Britain suggested that under certain conditions the vaccine could cause brain damage. As a result of this the proportion of babies being immunized against whooping cough dropped from seventy-nine per cent to thirty-one per cent, and subsequently a serious epidemic broke out with over 2,000 children catching the illness each week. More than thirty children died and many others have been left with lung damage. A national survey established that the chance of brain damage occurring after injection is about one in 330,000.

This is a subject which causes many parents a great deal of worry and their concern is understandable. To realize there is a possibility of damage, even though the statistics show that the possibility is slight, can be distressing. Medical staff are well aware of the dilemma parents face, and hopefully will take the time to discuss the subject with you. But it can't be stressed sufficiently that whooping cough in young babies may be a very serious illness indeed.

You should, however, not have your baby immunized if any of the conditions exist as listed previously. If, following the first injection, your baby cries in an abnormal way for a long period, or appears feverish or off colour, let your doctor know and he may decide to omit the whooping cough component at the next injection.

Do not be afraid to ask questions of your doctor or health visitor if anything worries you: they are there to help and you are there to do the best for your baby – so persist!

The risk of damage from vaccine is far less than the risk of damage from the illness itself.

POSTNATAL DEPRESSION

So much has been written recently about postnatal depression that you might think it is something that will happen to you as a matter of course. It is quite true that feelings of weepiness, inadequacy and weariness are quite common for a few days after the birth, but it is only when this tiredness and depression persist for weeks, and when they colour the days to such an extent that everything else seems meaningless, that you should recognize that this is a state which needs help.

The postnatal examination at six weeks could be a good time to talk about your feelings, though if you are really concerned you may want to consult your GP before then. Ask him not to dismiss your symptoms as 'imagination' but to help you – perhaps by medication – or by discussing ways to help your baby establish a routine which enables you to relax more, or perhaps by arranging for you to talk things over with a psychiatrist.

Real postnatal depression, called puerperal psychosis, is a state where you really are so depressed that you are ill and not responsible for your own actions. Ask for help if you feel you are tipping over into such a state – talk to your health visitor or GP. Your partner should be aware of your feelings and be able to enlist help if you are too lethargic to make the effort yourself. It is rare for a mother to be so depressed that she has to return to hospital for treatment, but if that should happen then many hospitals nowadays make provision for the baby to stay with her (see page 230 for addresses of self-help groups).

What is 'normal'?
It is normal to feel tired – you have more to do. It is normal to wonder if you will ever again be carefree: normal to feel that you are tied interminably to house and baby: normal to hope that the baby sleeps from one feed to the next: normal to suspect that if your baby cries you are doing something wrong. Not only is your body adjusting to the changes made by pregnancy, birth and labour, your emotions are also adapting to a new lifestyle, and to yourself as a different person. In some ways nature helps, since hormones circulating in your body help you for a few months to think of yourself more as mother than wife.

The crying baby
You will not always know why your baby is crying: sometimes all you can do is cuddle and comfort. In fact it is not always crying that worries a parent – it is the unpredictability of not knowing when you are going to be summoned by that cry. Mothers are still tuned in to their babies' crying and it worries them much more than it does the baby-sitter who can switch off and go home for an uninterrupted night's sleep. And always at the back of the parent's mind is the thought that perhaps they are doing something wrong, that the baby 'ought' to be good.

Self-help groups (page 230) are a lifeline to new mothers. Through them you will meet mothers in the same situation as yourself and realize you are not alone in reacting as you do. Companionship brings reassurance. The National Childbirth Trust, for instance, has a service to help mothers who are having difficulty with breast-feeding. One of their members – who breast-fed successfully herself – will come to your home to talk things over and offer practical advice. Baby-sitting circles often evolve from joining an NCT group, and this means you are able to get out more often, either alone or with your partner.

Child abuse
A proud mother, accepting compliments on her daughter's wedding day appearance, agreed, 'Yes, she looks lovely – yet no-one knows how nearly I came to throwing her out of the window when she was a baby'.

Many parents, looking back on their children's early days, have confessed they were fortunate not to have injured them in the first weeks and months of parenthood. It may come as both shock and reassurance to know that the sometimes violent feelings you may have towards your baby have been shared by so many.

If you become aware that your irritation is building up and becoming almost uncontrollable then go to your doctor and tell him about it. He will not be at all surprised or dismissive. Of course you may be able to fool him. You may keep going to him with trivial ailments while all the time trying to get to the point of telling him that you are an 'unnatural' parent – you would like to give your baby an almighty swipe. He may see through this but do not rely on it. Just tell him your real feelings and fears – and ask for help. As an immediate measure, if your baby's crying so irritates you that you fear you will lose control, leave him in a room as far away from you as possible – making sure he is safe. Make yourself a cup of tea. Ask someone to listen while you walk round the block. Hit a cushion. Phone your health visitor, the NSPCC or local group affiliated to Opus (see page 230).

Don't ever give in to smacking or shaking your baby. One reason, of course, is that even a mild smack could injure him, but another is that if you did once give in to your anger, you might find you couldn't stop, and you could then cause him severe injuries.

Why, you wonder, should you want to harm him? For a number of reasons – he may not be 'behaving' in the way you would like: you may want a son and have a daughter: you may imagine that if he wets the bed he is doing it on purpose, that all the time by his crying and his failure to be the model baby you had dreamed of he is showing the world what a bad mother you are. Quite suddenly, all these partly hidden thoughts may come to a head – you are trying to manoeuvre him into a high chair and he will not bend his legs – and something snaps. If you force him you could very easily break a leg.

Some of the injuries inflicted on babies are due to overcrowding, immature parents, shortage of money – but not all the injuries are by any means to those less privileged babies although if you have money the chances are you can 'buy' help from childminders, baby-sitters and nannies, so you have more respite from daylong babycare.

A parent who batters a baby does not necessarily hate the child: deep down it may be an expression of the fact that he or she wants attention for him or herself. You have to be prepared – with parenthood – to give love and attention without expecting anything in return.

Not all battering may be physical. A withdrawn, cold parent can emotionally batter a child just as surely as the bruises and abrasions of less subtle injury. The result may be a withdrawn, passive child who fails to thrive and grow. Often this is because the parent concerned has not been given love as a child and is now lacking in the ability to give love to others.

How common is baby battering?

More than one child a week in Britain is known to be killed by its parents – and many more must be so without it being discovered. The National Society for the Prevention of Cruelty to Children handles between 40,000 to 50,000 calls a year, and a third of those calls are from the parents themselves who recognize their feelings and ask for help.

This aspect of the Society's work is not always realized. The inspector today is not 'the cruelty man' who wears a uniform and comes in to take the child away and the parents to court. He is a trained social worker who recognizes the stress and will

Extra work and the new responsibility can weigh heavily on the mother. If your depression is severe, ask for help.

support the parents sometimes for months or years by visits, by listening, by explanations. He will not blame, he will help.

Moreover, if you suspect that a child is being badly treated and feel you must inform the Society, then your anonymity will be preserved. You can be sure of that – some time ago the Society pleaded this privilege before the House of Lords who upheld its right to privacy.

In some districts a Crying Baby Service has been set up by local health visitors who keep a twenty-four hour telephone rota. Any parent who is distressed beyond control by a crying baby can ask for advice. If necessary the health visitor will come to the house.

Do not let irritation or resentment grow to danger point: there are societies and services able to help, and a telephone call could make the difference between an unharmed baby and a lifetime of remorse. (See page 230 for useful addresses.)

CHILDREN WITH SPECIAL NEEDS

The birth of a handicapped child is a traumatic experience for his parents and for the whole family. Feelings of guilt, anger, disbelief and above all, perhaps, the realization of the added responsibility they will have to undertake, may be overwhelming.

Much of the parents' reaction will depend on the manner in which the news of the child's birth is told to them by the medical staff. It is now generally agreed that whatever the disability it is better that parents should be told as soon as possible, and that they should be allowed to see and hold their baby without delay. Being told that their baby is 'not quite right', and not being allowed to see him, inevitably suggests that their child is some sort of monster, whereas the truth may be that he has some minor condition. Parents of completely healthy and normal children who for some reason do not see their baby for some days (which used to be the practice with babies delivered by forceps) often imagine that there is some conspiracy of silence about a handicap, and suffer greatly from the lack of understanding of their feelings.

As with the usual process of 'baby bonding' the sooner the parents can see and hold their baby, the sooner will they accept their child.

The parents of a handicapped child are bereaved parents for they are bereaved of the perfect child they anticipated. Not only are the parents bereaved – so also may be the brothers and sisters, the grandparents, the relations and friends who looked forward to the coming child. As such, they must pass through the stages of loss – disbelief, anger, sorrow and finally, some kind of acceptance – and in these stages they must be supported by information and care. Much of this support may come from the intuitive sympathy and sensitivity of those closest to the family, but outside this framework is a vast and growing army of professional and qualified groups, whose expertise is directed specifically towards helping and understanding particular problems. At no time has there been more help available, though paradoxically it might be claimed that at no time has the help been less needed, because so many of the disorders that afflicted children even fifty years ago have been eliminated or are being controlled. Against this must be reckoned the number of children, frail at birth, who now survive but who would not previously have done so.

The existence of such help points to a radical rethinking of the attitude towards children with special needs: the acknowledgment that a 'handicapped' child may mean a 'handicapped family', and the recognition that a child whose physical, emotional or intellectual growth is limited may not be limited in all directions.

A child in a wheelchair may be treated as though he is deaf: an undersized adult as though he is mentally undersized: most people, when speaking to the blind, raise their voices, even though it is well known that blindness often results in a sharpened sense of hearing! The obese child is considered different and less socially desirable: the scarred child may be isolated. The handicapped person or child presents a personal challenge: can we accept him without reservation, fairly and without condescension, acknowledging his right not to be discriminated against? Can we acknowledge that perhaps he makes us feel uncomfortable, or guilty so that we react either with avoidance or with unnatural concern?

Handicap may be physical or emotional: sometimes one overlaps another or may cause another: the deaf child, if not given special care, may find it difficult to keep up intellectually with children of his age group and so become isolated and withdrawn.

Physical handicaps are now usually diagnosed earlier through developmental checks and greater awareness of what problems may exist. Mental handicap may not be recognized until the baby fails to react in ways which would be expected of his age and this is also true of emotional handicaps. The earlier the diagnosis of any handicap, the better the chances of effective treatment.

A sophisticated hearing aid gives freedom to this small boy – born blind and deaf through rubella injury before birth.

The strain on the family

A child who needs extra care and attention imposes strain on a marriage and on the family. Father and mother do not always agree on the treatment and may find themselves in conflict about the child's prospects: other brothers and sisters may resent the extra attention the less able child needs. Where it is practicable the child should not be overindulged or overhelped. It is just as much a mistake to expect too little as to expect too much. Even a child with quite a severe physical or mental handicap can become part of a family, contributing to the best of his ability, if he is given the right support and upbringing. In these matters the specialists dealing with the child can give invaluable guidelines: if the child is being cared for by several specialists for various conditions there will still be one who acts as coordinator and with whom the parents can discuss their problems.

It could be that a child's disabilities are so severe that his parents fear they will not be able to look after him adequately at home. The decision then has to be taken whether the child should be cared for in an institution. Such a situation is inevitably distressing and may cause great heart-searching to the parents. If they decide that an institution is the best solution for their child they may still feel that somehow they ought to have managed at home. They may even feel that somehow they are responsible for the child's handicap and now they are further adding to their 'guilt' by abandoning him. There is a further burden if the parents do not agree on the decision.

In such a situation the supportive advice of doctor, psychologist or other medical staff is

A handicapped child puts a strain on all the family but older children are often of enormous help.

Supervised play for the handicapped child relieves the burden on the home – and helps the child to adjust socially.

invaluable and necessary, not only to help the parents with their decision, but also to help them recognize that caring for the child could well be beyond their resources, and could lead to the further disruption of the family. A self-sacrificing decision to keep their child at home may well not be the best solution for the child himself. It is perhaps worth remembering that the majority of support-systems, organizations and self-help groups for children with special needs have been originated by parents with experience of such a child; that from their suffering has flowered a remarkable harvest of sympathy and practical aid.

It is an easy mistake to attribute all the child's behaviour to his specific disability: a frustrated child can scream with tension whether he is handicapped or not: very often it is a question of trying to separate cause and effect. A child who cannot move will not be working off his energy with physical exercise, and will need other outlets. 'Bad' behaviour need not be excused solely on the grounds of handicap: if it has caused the behaviour then that is a different matter: a deaf child could appear disobedient when he hasn't heard what has been said to him.

It is on subjects such as this that the experience of parents who have been through the same kind of situation can be invaluable. Your health visitor, social worker or doctor may be able to put you in touch with any local group, or branch of national organizations, which could be of help. Members begin with a mutual built-in sympathy: children are accepted with understanding, and it may be possible to arrange baby-sitting so that housebound parents have some respite while knowing that their child is being cared for by those who understand the specific problems.

Over eighty per cent of handicapped children (1984) are now living at home for most of the time. Facilities for part-time care – whether in the child's own home for a few hours, or in holiday homes for a few weeks – are essential for the relief and well-being of the family. The National Children's Bureau (page 230) has published a list of such facilities called *Respite Care Services* – ask at your library or buy direct from the NCB.

In some areas adventure playgrounds for the handicapped have been set up. This allows children with disabilities to have some of the advantages of adventure play while being cared for by trained staff who will see they come to no harm. Where possible, handicapped children should mix with all children, in playgroups and mother and toddler groups, as equals. It could be that the parent of a handicapped child may feel uncertain of the welcome she would get at such a group, but a preliminary talk with the playleader and other mothers could do much to introduce her to activities and friendships of benefit both to herself and her child. It is not only the handicapped child who may feel isolated: it is also his parents.

The education of handicapped children is now administered by the Department of Education (DES) and not, as previously, by the Department of Health and Social Security (DHSS). This is in keeping with the policy of integrating such children into ordinary schools unless their frailties are such that a special school (for instance, for the blind) would be of more help to them.

One of the main worries of parents of a handicapped child is what will happen when they can no longer care for the child. Mencap (page 231) has a scheme through which parents can set up trusts for their children so that they are provided for at that stage.

Some of the specialists trained to help a handicapped child:

- teachers
- psychologists medical staff
- occupational therapists physiotherapists music therapists
- play specialists
- speech therapists

Feeding

Sleeping and waking, washing and feeding – for the first few weeks these must seem your main occupations and preoccupations if you are caring for a new baby. And since a baby with a satisfied tummy is usually a contented baby, the fourth factor nearly always influences the first.

This is not to suggest that a baby's stomach should be kept so full that, between feeds, she is in a perpetual daze of sleep or half sleep. As her senses develop so that she is able to take more interest in the world around her, the periods of wakefulness will gradually increase. But in these early days the baby who is neither lonely, uncomfortable nor hungry will usually be a relatively trouble-free baby.

Before your baby's birth you probably made up your mind as to how she would be fed: breast or bottle.

BREAST-FEEDING

Breast-feeding – the 'natural' way – sometimes provokes quite unnatural reactions. 'Too tiring, too trying, too much trouble ... and formula milks today are so good and so well-balanced ...'

All the same, there has been much greater emphasis of late on the merits of breast-feeding, and hospitals and midwives today will be ready to help you to establish this successfully.

The reason for the change of emphasis is largely due to greater recognition that breast milk provides for the baby certain benefits that even the best formula can't. To begin with, it has been specially produced for your particular baby, it is always available at the right temperature, and it is more or less fuss-free. It's not entirely free as the mother needs to eat more and maintain a nutritious diet, but it certainly seems to cost less than formula milk. You need no bottles, there is nothing to mix, and it provokes no allergy in your baby (although you could eat food that the baby is allergic to and this you will only discover when you have done so). Moreover, it provides your baby with valuable protection against infections, while colostrum – the liquid secreted in the first day or two after birth – is rich in protein.

For the mother, breast-feeding has advantages and disadvantages. It helps her to lose weight and regain her figure more quickly. Most mothers find it a pleasurable sensation and that it makes them feel very close to their baby. It helps the uterus to contract. The disadvantages – though these are not inevitable – are that she may get sore nipples, she may resent being tied to the baby (though she can express her milk into a bottle and leave it for someone else to give), it is a physical strain, and she may feel tired.

Breast-feeding is not in itself a contraceptive and if you become pregnant again during the first three months then your doctor may advise you to stop breast-feeding if it is felt this is making too many demands on you.

Medication can be secreted into your milk, though probably only in small amounts, and it can also be affected by birth control pills. While the effects of alcohol and drugs on milk are not fully known, it would be unwise to indulge too much in the first, and may be dangerous to do so in the second.

Some food that the mother eats may upset the baby, and you may have to think back to what changes in your diet may have been the cause of pain or distress in your baby. Onions, cabbage and tomatoes sometimes have this effect.

If it is 'natural' why are there difficulties?
Establishing successful breast-feeding may take some little while. After all, you are both probably inexperienced. Babies like to suck but they cannot draw off milk unless they get not just the nipple but the whole areola (the brown skin surrounding the nipple where the milk ducts are) into their mouth. Some babies suck without feeding but you can tell when they are really feeding by watching if their jaw moves strongly and rhythmically just under the ear. Sometimes babies who have taken enough milk like to stay there, dozing and sucking. If you have to call a halt and baby will not let go, put one finger very gently into the side of her mouth alongside the nipple – that will do the trick.

Some babies get the idea of breast-feeding right away. Others fuss and fidget and make a performance of it and you both get very agitated when she does not get any milk. The nurse in hospital will help you cope, and by the time you come home you will probably be managing very well. If not, your midwife or health visitor will take over during their visits.

Milk comes in on the third or fourth day after birth. Before then colostrum is present

Once established, breast-feeding can become a time of pleasure and mutual satisfaction. Worries that 'the baby is not getting enough' are groundless if she continues to thrive and seems contented.

and your baby will be given to you for short times so that she can get used to the idea of sucking, and you can enjoy each other's company.

The 'let down' reflex of milk into your breasts is something you will soon learn to recognize. The flow of milk is stimulated into the breasts by the pituitary gland in the brain. This releases oxytocin into the bloodstream which in turn forces milk from the milk glands into the ducts. This reaction can be caused by your baby's sucking or even by hearing her hunger cry or her presence in the room. It is an emotional reaction and you will feel the breasts tingle as the milk flows in to satisfy her hunger.

It's an enjoyable time

Make yourself comfortable to breast-feed. Find a position that suits you – with your back supported and your feet on a foot-stool perhaps. And support the baby's head so that she can reach the nipple. If your breasts become too full the nipple will be flattened and you may need to express a little milk

Don't exclude an older child when you are breast-feeding. She could already find it hard enough to accept the new baby.

Breast milk can be expressed, stored in the refrigerator and given later by bottle.

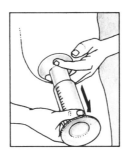

before the baby can suck properly. Sometimes a baby falls asleep during feeding which is annoying if you know she is going to wake up again in half an hour for more. Try touching her cheek, or making her a little less comfortable by unwrapping and re-arranging her blanket; it may do the trick.

This sleep business is particularly annoying if it happens for the last feed. You have sat up waiting and then when you try to feed her she will not wake up. Eventually you crawl into bed – and just as you are dropping off she wakes. If she persists in this habit try going to bed earlier: if she doesn't wake for the last feed until one or two in the morning you'll have got a few hours sleep in and the chances are that after a few days she will then go through until about six.

Human breast milk contains less protein than cow's milk and breast-fed babies may like to be fed very often – the idea of four-hourly feeds derives from the use of cow's milk, as this is how long it takes to empty from the baby's stomach. If your baby wants the breast again after an hour or two, let her have it and enjoy it. This does not mean you are not producing enough milk, it is just how human babies behave. Much crying and unhappiness stem from a failure to understand this.

Your baby may be restless in the evening and with breast-feeding this could be because you are tired at the end of the day and she is not getting enough milk. Try to rest for an hour or two before that feed. Many mothers like to have a cup of tea or milk while they are feeding: you'll probably find you get extra thirsty anyway, so drink as much as you want, although extra fluid will not actually make more milk.

Most breast-feeding mothers wonder if the baby is getting enough milk – after all, in a bottle you can actually see the contents disappearing. If your baby is thriving and appears contented then she is getting enough. She may want more at some feeds than others. She will suck strongly at first if she is hungry, and may get enough in the first few minutes. She may not want to suck at all from the second breast, but make sure she begins on that alternative breast at the next feed.

Always resist the temptation to 'test-weigh' – that is weighing your baby before and after every feed. This will only worry you if she takes very little at some feeds.

Nowadays it is recommended that mothers 'feed on demand' – but if your baby demands every hour that can be wearying. However, remember that the more the breast is suckled, the more milk it will produce; also that all the milk a baby requires may be taken in the first few minutes. But, baby may not be hungry: she may want a cuddle. She may have a stomach-ache so you could try her with a spoonful of water.

In the first days at home if you have been in hospital, or up and about if the baby has been born at home, there may be a falling off in the milk caused by the extra work you are now doing. Don't give up and give supplementary bottles of formula milk, because without the stimulus of feeding, your milk will gradually dry up. Suckle your baby little and often if necessary.

And if you have some initial trouble breast-feeding and temporarily give up, don't accept injections of milk-drying drugs in hospital: the difficulty could be cleared in a day or two and then you will be able to return to breast-feeding (see page 79).

A man may feel excluded when his baby is young and so much of his partner's attention must necessarily be given to the needs of the child. Taking his turn with bottle-feeding – whether from expressed breast milk or from a formula solution – is a first rate opportunity for father and child to become more closely involved. It will also give the mother time for herself or allow for her to get on with other jobs.

BOTTLE-FEEDING

Babies thrive and grow on bottle-feeding, and if you choose to feed your baby this way from inclination or necessity you should not worry that she will not remain healthy. Most formula milks suit most babies and you will not find it necessary to keep changing them, although you will need to buy for the right age-range, which will be specified on the pack. Parents sometimes worry unnecessari-ly about choosing the 'right' brand of milk.

One of the advantages put forward with breast-feeding is the closeness which can develop between mother and child during that time, so make sure you make the bottle feeds just as enjoyable. Cuddle your baby up closely and talk to her in just the same way. Bottle-feeding also means that father can take a turn with feeding.

HOW TO PREPARE THE BOTTLE FEEDS

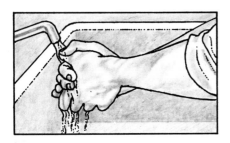

Boil a kettle and while it is cooling wash your hands thoroughly.

Stir with a sterilized spoon until all powder is dissolved.

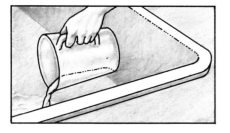

Remove the equipment from the sterilizer and drain into the sink.

Fill bottles to exact level required. Never overfill.

Pour the exact amount of boiled water into a sterilized jug.

Place the teats on upside down and then screw on the bottle lids.

Using a knife level off the exact number of scoops and place feed in jug.

Put the covered bottles into the fridge straight away.

STERILIZING THE BOTTLES

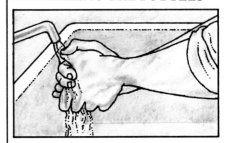

Wash your hands and fill the sink with warm soapy water.

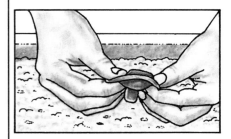

Turn the teats inside out and rub them with salt.

Use a bottle brush to remove all traces of milk from inside the bottles.

After rinsing immerse equipment in fresh sterilizing solution.

Formula milk is prepared from modified cow's milk, that is, cow's milk which has been dried so that it is more easily digested, and to which boiled water (to dilute the milk) is added. Sugar is also added to bring up the calories. Sodium and phosphate are found in cow's milk in high quantities and these must be reduced to make them approximate to the low content in breast milk. All formula milks have been fortified with vitamin D. Instructions on the packet must be followed exactly. Do not give an extra scoop 'to make it extra nice', and if the instructions say 'flat spoonful' then make sure it is just that by flattening it off with the back of a knife. Don't add sugar unless the instructions tell you to.

You will probably feel that your baby will enjoy warm milk more than cold, and in that case you can stand the prepared bottle upright in a container of warm water for a few minutes. Then shake it to distribute the heat and try it on the back of your hand for temperature. Giving your baby cold feeds does not make them less nutritious or palatable – she'll take them just as well from the refrigerator, and it will certainly save you trouble during the night if you don't have to warm the bottle.

How much should baby take?

Your baby will probably not always finish her bottle and if she is not hungry then don't try to force her. Bottle-fed babies tend to put on more weight than breast-fed, and this could be because parents urge them to 'finish it up'.

Your health visitor or the clinic will guide you on the amount your baby needs which is according to weight, but an indication would be for each feed.:

New baby 60-85 g (2-3 oz)
By four months 170 g (6 oz)
By six months 200-230 g (7-8 oz)

If your baby leaves some milk in the bottle it should be discarded and not saved for the next feed because of the risk of contamination. If she consistently does not finish bottles it would be more economical to make up smaller amounts and have standbys in case she suddenly develops an appetite.

Fresh milk is unsuitable for young babies because of its high sodium and phosphate content. It contains too much protein for the baby's immature kidneys to cope with, and its fat is too difficult for her to absorb. It is also low in iron.

Complementary feeds

If, despite your efforts to breast-feed your baby, you are sure she is not getting enough milk, then you can offer her a bottle of formula milk after she has finished her breast-feed. It could be, for instance, that your baby does not settle during the evening and you suspect your milk is inadequate. A complementary bottle at this time could settle her, but make sure that she sucks first at the breast so that your supply is being stimulated.

If your baby develops an allergy to cow's milk then you could try goat's milk, but only when your doctor recommends. There are special formula milks if needed and your doctor will suggest these alternatives.

COMPARATIVE CONTENTS OF BREAST AND BOTTLE MILK

CONTENT	BREAST	FORMULA BOTTLE	COMMENT
Water	Same	Same	Babies' immature kidneys need more water than adults'
Calories	Less	More	Energy for growth
Protein	More (colostrum also protects against infections)	Less	Building blocks of growth
Fat	Variable on mother's diet	Adequate	Provides energy, carries vitamins A, B, E and K into blood stream
Carbohydrates	Lactose	Sucrose or lactose	Lactose is better than sucrose. For energy
Vitamins	Deficient. Vitamin D supplement may be prescribed	Enriched to provide	Maintain growth
Iron	Usually adequate unless mother is anaemic	Deficient unless fortified	For blood
Salt	Adequate	Sometimes too much	Health and growth

It should be noted that formula milks vary in content. Information listed on the pack will show where there have been additives.

WEANING

Getting your baby on to solids is not the complicated process you may have been led to expect. Your baby will naturally still need the comfort of breast or bottle for some time, but she will also soon get used to taking small amounts of food from a spoon.

Don't delay in starting mixed feeding beyond the sixth month because by then the baby's natural stores of iron are running out. If your baby seems very hungry at three or four months you can begin to offer her a spoonful of cereal after a bottle or breast-feed. Baby rice is best to begin with. Use a plastic spoon. At first she will probably push the food out with her tongue because she is quite unused to this method of feeding and will wonder what it's all about. Most of the food will be wasted but just a little will go down. She will be getting used to different tastes and textures, but still getting her main nourishment from her milk feeds.

What is important is not to make feeding a battleground. This has previously been a time of great enjoyment for your baby, and you will not now want to make it miserable.

Beginning mixed feeding is probably more convenient at the morning (ten o'clock) or afternoon (two o'clock) feeds, as you will have more time then. You can offer the spoon before, during or after the milk feed – use your judgment as to when your baby is most cooperative. If she is overtired or over-excited, go straight to the breast or bottle, then offer a solid when she is calmer.

It's a messy business all right but learning to chew and swallow instead of sucking isn't particularly easy.

THE MERITS AND FUNCTIONS OF FOOD

Protein	Body builder	Meat, fish, cheese, eggs
Calcium	Bones, teeth etc., blood-clotting and muscles	Bread, flour, cereals, milk
Carbohydrates	Energy	Sugar, root vegetables, flour products, potatoes
Iron	Prevents anaemia	Egg yolk, liver, meat, green vegetables
Fats	Energy	All animal and vegetable fats★
Calories	Growth and fuel	Sugar and fat-rich foods contain most
Vitamins	Normal functioning of body metabolism	May be recommended as dietary supplements by your clinic in the form of tablets or drops

★Recent research has highlighted the danger of too much animal fat in the human diet, so be aware of this in your child's diet (and your own) and try to maintain a healthy balance.

Introduce different foods gradually. If she seems to dislike one, go on to another and return to the first in a week or two. Introducing foods like this also has the advantage that if one food seems to disagree with her, you can quite easily isolate which one it is. Do not try new foods when your baby is unwell.

Too much cereal may make her fat, so balance with the proteins and fresh vegetables (see chart below left).

Some babies eat methodically and reasonably steadily: others dawdle and dream. Your baby will also attempt to feed herself – the first sign is probably when she smacks her fist down on a plateful and gets it over the wall. Now's the time to cover the floor and yourself – independence is rearing its messy head. Give her her own spoon, but you will find you can probably still do the feeding yourself: she will be so busy examining and playing with her spoon that she will take food from yours at the same time.

Up to seven or eight months the food should not be lumpy – at this early stage she will prefer a smooth mixture. If you are using tinned foods, which are very convenient, use the strained type which is smooth. Try not to let all meals in a day be tinned or bottled: your baby can have the same food that the family has, provided it is well mashed or sieved.

Around seven or eight months introduce slightly lumpier foods as she may otherwise get so used to the bland, smooth type that she will not want to change. By this time too her gums are hard and adequate for chewing and crushing. By now some of your baby's mealtimes will be coinciding with your own, and she will begin to notice what you are eating and want to join in. She will already be able to hold a rusk for herself (or finger of bread hardened in the oven) and enjoy chewing (see page 210 for Choking).

Babies will not starve themselves: if they see they can get a reaction from you by playing up at mealtimes, or refusing foods, or spraying a mouthful over you, then they may well do so. The food play is merely a means of getting your attention. Ignore it as much as possible: real distaste for one particular food is quite different and easily recognized.

If your baby refuses food consistently, try something else and come back to the first food later. You can always 'hide' ingredients like milk or eggs in cakes or puddings, so she will not be lacking in these. Showing a distaste for food like this is different from the years ahead when children suddenly announce that they've 'gone off' something they have previously eaten with relish.

In some ways it is important not to take too much trouble over preparing special food for your toddler, because if she rewards your efforts by spitting it out you will naturally feel resentful – which will show. The battle of mealtimes can begin with your perhaps wondering if this child is 'grateful' enough for all you are doing for her. She does not have to be grateful – she doesn't know what it means.

If your baby or toddler prefers pudding first, then let her have it – sometimes. If you refuse you are giving her the idea that pudding is the reward for being good *after* she has finished off the nasty old meat and fish. Of course you can keep the pudding out of sight if you wish until the first course has gone. It also would not be wise to fill her up with a large helping of pudding first so she has no appetite for the meat course, though a milk and egg pudding will be nutritious.

DO NOT
- Add salt or sugar to prepared baby foods unless directed
- Give more than one cereal a day
- Make the food too hot
- Leave baby alone to eat
- Give sweet foods or drinks between meals.

Adapted from Health Education Council Leaflet *Starting Your Baby on Solid Food.*

HOW TO 'HIDE' INGREDIENTS YOUR CHILD MAY DISLIKE

Milk
In mashed potatoes, soups, milk shakes, puddings, sauce (cheese), custards, milk jellies and blancmanges, ice cream, any creamed fish

Eggs
Put in mashed potatoes, scramble, in pancakes, omelettes, in sauces, biscuits, cakes.

Cheese
Sprinkle grated over vegetables, in sauces, sandwiches, uncooked on toast.

A baby enjoys company. Raised to the height of the adults' table she will be able to take part in family mealtimes.

Stages of weaning

	EARLY MORNING	BREAKFAST	LUNCH
At four or five months	 Breast or bottle	 Breast or bottle plus teaspoonful of baby cereal	 Breast or bottle
Between four-and-a-half months and five-and-a-half months.	 Breast or bottle	 Breast or bottle plus cereal	 Breast or bottle plus strained broth
Between five and six months	 Breast or bottle	 Breast or bottle plus scrambled egg	 Puréed meat or fish with vegetables and stewed fruit Try water or fruit juice

You can prepare puréed food yourself in large batches and freeze it in small portions for later use. Foods with a smooth and creamy texture are most readily accepted.

Between six and seven months	 Breast or bottle	 Cereal and scrambled egg, milk, vitamin drops (ask health visitor)	 Minced meat or fish with vegetables, milk pudding or egg custard or jelly, water
Between seven and eight months	 Water or fruit juice	 Cereal, scrambled egg, wholemeal toast and butter, milk	 Cheese, fish, minced meat, chicken or liver with mashed vegetables. Milk pudding, stewed fruit, water
Between nine and twelve months	 Water or fruit juice	 Cereal, boiled egg, wholemeal toast and butter, bacon, milk	 As before but try chopping instead of mincing

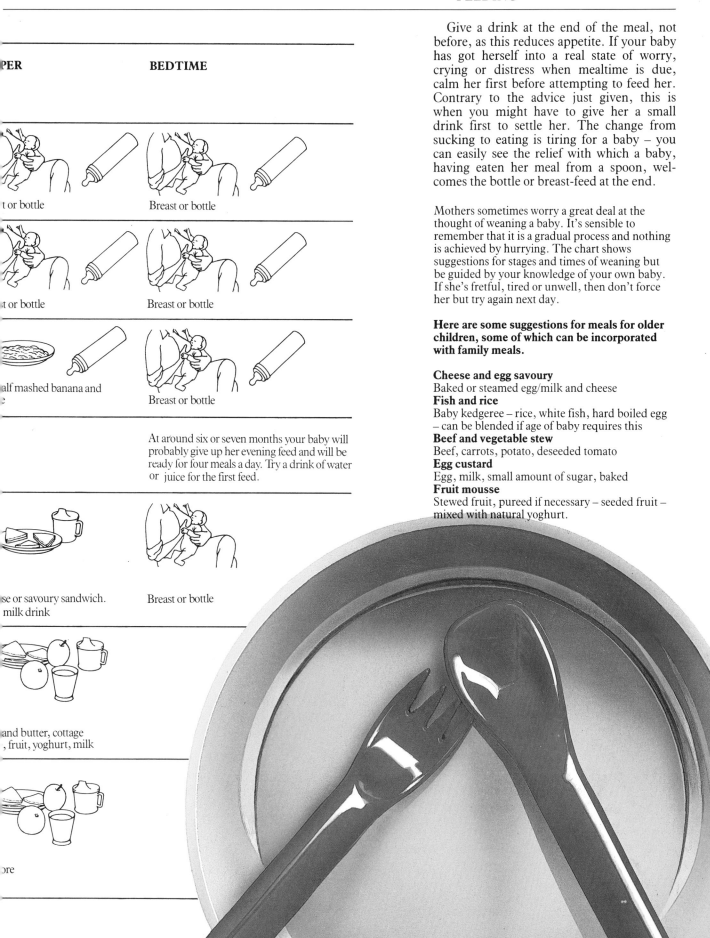

PER	BEDTIME
t or bottle	Breast or bottle
t or bottle	Breast or bottle
alf mashed banana and	Breast or bottle

At around six or seven months your baby will probably give up her evening feed and will be ready for four meals a day. Try a drink of water or juice for the first feed.

se or savoury sandwich.
milk drink — Breast or bottle

and butter, cottage
, fruit, yoghurt, milk

ore

Give a drink at the end of the meal, not before, as this reduces appetite. If your baby has got herself into a real state of worry, crying or distress when mealtime is due, calm her first before attempting to feed her. Contrary to the advice just given, this is when you might have to give her a small drink first to settle her. The change from sucking to eating is tiring for a baby – you can easily see the relief with which a baby, having eaten her meal from a spoon, welcomes the bottle or breast-feed at the end.

Mothers sometimes worry a great deal at the thought of weaning a baby. It's sensible to remember that it is a gradual process and nothing is achieved by hurrying. The chart shows suggestions for stages and times of weaning but be guided by your knowledge of your own baby. If she's fretful, tired or unwell, then don't force her but try again next day.

Here are some suggestions for meals for older children, some of which can be incorporated with family meals.

Cheese and egg savoury
Baked or steamed egg/milk and cheese
Fish and rice
Baby kedgeree – rice, white fish, hard boiled egg – can be blended if age of baby requires this
Beef and vegetable stew
Beef, carrots, potato, deseeded tomato
Egg custard
Egg, milk, small amount of sugar, baked
Fruit mousse
Stewed fruit, pureed if necessary – seeded fruit – mixed with natural yoghurt.

Your child's teeth

DEVELOPMENT

Six weeks after conception your baby's teeth are already beginning to develop. At his birth, all twenty primary teeth are forming and the first permanent teeth may also be developing.

So it is obvious that, even in pregnancy, you need to be aware of how you can help those teeth to develop healthily. If the mother's diet during pregnancy is adequate (see page 14), her baby's teeth should develop normally. If her diet is grossly deficient – especially in calcium, phosphorus or vitamin D – the structure of her baby's teeth will be abnormal. The amount of calcium in the enamel or the quality of the enamel can be affected, and defects may appear as white spots or small depressions on the teeth. Infection or fever during pregnancy can also affect the baby's teeth in the same way.

Fluoride protects the teeth against cavities and some doctors prescribe fluoride supplements before birth. It has been queried whether this does very much good, but it certainly does no harm. Tetracycline, which is contained in some antibiotics, causes permanent yellow, brown or grey discoloration of the developing teeth. It can stain the primary teeth of the fetus and may also stain the permanent teeth. If your doctor knows you are pregnant he will not prescribe antibiotics containing tetracycline, but make sure you mention the fact to him.

FROM BIRTH TO SIX MONTHS
Your newborn baby has at least twenty invisible teeth developing in his jaws. Between birth and six months, ten to twelve permanent teeth also begin to develop. Occasionally a child may be born with a tooth, or one may appear within the first three or four weeks. These are called natal teeth, and are usually incompletely formed and lack adequate roots.

It is possible to breast-feed a baby who has natal teeth and this is frequently done. However, if the teeth cannot be tolerated, or if they are very loose, they can be taken out.

This may mean that when the primary teeth come through there will be one missing, since the natal tooth is a primary tooth that has erupted early. Later teeth are usually unaffected.

After birth, as before, your baby needs adequate nutrition for his teeth to grow properly (see page 79), and since breast milk

Decay can nearly always be prevented by proper cleaning and a good diet. Children up to about three do not have sufficient dexterity to clean their own teeth.

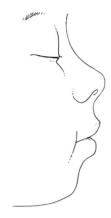

The position of the lower jaw in relation to the upper jaw at birth.

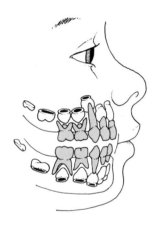

While the primary teeth are erupting the secondary teeth are already in the jaw.

may be inadequate in iron or vitamin D, your doctor may prescribe supplements of these and of fluoride.

FROM SIX MONTHS TO TWO YEARS

At birth your baby's lower jaw will be positioned quite a way behind his upper jaw. During the first year the lower jaw grows at a faster rate than the upper jaw, and by the time your baby has all his first teeth the jaws will have 'caught up', and the upper and lower teeth will fit properly.

FROM TWO TO THREE YEARS

By now all your baby's primary teeth have appeared and up to twenty-eight permanent teeth are developing within the jaws. Illness or high fever could result in defects to these permanent teeth. If antibiotics are prescribed, make sure they don't contain tetracyclines.

APPEARANCE OF THE TEETH

Dark or abnormal colour of primary teeth indicates that they have not developed correctly. Since the stain is within the teeth it cannot be removed by brushing, although there are bonding techniques through which a dentist can improve the appearance. Stains that appear after the teeth have appeared are not inside the teeth. They have been caused by germs sticking to the tooth surface. Correct brushing can prevent their forming but once they are there they can be removed by a dentist using a dental polishing paste, which is more abrasive then toothpaste.

Incisors may have small bumps, called mamelons, along their biting edge, but these disappear quickly as the teeth are worn by biting and chewing. If they are still there by the age of four, this usually shows that the child is not biting correctly: your dentist will advise you if correction is necessary. Spaces between the primary teeth are normal – in fact it has been said that they should be spaced like a white picket fence as this is necessary to accommodate the larger permanent teeth when they eventually arrive.

TEETHING

Teething is a normal and generally painless process, although a variety of signs and symptoms have been attributed to it – increase in salivation, thumb or fist sucking, irritability, and the need to bite on hard objects. What both parents and doctors must guard against is thinking signs and symptoms of illness are due to 'teething'. If your baby has a fever, diarrhoea, bronchitis or infection, he is sick and should be seen by a doctor. He may be teething at the same time, but the teething has nothing to do with his illness.

Teething rings will give him something to chew or bite: some of them contain liquid that may be cooled or frozen to relieve the mild inflammation sometimes seen with erupting teeth. Make sure the rings are safe, non-toxic, and that they can't be swallowed. A large carrot stick – too large for the baby to swallow – can be refrigerated and given to him to chew. Do not give hard biscuits – they soften once in the mouth, lose their effectiveness, and the softened crumbs might stick in your baby's windpipe. And don't rub a dissolved aspirin on the gums because it could burn the tissue.

There are a number of products available

How they appear

There are twenty primary teeth and thirty-two permanent teeth, including the wisdom teeth.

Most primary teeth are smaller and whiter than the permanent teeth that replace them. They used to be called 'milk teeth'. Teeth are used to chew food so it can be swallowed, and they are necessary for proper speech sounds.

Primary teeth keep the space ready for their permanent successors. There are ten upper and ten lower. Starting from the centre of each jaw, there is first a central incisor, lateral incisor, canine, first molar, second molar.

The lower central incisors usually erupt first at about six months though it may be

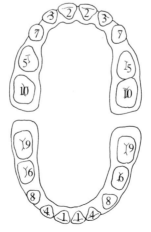

earlier or later. These teeth are usually followed by the lower lateral incisors. By one year, four lower and four upper incisors will probably have arrived. Within the next twelve months, the rest of the primary teeth erupt.

Don't worry if your baby's teeth don't arrive at the time suggested. As long as your doctor is satisfied everything is normal, lateness is not anything to be concerned about. Occasionally a primary tooth may not have developed and this may mean that the permanent tooth replacing it will also be missing. If a primary tooth is lost early, the movement of the adjacent teeth into the space can lead to crowding of permanent teeth when they erupt.

without prescription from your chemist which will help to relieve your baby's discomfort if teething worries him. Most of these contain benzocaine, a local anaesthetic which, when rubbed on the gums, helps relieve the irritation.

THUMB SUCKING

Various theories have been advanced to explain why children suck their fingers – emotional stress, early weaning, bottle rather than breast-feeding. But children who suck their fingers or thumb have been found to be as emotionally stable and secure as other children, and just as many breast-fed children suck their fingers as those who are bottle-fed, so none of the theories can really be supported. Probably most babies who suck their fingers or thumbs do so because they enjoy it and eighty-five per cent or more stop by the time they are four. If it persists beyond that age it may affect the position of the teeth – usually causing a space between the upper and lower front teeth, or the upper front teeth to stick out. However, the shape of the face and the position of the teeth is for the most part inherited. The amount of deformity produced by persistent thumb-sucking has been much exaggerated.

Sucking a dummy (pacifier) may have some advantages: it is not attached to the hand and arm so there are no muscles to pull the teeth forward, and it is often given up when it is lost or mislaid. There are different types of pacifiers but if you buy one, look for one with a large, firm shield to prevent accidental swallowing. If you tie it round the child's neck be sure that the string is not long enough to become entangled round the neck and cause choking. Never dip a dummy in honey or any other sweetener – the constant sugar will cause severe decay.

Most babies suck their fingers or thumbs just because they enjoy it. The fear that it may result in protruding teeth has been much exaggerated.

CLEANING YOUR CHILD'S TEETH

Your baby's teeth can decay as soon as they arrive and their care is almost entirely in your hands. Decay can nearly always be prevented by proper cleaning, a proper diet and using fluorides.

Cavities are formed because a sticky coating called plaque and consisting almost entirely of germs, adheres to the teeth. The germs use sugar from the food eaten to make acids that dissolve the enamel of the teeth.

Clean your baby's teeth every day beginning when he has just the one which – because it is in the front – will be easy to see. Clean the teeth every night before bedtime

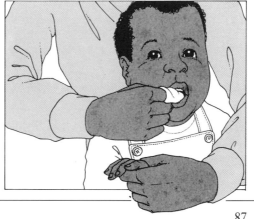

Prop the child on your lap or on a counter in front of you with his head against your stomach. Use moist lint or clean face cloth, cotton-tipped swab, piece of gauze or small toothbrush. Clean with gentle scrubbing action and include the gums where particles and germs also collect. If your baby cries, clean his teeth anyway.

Give snacks of fruit or baked breadsticks rather than candy, cakes or biscuits. Cut out sweet, sticky foods, such as jam and jellies that cling to the teeth and cause the beginning of decay.

or, if you want to do it more frequently, after feeding.

Children of up to three years do not have the dexterity to clean their own teeth, so a parent has to do it for them. When all twenty teeth are in the mouth make sure that you clean the back as well as the front ones – and all surfaces.

Fluoride toothpastes help prevent cavities but a word of caution: toothpaste is meant to be brushed on to the teeth, rinsed and spat out. Children under three usually swallow it so use only a small amount, not the thick ribbon you take for yourself. Just put enough on the brush to moisten the ends of the bristles and then spread it along with your finger, and teach the child to spit.

The effect of sugar on your child's teeth

Sugar causes dental decay and three factors affect its potential to do so: its type, its stickiness, and how often it's eaten. Sucrose, or the sugar on your table, is the most common substance to cause decay. Because the sucrose molecule is small it gets easily into dental plaque where it is transformed by germs into acid.

A sticky, sugar-containing food will adhere longer to the teeth and give more time for the acids to form. Sugar in sticky or hard sweets that must be sucked slowly is especially damaging because of the time it is kept in the mouth. Acids formed from sugar act on the teeth for about twenty minutes. If an amount of sugar-containing food is divided into five pieces and eaten at five different times during the day there will be five twenty-minute acid attacks. So the same amount of food can be five times as damaging

if taken at different times. That is why frequent sweet snacks are so dangerous.

How can you help?

Now you know why, how and when sugar damages the teeth you can make an informed choice about what to feed your child. Here's a guide. Use sucrose (common table sugar) sparingly in foods, drinks and snacks. Don't over-sweeten your child's food – it will give him a preference for sweet foods. Even baby food manufacturers have recently reduced the amount of sucrose in their products or eliminated it completely.

Give fruit, raw vegetable sticks, breadsticks as snacks – not sweets, cakes and biscuits. As your baby gets older, nuts and popcorn are healthy snacks that will not produce cavities.

If you must give sweets, choose sugar-free ones and chewing gum. These products contain sweeteners (mostly sorbitol or mannitol) which produce very little acid.

Be aware of 'hidden sugars' in processed foods. Some breakfast cereals contain as much as fifty per cent (by weight) of sugar. Read the labels and remember that the order of ingredients indicates the proportion: those listed first occur in greater quantity than those listed later. Processed foods sometimes contain several different sugars so the total can be large. All the following are sugar: corn syrup, honey, sucrose, fructose, glucose, maltose and dextrose.

Reduce or eliminate sweet, sticky foods such as toffee caramels, peanut brittle, lollipops, glazed popcorn and hard sweets.

Remember that flour and most breads don't cause decay in themselves, but, once chewed, bread becomes sticky and so helps to retain other decay-causing foods in the mouth. Jam or jelly spreads, for instance, will cause decay, butter, margarine or cream cheese won't. Some peanut butter contains sucrose – check the label.

Many medicines are made palatable by being blended in a sweet, syrupy liquid. If given several times a day for several weeks this can cause decay so clean your child's teeth when you use them.

Lemonade and other soft drinks are less cavity-producing than used to be believed – the rapid passage of liquid through the mouth and small contact with the teeth helps. 'Diet' soft drinks contain sugar substitutes or small amounts of sugar.

Sweets should be given only at mealtimes, not as snacks. During a meal the action of the tongue and extra flow of saliva will help clean the teeth but ideally you should also clean your child's teeth after a meal, especially if it contains a sweet or sticky dessert.

Discourage snacks of foods which contain sucrose. It is impossible and indeed not desirable to eliminate all sucrose-containing confections, but it is better to eat a whole lot of sweets or cake at once rather than at frequent intervals during the day.

Fluoride

All water contains some fluoride and in some areas the amount present naturally is enough to help protect the teeth against decay. Where it's not, the level may be adjusted by the water company. If necessary, your dentist or doctor will prescribe a supplement and you will be shown how to add it to water or fruit juice (but not to milk since the calcium in milk binds some of the fluoride and prevents it from combining with the calcium of the developing teeth). Only give your child the amount recommended: too much can cause discoloration.

Breast milk contains only a trace of fluoride, not enough to protect your child's teeth – tell your doctor you are breast-feeding and discuss this with him.

The first visit to the dentist

Between the ages of two and three is about the right time for this first visit, although if your child has injured his teeth or you suspect cavities either by seeing the holes or by toothache, he will need to have visited the dentist sooner. Choose a dentist who is used to working with children and tell your child about two days before the visit. Tell him the dentist looks after people's teeth, that he will count his and may clean them with a special toothbrush. Don't tell him that 'it won't hurt' or promise a toy if he is good. Children interpret this to mean that there is something threatening: they can also read facial expressions, so if you're afraid of dentists don't convey this to your child. Some dentists will let you go into the surgery and if you do, don't talk to the child or grimace as if something unpleasant is going to happen. Ask the dentist if you may hold the child's hand.

Most dentists will tell the child what they are going to do, then explain as they are doing it. They examine for cavities and check the general number, shape and state of the teeth and gums. They will take x-rays if needed, but only if needed: the small amount of radiation used for dental x-rays has not been proved harmful, but neither has it been conclusively proved safe. The dentist may give your child a small present – it is a 'positive behaviour-reinforcement' – rewarding for good behaviour, but not the same as a bribe to be good.

The next appointment will probably not be for another six months or year.

The first visit to the dentist should be made when your child is between two and three years. Don't convey anxiety to the child before the visit and choose a dentist who is used to children.

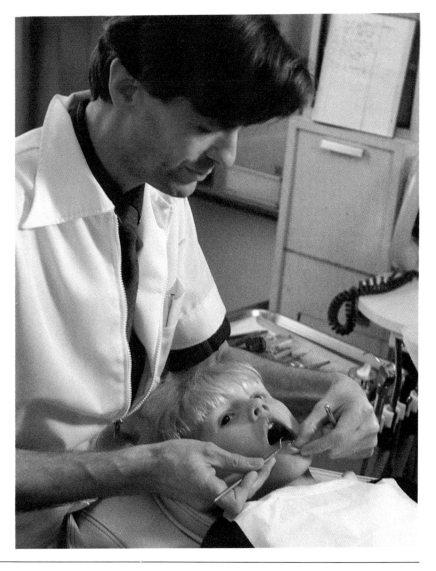

Sleep and bedtime

Do you only feel 'safe' when your baby's asleep? Sleep is one of the most mysterious benefits conferred on mankind and, like most benefits, usually remains unrecognized until you can't have it.

It is regulated by a monitoring centre the size of your fingertip, deep in the base of the brain and its purpose, obviously, is to protect against overtiredness and loss of alertness. It renews energy but it also gives the chance to withdraw from unpleasant and distressing situations. Dreaming during sleep allows us to explore new and imaginative experiences, and it especially helps children to enter worlds generally unknown to them. It also provides an escape from boredom.

A new baby in the family entails so much extra work and fatigue that it is only really possible to get through it all if the baby sleeps a reasonable part of the twenty-four hours. So the whole subject immediately becomes two-sided: how much sleep the baby takes inevitably affects how much sleep the parents get – and the habits of the baby don't always coincide with the wishes of the parents.

Your young baby will not stay awake and cry just to be awkward. She has not enough sense. She may be uncomfortable or unwell or need a cuddle, but when she needs to sleep, she'll sleep. Each baby may vary in the amount of sleep she needs, so time charts can only be indications. Although there are patterns of sleep – that is times when most babies sleep and wake – each baby may vary within that pattern.

The types of sleep
For both children and adults there are two kinds of sleep – the first is deep and 'inactive': it goes from light to very deep, and it is very difficult to wake anyone who is sleeping very deeply.

The second type of sleep is known as Rapid Eye Movement (REM) sleep, and it is called that from the rapid eye movements which take place and which indicate that the sleeper is dreaming. This is a lighter sleep. In children up to the age of five REM sleep is longer than the deep or inactive sleep.

Age of baby	Amount of REM sleep
Fetus	usually total
Premature newborns	75 per cent
Full-term newborns	50 per cent
Up to age of 5 years	steady decline to 25 per cent, thereafter little change

We can only guess that babies dream because they are not able to tell us when they do. If you watch your sleeping baby you will be able to see quite easily the difference between the inactive and the REM sleep. In the latter the face may twitch, there is irregular breathing, restlessness and you can see her eyes darting beneath her lids. Non REM sleep is more peaceful. Scientists can measure the two patterns of sleep with an electro-encephalogram which records brain activity. In inactive sleep there are slow and regular brain movements: in active sleep there is sharp activity with special 'spike waves'. These are similar to the brain-wave patterns found in epilepsy, but they in no way indicate brain abnormality.

How much sleep does a baby need?
The books used to state firmly that, apart from feeding, a new baby slept for most of the twenty-four hours. However, a great many babies had not read the books and their parents not unnaturally thought that either they were handling their baby badly, or that there was something wrong with her. Babies may not need as much sleep as we once thought: a newborn baby stays awake for as much as an hour after birth, and the needs of individual babies vary as much as the babies themselves. An indication – and indication only – might be:

Average newborn	sixteen to eighteen hours a day
At two months	about fifteen hours
At one year	about fourteen hours
At two years	about twelve hours
At five years	about ten hours

It makes little difference whether your baby takes her sleep continuously, or in several shorter periods. Little difference to the baby, that is. She won't need silence to get to sleep, but sudden loud noises will startle or wake her. The rhythm of voices, radio, the sounds of home will not disturb her and in a half-awake state will be comforting. If you insist on silence for the baby to go to sleep you'll be setting a pattern for a long time to come. A baby will sleep soundly within yards of the brass band in the park, and while there's no need to introduce a brass band into your nursery, the background noises of home – the whirr of a lawn mower, the sound of a sewing machine – will make a reassuring link between a toddler in bed and the adult life going on elsewhere.

A baby sleeps when she needs to and gradually evolves her own pattern of sleeping and waking times.

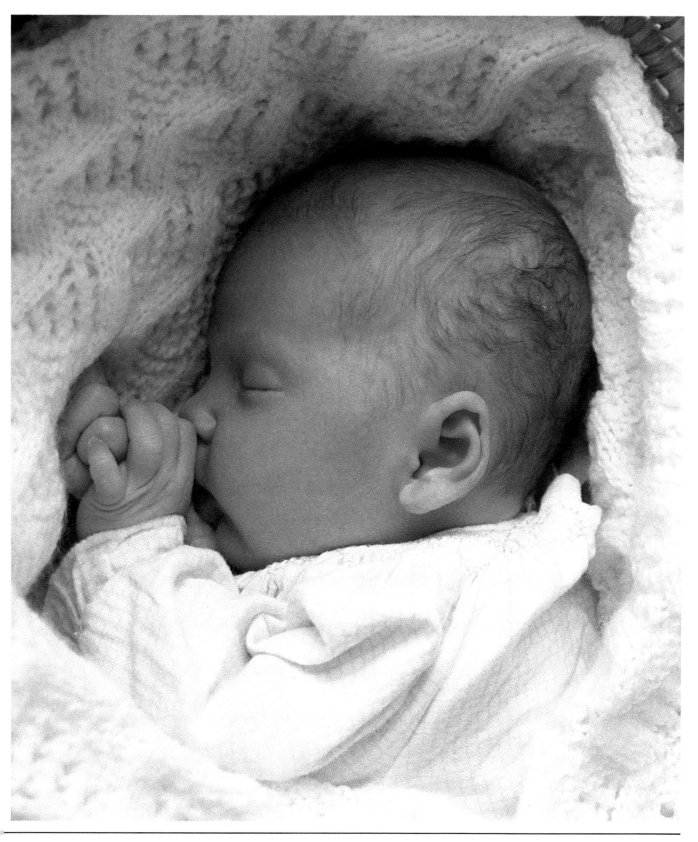

As we said – when a baby needs to sleep, he sleeps, whatever the situation – here he's safely tucked up in a back pack carrier.

Warmth, comfort, security and a full stomach induce sleep. A new baby feels safer when firmly wrapped – it mirrors the safety of the uterus: as she begins to move her limbs more she will want to be free of the restrictive wraps. A sheepskin fleece for the baby to sleep on has been shown sometimes to help a baby to sleep more soundly.

Your small baby can't decide in what position she will sleep: you decide for her – on her back, side, tummy. She may have a preference and your experiments will show which she likes best. She may sometimes want her position changed. Sometimes she may wriggle her bedclothes off and be uncomfortable and chilly. She may want the reassurance of a cuddle, and once she knows you are around she'll settle again. Even your voice may do the trick.

To fit in with the rhythm of family life it would be most convenient if your new baby awoke regularly for feeds, and slept most of the time in between. Some do – lots don't. Babies have an inborn sleeping pattern and it may take time to adjust this to the habits of the family. Practical ideas to help fit the new baby into the family routine are given in Daily Care (page 93). It has been shown that if a crying baby is attended to reasonably promptly she cries less because, presumably, she knows that reassurance is always at hand. Although you cannot and should not leap into action at the first whimper, 'crying it out' is not a good idea. It is distressing to both baby and parents who will often have to 'give in' in the end.

By six weeks or so your baby probably has one wakeful time a day – usually late afternoon – which is about the most convenient time she can choose as she can then kick, watch what's going on, and generally tire herself out for the evening feed and bed.

Naps decrease as your baby grows but this is compensated by her being able to amuse herself while she is awake – she will increasingly like company or watching the world go by. It takes time for parents to get used to the fact that wakeful babies are not always crying babies.

Some babies – when they are giving up some of their daytime naps – sleep all the afternoon and stay awake all the evening. Not a good idea – you need some time to yourself, much as you love her. Bringing lunch forward or an afternoon walk might keep her awake so that she can still have a nap, and then have a time to be awake.

Babies sometimes cry during the evening and this could be because the last feed (particularly if it is a breast-feed) is given when you are tired and possibly trying to cope with an evening meal. The baby may sense your tension and fatigue and there may also be less milk because you are tired. Some ways of coping with the early evening rush are suggested on page 54. Babies learn when they are being 'dumped' in a hurry surprisingly early, and may raise the roof to let you know their thoughts.

When do babies begin to react against bedtime?

During the first few months your baby will probably settle herself into a favourite way of going to sleep. She may begin to suck her thumb or a piece of her blanket, or there may be some other comfort habit she has devised for herself or you have suggested to her. Because she begins to be able to turn over or change her position she will probably go to sleep in her own chosen position. But at about nine months changes take place. She begins to realize it is pleasant to be with company and in an atmosphere where plenty is going on: she loves you so much she can't bear to be separated from you, but – and this is the sinister part – she is able to keep herself awake if she wants to. Tension, overexcitement, overtiredness – whatever the cause she will begin to be able to keep herself going.

It may be that the abrupt 'bath, bed and lights out' routine is no longer acceptable. She cries and you go back to her: she smiles and you settle her, you begin to worry about the evening meal overcooking and make a move towards the door. She opens one eye, takes her thumb out of her mouth and bawls. It is enough to try the patience of a saint.

So you too have to be wily. A regular bedtime is a good idea – it makes the point that daytime is different from night-time and anyway you need some time to yourselves. So what you now have to do is – for your daughter's benefit – begin to merge her day into her night. Make the transition less abrupt.

Begin the bed preparations reasonably early so that you're not rushed at the end (see page 95). Perhaps the last feed can be leisurely, there may be gentle talk and play. If she sleeps upstairs, give yourself time to potter around within earshot or even eyeshot ... tidying away bath things and so on. She may watch you through an open door and it could be a good idea to have a low light on the landing and none in her room. You'll know what proves best for your daughter. You could hum to yourself or sing and make small domestic noises ... and hopefully she will drift off to sleep contented because you are near and she hasn't been abandoned.

And if she doesn't?

Well, don't leave her crying. Go in to her, reassure her – sometimes you can call up to her while you juggle with the evening meal downstairs. Reassure her that she isn't deserted, because that's probably why she's crying. If voice alone doesn't help, go in to her and talk to her but don't bring her down. If you do you will have confirmed her suspicions: that it really is better to be with the family, not left alone in that room of hers.

It takes time and it can be maddening if you want to get on with things elsewhere. The only consolation may be to think that the phase will not last forever.

It can be small comfort, but she really will learn in time, especially if you're able to stay calm and unfussed and make the hour or two leading up to bedtime relaxed and peaceful.

Then again recognize that your baby may be genuinely frightened at being abandoned. She may also, of course, be 'trying it on', but you will be able to distinguish between the two: real distress carries on into small frightened whimpers and only gradually subsides as you comfort her; 'trying it on' can nearly always be turned off like a light, unless you have left her so long that it has turned into real distress. As always, when coping with your own baby try to think back to what *you* felt as a child.

One useful ploy if you're comforting a toddler is not to take the child out of her cot but to kneel down beside her and comfort her through the bars. Gently persuade her to lie down again if she's sitting or standing, find her cuddly toy, cover her up again, sing her a lullaby. This gets over the idea that the cot is not a bad place to be taken out of in order to be comforted, but a place where comfort can come in.

The same basic principle of giving attention promptly but not abandoning cot and bedroom carries on throughout the toddler years. An uncertain or frightened small child may be reassured by the sight of your knitting or your book left in her room – a talisman that you are still there and will return. The words 'back soon' can also be reassuring, particularly if you use them during the day and *stick to their promise*. One desperate father was known to settle his daughter with the phrase 'see you in about fourteen hours, eh?' in the hope that he could hypnotise her into the habit …

And it is never too early to begin lullabies, bedtime rhymes – and stories …

Cuddlies, comforters and things that console in the night

There is a suburban railway track just outside London where trains run over a bridge across a steep cutting, the sides of which are thick with tall spindly trees. They are so tall and the cutting is so deep that the treetops are just on a level with the train windows. And in one of those treetops – inaccessible except from the trains – hangs a teddy bear.

It could only have been flung from a train window – probably in a moment of wild toddler excitement – but imagine the agonizing loss … imagine bedtime and shudder.

Some babies find it easier to fall asleep if an adult stays quietly within sight while they're settling off, so that day blurs into night.

And the moral is ... if your baby has a cuddly, then duplicate it without delay. It is easiest if she chooses a nappy or piece of cloth, but make sure the standby is sometimes used because it will be the familiar smell, as well as the feel that comforts her. With a standby to fall back on it won't be so traumatic if the original gets lost or left behind.

Bedtime rituals usually develop gradually. The ceremonial folding of the cuddly – sometimes this is a very elaborate process –

the placing of teddy in bed, or the arrangement of about sixty-four toys without which, it seems, bedtime is not bedtime. Part of the time of course she is having you on and you both know it, but you should be able to manipulate it into a fairly good-humoured relationship.

Don't call me, I'll call you

A face appears round the door. The smile may be a little uncertain, unsure of the welcome. Or it may be utter triumph – 'Look, I've saved you the journey upstairs. I've come to you. Aren't I clever? *Admire* me!'

Greet her with politeness, patience and, if possible, a straight face. 'Did you want something? A drink of water, or (unsweetened) fruit juice? Yet another goodnight kiss?' Then back she goes. If she comes again, repeat the treatment but show her you really mean what you say by a calm firmness.

She may also appear at your bedside during the night. Advice about what to do has become more relaxed recently – or perhaps returned to previous habits. Most paediatricians now would advise you to let her come in when the comfort of your body and warmth will send her off to sleep. You may worry that the habit will continue indefinitely but if you have established that you are always available then the security you have instilled will free you to say, 'Look, I'd rather you stayed in your own bed, so could you please?' As she wants your approval as well as your presence, she may well do so and when she does, praise her and thank her in a matter-of-fact way.

The occasional evening out does not harm a toddler so long as she is not so overtired she can't sleep. She will feel immensely pleased with the privilege and you are giving her new experiences and enjoyment.

Make bedtime pleasant – for all of you

If, as your toddler grows, you make bed a threat or a punishment – 'Any more of that and you'll go straight to bed' – then you are certainly building up trouble for yourself. 'Bed is a bad place to which I am sent when I'm naughty.' So, she will reason, when bedtime comes that too must be a punishment.

The trick is to make bedtime almost a natural privilege ... the day must be geared to wind down gradually. There should be one or two warnings given about bringing a game to an end, or putting toys to bed; there should be a ritual of storytime, bathtime, last-minute kisses.

And one of the absolute necessities is to make the bedroom and the bathroom comfortable *for you*. While your two to three year

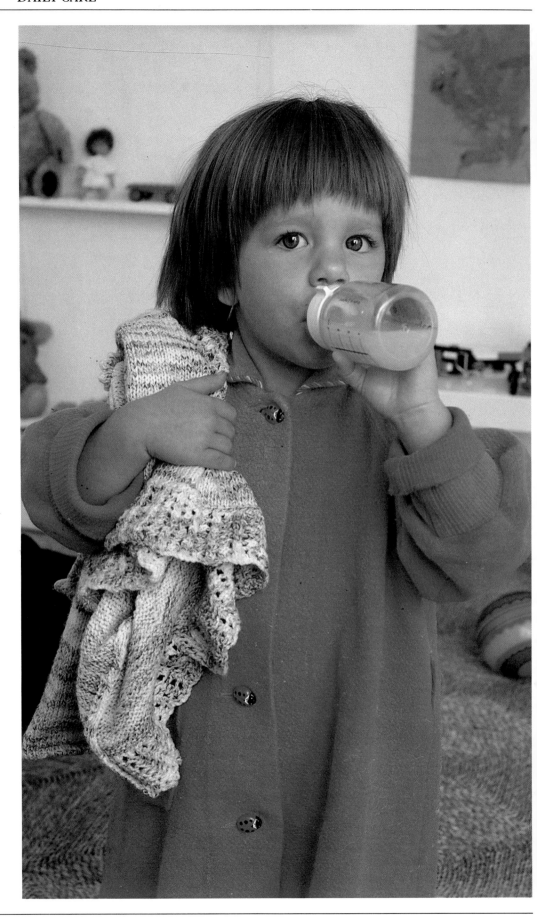

A drink at bedtime may be comforting but make sure it is not sweet and sticky and that teeth are cleaned afterwards.

old plays at submarines in the bath, you don't need to perch on the edge of the bath, or hop from one foot to the other waiting for the flotilla to be sunk, so you can get her out. Take a cup of tea in and sit on the bath stool. Some really artful parents begin the bedtime story in the bath – the echoes inspire dramatics in the reading – and finish it when the child is towelled, warm and tucked up in bed.

Don't play overexciting games just before bedtime: your child won't be able to wind down suddenly. If bedtime coincides with mother and/or father returning from work, taking turns with the last stages, or even the whole bathing procedure, becomes a very special time when parents and child deepen their own relationship. It also means that the child accepts comfort and care from both parents – because if mother is spending most time with the child there may be a tendency for 'only Mummy' to be the one to be able to help in emergencies.

Although the young baby usually wakes in the night from hunger or discomfort, and once that is attended to, will fall back to sleep, the baby from about nine or ten months onwards will often wake during the night, may whimper or resettle herself and then go off again without attention. If you need to go in, however, don't turn it into a chat show: deal quietly with what seems to be the trouble and then go back to bed. Children often wake in the night, play quietly with their cot toys and then go back again. The same happens early in the morning – children may amuse themselves for some time before calling for you. If they learn through your response that you'll come when they really need you, then they will need to call you less frequently.

What about baby-sitters?

Nights out are good ideas for parents. A grandparent or friend whom the baby or child already knows is the best baby-sitter, so that if she should wake she won't be greeted by a complete stranger.

Leave your telephone number, the doctor's, ambulance, and health visitor's if you have a twenty-four hour service in your area.

Tell the baby-sitter about any particular name your child has for her cuddly, comfort toys, wanting to go to the lavatory, drinks and so on – or any special habits she has. Explain your usual practice about responding to cries and requests so that the baby-sitter can be consistent.

Leave a bottle-feed prepared or expressed breast milk or any other drinks your child may need.

Come back when you say you will – and if your child has woken then don't feel so guilty

that you never go out again. A baby-sitter is not as emotionally involved as parents and won't have minded being disturbed during the evening in the same way that you would.

Should you tell your child you are going out? Honesty is usually the best policy, but don't make such a song and dance about it that your child suspects it's something she's meant to react against. If she really does sleep every evening and all evening you may be tempted not to tell her – this is something to decide for yourself. But just as you enjoy an evening away from her, the chances are she may enjoy an evening away from you with someone else to put her to bed and read the story – particularly if it's someone she already knows and loves.

In Britain it's illegal for anyone under sixteen to be left in charge of a child under twelve. Of course, a sixteen year old used to young children could no doubt cope better than an adult who's never held a young baby before, but that is the law. It is sometimes possible to overcome this by having the competent adolescent to baby-sit while an adult neighbour is nearby and on telephone call if something should happen the baby-sitter can't immediately deal with.

Baby-sitting circles are an excellent idea, particularly if the children know each others' parents, possibly through a mother and toddler group (see also page 20).

Three in a bed? Some parents find it a peaceful solution to broken nights. The habit is usually broken by the child herself.

Toilet training

A first-time father one day presented his toddler with a round, hollow object. It was blue and had a handle at one side and very sensibly the child put it on his head and looked for approval. Tolerant smiles and laughter greeted this achievement (father had read the baby books too), and then the real purpose of the present was demonstrated. A little thump on the inside of the container – such as might be caused by a small jet of water striking it – produced a little tune. Humpty Dumpty. Father had brought his son a musical potty.

The child was enchanted and refused to move without it. He was prevented from demonstrating its powers in supermarket aisles, but certainly many a peaceful picnicker was astonished to hear the strains of Humpty Dumpty with full orchestral accompaniment issuing from the bushes into which Junior had just disappeared.

Pleasure was tinged now with anxiety: would the association of music and action become so linked that every time that tune was played the child would react? Did the dog ever wag Pavlov? The answer came when the familiar tune was heard issuing from the next room and going in to congratulate their son the parents found him sitting peacefully beside a puddle while firmly holding a toy brick inside the potty. Boy Wonder was pushing back the frontiers of science. Babies are naturally lateral thinkers.

How the plumbing works

There are few subjects which cause parents such concern as toilet training, yet it may take up to three years for a child to learn the control an adult takes for granted.

The anxiety is understandable: a baby who can look after his own toilet is much more socially acceptable than the one who can't. And there is perhaps a more subtle anxiety because – apart from the amount of work a young baby causes at this stage – getting a baby clean and dry somehow seems more of an achievement for the parents than for the baby. Probably this is linked with our ideas of what is 'nice', but your ability to take toilet training in your stride and regard it as an almost casual part of the whole miracle of growth will have a lasting effect on your baby. This becomes obvious with the second, third or fourth baby who nearly always largely trains himself through watching his siblings. So good luck with the second, third or fourth, but meanwhile consider the first – and his plumbing system.

Some toddlers are distressed by being asked to sit on their potty – distraction with a toy or by talking to them will usually help.

A baby has been described as a padded alimentary canal with an entrance at one end and an exit at the other. This is also an assembly line in reverse because as the tract or gut goes through, it takes on different shapes, designed for the job it has to do. So the mouth is made for sucking and later chewing, the next part has muscular control which propels food from the mouth to the stomach. The stomach mixes and passes processed food into the small intestine where most of the nutrients are absorbed. The small intestine empties into the large intestine whose job it is to absorb water and temporarily to store the now depleted food before it is eliminated as faeces. So along its length the gastrointestinal tract has crushed, mixed, digested, absorbed and finally eliminated.

We do not have to think about the process: once food has gone into the mouth the system will take over, and our first indication of its progress is when discomfort signals it is time for a bowel movement. This is where the adult does have control – but the baby and young child do not: it has to be learned in much the same way that a child learns other skills – walking, talking, climbing.

Do not be obsessive
Within the first two to three days of life your baby will pass a green/black stool called meconium. This is formed from accumulated material produced by him before birth since, although he urinates frequently, the baby in the uterus does not normally pass stools. If you are in hospital the passing of meconium will be monitored, and if you are at home you should watch for it yourself or the midwife will do so. If it does not happen within three days you should tell your doctor as it might indicate an intestinal block.

Your baby may pass a stool after every

A baby's digestive system, and ours too for that matter, is a tube stretching from mouth to anus, modified along its length to perform various tasks. Food is propelled along by involuntary muscular contractions. Up until fifteen months the baby will move his bowels automatically but some time after this he will develop control.

Mouth
sucking, crushing

Oesophagus
propelling

Stomach
mixing

Small intestine
absorption of nutrients

Large intestine
absorption of water

Anus
elimination

feed for the first few weeks. Breast-fed babies tend to pass less frequently than bottle-fed babies, but as long as your baby is healthy and contented, there is no need to be concerned about the number of times in a day that your baby has a bowel movement. It could vary from three to twelve, and then again he might very well miss a day or two. Breast-fed babies always pass soft stools, usually yellow: bottle-fed babies produce firmer stools, more like an adult's in colour. The difference is due to the different composition of the milks.

A breast-fed baby does not get constipated and diarrhoea is uncommon because your milk has been specially made for his digestive system. If your bottle-fed baby is constipated, a few sips of water (tipped in with a spoon) between feeds will help. Ask your health visitor if the condition persists.

It used to be a preoccupation to study the colour of the baby's stools. Don't let yourself fall into this habit: if your baby is thriving there is no need to worry about that as well as everything else, although it may help you to know that green stools are caused by the bile in the digestive system and need not worry you. When the baby begins solids some of his food – beet and tomato for instance – may colour the stools. Watery stools should, however, be reported to your doctor. Traces of mucus and slime need not concern you.

The stools of a breast-fed baby are acid and consequently are unlikely to cause nappy rash (see pages 58 and 221) since the bacteria which produce the rash thrive in an alkaline environment. The bottle-fed baby will be more prone to nappy rash since he will produce alkaline stools, and the use of a barrier cream may be necessary. Curds in his stools will be undigested protein and are of no concern.

By two or three months your baby may be having a bowel movement perhaps only twice a day, and this will decrease until, by the time he is one, he will probably only have one a day – and not always that. Do not get preoccupied about bowel movements: if your child is healthy and contented forget the subject! (See constipation and diarrhoea on pages 211 and 213.)

Can you toilet train a young baby?
No way: you can catch him in time and that could mean you have saved yourself a nappy change, but do not fool yourself: just be glad you have managed it once. Some parents claim they have trained their baby by a few months: others think that too-early attempts will set up emotional difficulties later. Take the middle path – and relax.

The reason why you can't train a young baby is because he doesn't have the physical or emotional maturity to control his movements.

If your baby has a bowel movement after every feed then you will probably think it worthwhile to let the pot catch it. Hold the pot on your lap and hold the baby on it with his back supported by your stomach. Make sure he feels safe and is warm – and the cold rim of the pot may do the trick. He is, however, not consciously opening his bowels – he is responding with a reflex action.

You may have quite a lot of success this way and feel very pleased about it. And then – at about nine or ten months when he is beginning to have views on life – he will probably refuse. He may cry, squirm, go red in the face with anger, but he will not use that pot. So don't make him.

You may decide to begin again when he is about fourteen or fifteen months, or you may decide to wait until even later. He will of course be aware that you both go into the

A baby takes great interest in the whole business of potty training – when she begins to understand what's expected of her.

Success! Bladder and bowel control are not easy to achieve and your toddler deserves praise when it's due.

lavatory and that things happen in there, and sooner or later he may dimly get the idea that he would like to copy you. It is incidentally very important that you don't lock a child out of the lavatory when you go in. He need not come in with you and you can pull the door to if that is what you want, but locking a child out implies rejection and that something mysterious is going on inside.

By about fifteen months most toddlers will squirm or screw up their faces when they are about to have a movement, and you can act to make sure it goes in the right place. By now the child is beginning to associate the feeling with the action, and this is a good time to find a family word to describe what is going on. Using the word in connection with the feeling and what happens links all three together, and makes a connection between cause and effect.

Elimination may be messy but is not 'dirty'

There is one aspect of toilet training which cannot be sufficiently stressed. You should, of course, be relaxed and matter-of-fact about the whole business, but don't show by your words or actions that you find your child's faeces offensive. If you do then you are giving him the message that this particular happening is bad and dirty – and moreover you do not like it and therefore, to his way of thinking, you do not like him. This will lead to battles, tension on his part and bewilderment. If, furthermore, he doesn't manage to produce anything in his pot but, after sitting there patiently and docilely at your request he then gets up and fills his pants, you will naturally feel somewhat defeated – but do not scold: he will think it is the movement which is provoking your anger, not the fact that he did not get it in the right place. The aim should always be 'better luck next time', otherwise he may try to hold on and this can lead to constipation. Always praise if he succeeds in getting it right: your child wants and needs your praise and will get the message – and the control – in time.

The fuss that many parents make about their child not 'being clean' is really a reflection of their own embarrassment: that is natural, and the opposite – being rather too complaisant about other peoples' inconvenience and distaste – is equally to be avoided. But it is possible to maintain dignity, and that goes for your child's too: don't make him a scapegoat for lapses in public just because you happen to feel self-conscious.

When and on what?

By eighteen months or possibly a month or two earlier your son may be having a bowel movement at a regular time each day. Regularity is something to be aimed at so at this observed time every day – or after every meal

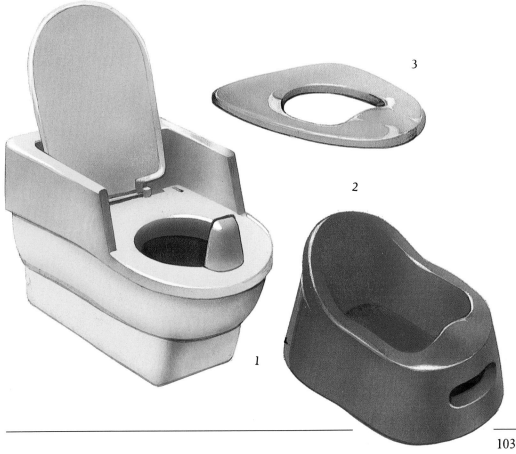

Pots and toilet seats come in all shapes and sizes. A child will feel secure on a pot with its own firm base (1*) and the removable splash guard will be useful for small boys. Simpler styles (2) are perfectly adequate, however, especially with a high back to help the child feel safe. Eventually you will find that a seat fitted to an adult-sized toilet (3) is more suitable for an older child.

*Available only in the United States of America

if that is more appropriate to his particular toilet habits – he can be assisted to sit on his pot. Pull his pants down and if he wants to he can look at a book or eat something or sing to Ted. The idea is to get him used to sitting on his pot so that it holds no fears for him. Nothing may happen of course, but he is becoming familiar with the regularity and what he is meant to do. Never hold him down on the potty, and don't get ratty if he begins to use it as a scooter, which he may well do if you buy the kind of potty that stands on the floor. Sometimes this is incorporated into a chair which cannot be moved so easily and which makes him feel safe. It is a good idea for little boys to use the kind of potty which has a small shield in front which will save them from spraying the floor. One advantage of the small potty is that it can be taken with you if you are travelling. Children often get extremely possessive about their pot and will not perform without it.

You can also buy a seat to fit over an adult-sized lavatory seat which will make it smaller. Children can sink into a large seat so that their legs wave about in the air and they cannot haul themselves out. Put a stool for him to rest his feet on also – it makes elimination easier.

When to praise and when not to

A child encouraged by your praise when he manages to achieve what you want may well become so delighted that he will bring you – and any visitors around – the contents of his pot so that he can share his pleasure. Don't react by expressing distaste or anger, even if you are embarrassed. All the same you don't want to encourage him, so the best idea is to take it rather casually but imply by your mild reaction that this is not quite the thing to do. Act in the same way if he wants to handle faeces. To a child the movement is still part of him. There is no need to imply this is the right thing to do and you can point out that it is making you a lot of work if he smears it on his cot; but if you overreact then he will realize this is yet one more way of getting your attention.

In the meantime try to make sure he does not have the chance to begin the habit. A calm 'there's a good boy' and then tipping the contents of his pot down the lavatory will help.

On the other hand this may well surprise him. You have just praised him for producing the movement and now you are throwing it away. Contradictory behaviour? Reassure yourself by remembering that all children learn control in the end, it just takes a lot of time and patience.

Not just clean – also dry?

Bladder control comes after bowel control. Your child may well urinate at the same time as he has a bowel movement so he is learning that there is a right place to put them both. During mild weather if he is able to play outdoors, leave off his nappies and put him into trainer pants or ordinary pants. You will then be one stage nearer 'catching him'.

It usually takes a month or two longer for boys to learn bladder control than it does girls. Offer the pot after a meal or a drink, or at intervals when your observation tells you he might be ready. And keep on praising – the technique is always to praise the 'good' behaviour and to ignore the 'bad', but not to make such a song and dance about it that it takes over his world. Too much insistence will only distress him and make you a nervous wreck.

Have the potty handy so that your child can use it himself when he begins to recognize the need. If he does it on the carpet, or the floor, which of course he will, you can be mildly exasperated, but not enough to disturb him. Some toddlers get very good at coming for the cloth to wipe it up! Once again, it is a question of patience and not hurrying, and he will eventually get the message. The average age for children to be dry during the day is two years two months.

Staying dry at night takes longer. Get your child to urinate before he goes to bed, and if he doesn't want a drink, don't give one. If he does, do – otherwise he'll keep awake saying he is thirsty. It is a good idea – even when he's dry during the day – to put him in a nappy at night. This saves wet sheets and also helps him not to get too worried about wetting the bed. You can lift and pot him just before you go to bed – or, if he urinates earlier, learn the approximate time and catch him then. Don't have a chat or turn on the light … the feel of the pot will stimulate him into using it and he probably won't even wake up. The same goes for the early morning. Many children urinate just as they are waking up so if you can get up first you could catch him, save yourself a wet nappy and give him a feeling of satisfaction and achievement.

Many children are not dry at night until about three: this does not matter – they will learn not to urinate in their sleep if you pot them and control does come. If bed-wetting recurs it may be associated with some anxiety (see page 200), needing different handling.

It is a good idea to teach your child to wash his hands after going to the lavatory since it is instilling good habits – but it should not be implied that hand-washing is because the operation is 'dirty'.

When your toddler is old enough to use the adult lavatory, her feet must be supported, otherwise she will have difficulty in passing a motion.

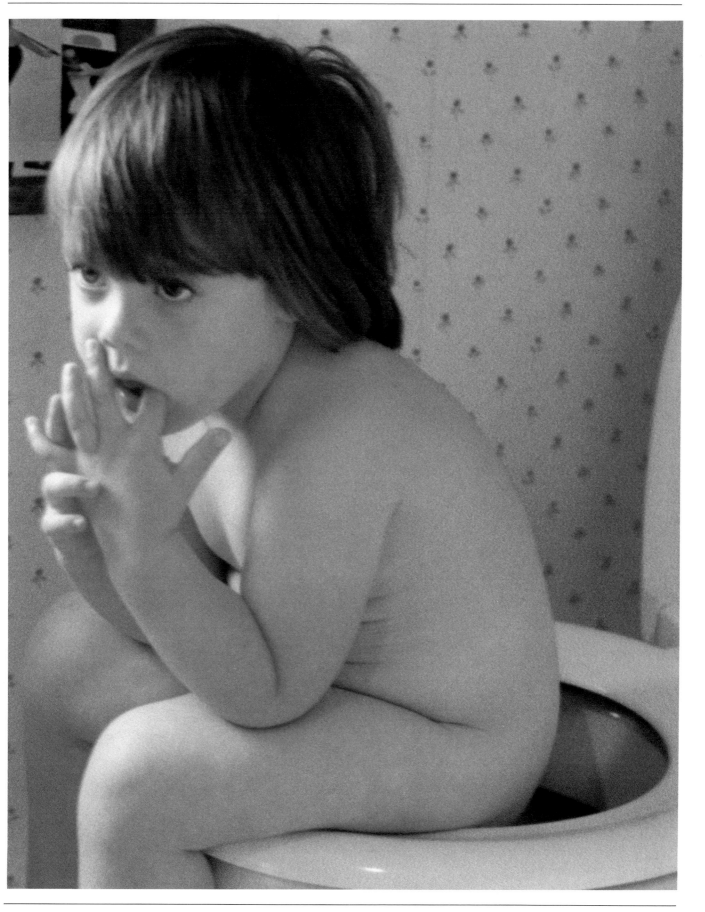

Your sick child

AT HOME

Thanks to medical advances, many illnesses in children which previously needed hospital treatment can now be treated at home. Provided the care is satisfactory this is obviously better for the child who does not have to suffer the emotional trauma of being separated from the family and subjected to procedures at the hands of strangers, however kind (see page 108).

Your doctor will tell you if your child should stay in bed, but generally speaking if the child feels well enough to get up, then let her. She will be happier being near you and still being part of the family instead of being isolated in bed. Usually if she gets really tired she will go back to bed on her own. In the meantime, a couch or easy chair in a room where she can see what's going on will make her comfortable. Make sure she is out of draughts and that the room is kept warm enough.

If she has to stay in bed, make sure the bedroom is inviting and interesting enough – and that goes too for the parent who will probably be expected to keep her company for some of the time. It is often possible to take some of the household jobs into her room but you will also need an easy chair for yourself and any other visitors who drop in.

If your child is feeling under the weather, she will probably drop off for naps during the day, and when bedtime comes she may not be ready to sleep – which you no doubt will be. Keeping her interested enough to stay awake – within reason – makes sense, particularly towards the end of the afternoon or early evening. A television or radio in the bedroom will help and so will toys, books, games and pets. Telephone calls to grandparents or favourite friends and relations can be a great treat, provided they don't go on so long they send the bills skyhigh. Jigsaws, scrapbooks, cutting out and sticking, construction toys can all be done in bed and so can colouring (coloured pencils and stick paste are kinder to the bedlinen than paints and glue). Cutting up old magazines with blunt-ended scissors passes a lot of time.

What about visitors – and other members of the family?
Infectious or contagious diseases are usually passed on during the first day or two of illness, before you actually know what illness the child has. If other children in the family have been immunized against the sick child's malaise then they probably won't catch it, or, if they do, it will be in a mild form. If they have not been immunized then you should ask your doctor what to do about isolation, which will obviously depend on the severity of the illness.

Provided they are not too tiring, or disturbing, or don't stay too long, visitors are invaluable. A sick child can even be comforted simply by the sight of people they are fond of – grandparents or older children who are chatting quietly in the room. Try and arrange for a sick child still to be involved in what is going on in the rest of the family.

Medicines and pills
These are usually made palatable for children and it will not be difficult to get them to take them. Assume they are palatable and don't transfer your uncertainties to the child even before she opens her mouth. When she has taken the pills or medicine, take them out of the room: she may like them so much she will try and scoff the lot at one go. If the medicine is unpleasant, crush a tablet in a spoonful of jam or fruit juice or – after strong medicine – give a reward of a sweet. Special measuring spoons are often supplied with liquid medicine, and these make it easier for the medicine to be given.

Special food
Unless your doctor advises differently, your sick child probably won't need any special diets. Naturally if she has a sore throat she will like softer, easily swallowed food, but don't be alarmed if she goes off her food. Help her to drink as much as possible – fruit juices, beef extracts, milk or flavoured milk drinks. Expensive glucose drinks are not usually particularly good value for money unless they are the only thing your child will drink, in which case she is at least taking liquid. An egg beaten in milk provides calories and protein.

A sick child will probably want to eat little and often: prepare food that is attractive to look at and rather 'special': this will not only help her appetite but also help to keep her morale up and make her feel cared for.

Taking her temperature
You can usually tell if a child is feverish by feeling her forehead or by her flushed appearance, but a high temperature is not always a guide to a child's health as many

A sick child needs some company and the reassurance that she's still part of the family.

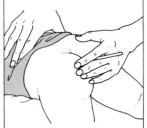

The normal shaped thermometer can be used in the mouth or under the arm. In all methods the thermometer must stay in position for at least a minute.

Use a stubby ended thermometer for taking the rectal temperature of a young baby or an uncooperative toddler.

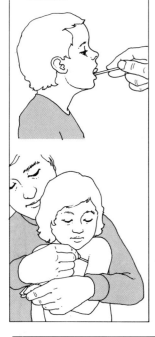

Three methods of taking a young child's temperature. By two years most children will cooperate with the oral method or if not the armpit method.

children can tolerate a high temperature (up to 39°C, 102°F) without being ill. In the same way, a normal or subnormal temperature is not an infallible guide as to whether she is well or not.

You will learn from experience what rise in temperature your own child can tolerate, and there are comparatively few occasions when you need take a child's temperature. If you do, there are three methods of doing so by thermometer: by mouth, under the arm or by rectum. You can buy discs or bands of a heat-sensitive material which can be pressed on the child's forehead and which will very quickly change colour or give a reading to show the approximate temperature: these, however, only show the skin temperature.

Hold a thermometer by the stem end – not by the bulb end – and flick down the mercury to below the arrow for 'normal'. When reading the temperature you may have to twist the thermometer between your fingers so that you can see the reading. After every use, wash in cold water and don't transfer from one child's mouth to another without washing first.

Never use hot water to wash – it may cause expansion sufficient to break the bulb. (See Fever on page 217.)

IN HOSPITAL

It could be that at some time your under-three might need hospital treatment – either as a stay-in patient or in the casualty department. Although it may never happen it is well to be prepared and to prepare your child also. As opportunities arise let her know gradually that a hospital is a place where people get better. In the same way that you read stories about farms, shops, garages, read also to her about hospitals. Point out your local building as you go past. Don't refer to the place as somewhere mysterious, nor talk in hushed tones to other adults about what dreadful things go on there.

A child doesn't need to be a patient before she visits hospital: many hospitals now allow and welcome children as visitors so if this situation arises naturally, take advantage of it. If another child in the family has to go to out-patients, take the younger child too. Jigsaws, books or similar quiet games will keep them both occupied, and if they have comfort blankets or toys, take them too. Some hospitals have small playgroups in the children's out-patients. Many books for very young children bring in visits to a hospital as a matter of course (see page 228) and there are also several books which specifically prepare a child for a visit. The National Association for the Welfare of Children in Hospital (NAWCH, page 230) can give additional information on all aspects of this subject.

Playing out fears

Children love playing at doctors and nurses – so encourage them with the emphasis on patients who get better, and are treated kindly and made comfortable.

If you know your child will have to go to hospital prepare her gradually by mentioning it from time to time as casually as you can. You can explain about anaesthetics in as simple a way as she can understand, and assure her you will be there when she wakes.

Try not to be tense as this will communicate itself to your child and don't deceive her by saying 'it won't hurt' if you know there is going to be an injection, for instance. Most nurses or doctors will say 'this will prick just for a moment' and hopefully will explain to the child, where possible, just what is happening. The doctor and nurse will know that you are worried also.

If you want to ask questions and think you may forget them, jot them down. Jot down too any symptoms you may have noticed, or conditions about the illness which you think may be helpful. It is better for some children that discussions with doctors take place without them – and if this is so, then taking another adult with you means that you can leave the child with her while you speak.

A stay in hospital

If the child has to be admitted, take some of her comfort toys with her, and of course her own nightdress and dressing gown. To the child, clothes are part of her and if possible she will want the clothes she went in left in her bedside locker. Unrestricted visiting is happily becoming more usual in many hospitals – this doesn't mean all relatives and family can drop in whenever they want: it should mean that mother or father can stay with the child for most of the time. On occasions, if medical procedures are necessary, then you may not be needed. Talk to the ward sister and tell her you would wish to be there when the child comes round from an operation, and ask if you will be able to accompany her to the operating room until she is given her anaesthetic.

Sitting by a bed can be very boring – especially if your child is playing happily with the child in the next bed and takes no notice of you. Visiting little and often may be better because the child can be told that you

are now going shopping, or picking other children up from school, and this has probably been part of her home routine and is acceptable to her.

The mother who stays in hospital with her child is often of great help to the nursing staff. She can help to amuse other children whose parents are not there – or take turns generally with feeding, taking round meals, with bathing, undressing and perhaps giving medicines. Much of this will depend on the attitude of the sister in charge, of course.

The practice of allowing mother or father to sleep in hospital with their sick child is now happily becoming more widespread. Some hospitals, regrettably, make difficulties but parents should always state that they wish to stay. Britain leads the rest of the civilized world in giving parents this right and in recognizing the invaluable role they can play in being with their child. The support and comfort given by the parent's presence immeasurably aids the child's progress, while the parents will feel they are not 'cut off' from their sick child but are playing a major part in her care.

It can of course be tiring for a parent to stay for long periods in hospital, particularly if there are commitments such as other children at home, so it will help if father and mother take turns to stay. Some hospitals allow pets in the ward, sand and water play, noisy games: silence and clinical order are not now regarded as essentials, but rather as deterrents, to recovery. A trained hospital play specialist will help a child to 'play out' her fears – giving teddy an operation, an anaesthetic, etc.

The convalescent child at home
Many children are so occupied and busy in hospital that they find home a very dull place when they get back. There may be no constant companions and no life of the ward going on around them. But your child could also feel that hospital had been some sort of punishment and now she may react by disruptive behaviour, anger or coldness towards – usually – her mother. Patience and understanding of this new aggression are the only solutions. It could be that talking to the ward sister, the play specialist or the hospital social worker before your child comes home could help you to prepare yourself and the rest of the family for what may – or may not be – the child's behaviour. (For organizations and books dealing with this subject, see pages 228 and 230.)

Unrestricted visiting is now usual in most children's wards. Parents can help to amuse, feed and sometimes give treatment to their children.

YOUR GROWING CHILD

No baby is an island. She cannot grow in isolation.

At birth her small computer has been programmed with the ability to progress – walking, talking, understanding: it takes a severe breakdown in the mechanism to interrupt this pattern of what we call 'normal' development.

But it is environment that launches the baby into the deep and delightful waters of living – and you are the chartmasters here, providing the compass, marking the reefs: you are the lodestar of your child's development in the early years. It takes a genius, of course, to bring up a baby but then that is what parents are. Although it's the parent who is the expert on his own child, acquired knowledge will also guide and help – and this is where the experts come in.

Few subjects have been so studied today as child development. Does that make today's parents lucky or unlucky? Will they end up totally confused by conflicting 'expert' opinions, hopping from one theory to another as yet a further page of research is turned and yesterday's gospel becomes today's mistake?

It is a question that bewilders parents more than researchers who are probably sleeping soundly through the night while mother and father are turning up the index in the baby book *Night crying: causes and cures*. Charity being at a low ebb at two in the morning you will be forgiven for wishing the author vociferous triplets.

But however much it may disconcert you when your baby does not conform to 'what the book says', the underlying principles of developmental behaviour are constant. They are the tram lines. Admittedly your baby may be a bus, taking odd little detours down byways where the view seems more pleasant, marking time at corners and then speeding full ahead on the wrong stretch of road with you in agitated pursuit.

It helps to remember that a baby is human. That means possessing all the inconsistencies. preferences and frailties which make a human being. And also all the glories, talents and potential. If the glories seem a bit thin when you are picking up the rattle from the pram side for the seventeenth time or manfully ('womanfully' probably) masticating a grey pastry jam tart 'cooked' by your three year old, take heart. As the politicians say, you are doing a splendid job.

But knowing *how* you are doing a splendid job does help with the eighteenth knee bend for the rattle, and this is where the experts' knowledge is invaluable. Knowing the general pattern and principles of your baby's development is like having a guide-rail over a precipice: you can hang on while you admire the view.

Although it is practical to write about different areas of development in separate sections – seeing, moving, talking – it is obvious that your baby won't grow like that in a series of isolated steps. Each area of growth affects another in a shifting pattern of development. Sometimes growth in one area supports growth in another. Sometimes there is a slowing down in one skill while there is a spurt in another and then again you will find a baby who progresses steadily and calmly in a near-textbook pattern.

Nature has artfully loaded the dice. Just as it seems life is all broken nights and feeding, your baby will stare at you for a long, considering moment and – deliberately and devastatingly – *smile*. When you are worn out with lumping her about she will begin to walk. Along the long

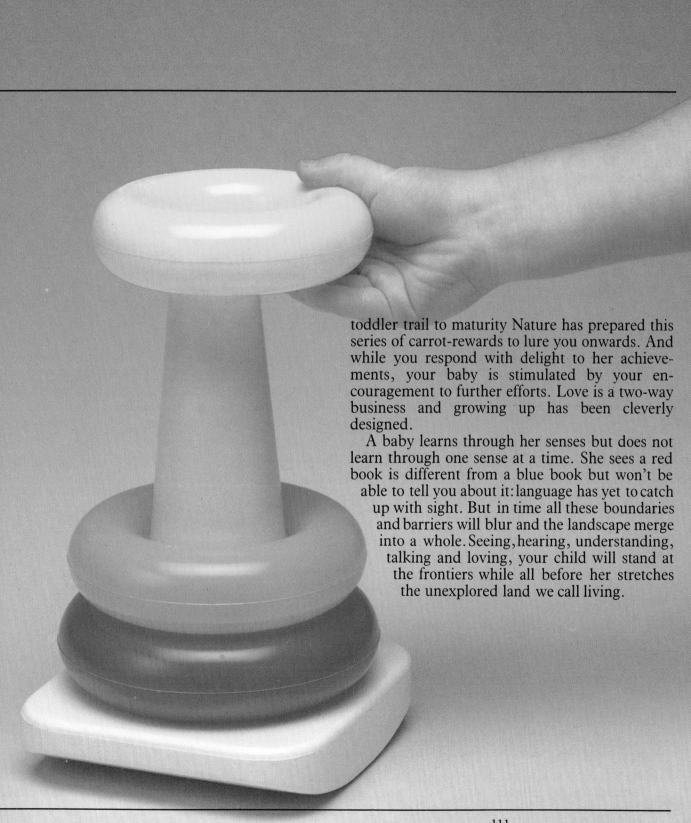

toddler trail to maturity Nature has prepared this series of carrot-rewards to lure you onwards. And while you respond with delight to her achievements, your baby is stimulated by your encouragement to further efforts. Love is a two-way business and growing up has been cleverly designed.

A baby learns through her senses but does not learn through one sense at a time. She sees a red book is different from a blue book but won't be able to tell you about it: language has yet to catch up with sight. But in time all these boundaries and barriers will blur and the landscape merge into a whole. Seeing, hearing, understanding, talking and loving, your child will stand at the frontiers while all before her stretches the unexplored land we call living.

Seeing

'How many weeks will it be, darling,' asked the expectant father, 'before the baby opens his eyes?'

'A baby,' was the frosty reply, 'is born with his eyes open.'

Mother was right. From birth your baby is able both to open and close his eyes because a new baby's eyes possess an inborn sensitivity to light (photophobia). We have the same reaction when we go from darkness into bright light and instinctively narrow our eyes against the glare. As most babies come from the sheltered darkness of the womb into bright light, the ability to protect the eyes by closing them is very important. It's because of our increased awareness of the discomfort the glare may cause the baby that it's becoming usual in many hospitals to lower the lights as much as is practicable at the moment of delivery. In the same way – because we now know that a baby's hearing is more acute than was previously thought – voices are lowered and noises are kept to a minimum.

Until comparatively recently it was thought that the new baby could see very little, if at all, but now research confirms what parents have always suspected – that from birth the baby can not only see but also seems able to focus his eyes. 'He's looking directly at me. I'm sure he can see me.' How many mothers and fathers have thought that in the first moments of welcoming their new baby, even if they have been too inhibited to say so? Now observation has shown that a new baby, if left peacefully, may keep his eyes open for up to an hour after birth and that during that time he will appear to be studying the face of the person holding him – hopefully his mother or father.

Your new baby can see objects that are fairly big and bright and at a distance of between about six and twelve inches. He can focus for a short while and follow an object for a short distance – and there's also evidence that a baby is more attracted to curved rather than straight lines because it is noticeable that he will study an arc longer than a straight line.

If all these preferences and abilities are put together – a fairly big object without too much detail, a curved outline, a distance of about six to twelve inches – there is one object which meets all these requirements and which, moreover, is the one thing he is most likely to see in the course of his daily life: the human face. Nature's plan is specific, controlled and very clever.

By four months of age the baby is beginning to see colours and by six months he will begin to perceive depth: by twelve months he will be able to focus almost as well as an adult.

It is probably only the outline and not the detail of your face that your baby sees. Eyebrows and eyes seem particularly important and all parents know how, while feeding, the baby's eyes seem locked on theirs.

But looking is not all. Within a few hours of birth your baby will turn his eyes towards the sound of your voice: not the voice from the next bed or the midwife's voice across the room but to *your* voice. So it's not only sight and sound that are linked from the beginning – preference and association are also being shown.

By two to three weeks your baby's ability to associate sight and sound is even more dramatic.

The curved object that your baby stares at with such attention (and at which he also has the most opportunity to stare) is your face. But this face, blurred, curved, with dark shadows where the eyes are, is neither silent nor static. It nods to him, turns and shifts about a little and it also produces reassuring, gentle noises, for there can be very few mothers and fathers who don't talk to the young baby they're holding and these gentle words of encouragement and affection are nearly always accompanied by nodding movements of the head.

So your baby soon learns that the face he sees so frequently produces its own particu-lar voice and this is the face and the voice that he associates with comfort, warmth, security. This face and this voice seem to be a good thing.

But won't any face or voice do? Can your baby really tell when it's your face, your voice? Although other faces and other voices can comfort a baby, there is proof that the new baby can not only associate his mother's face and voice, he can also distinguish when they are separated. A series of simple tests carried out in Boston and London some years ago showed that it is the voice linked to the face that holds the baby's attention.

In the first experiment the baby was shown his mother's face but she didn't speak. Instead her recorded voice was played from behind the baby, who either took very little notice or else seemed quite cross.

In the next stage the baby was shown his mother's face but a stranger's recorded voice was played to him so that his mother appeared to be speaking with a different voice. Again the baby was uninterested.

The next stop was to show a stranger's face which mimed to his mother's recorded voice. Again, there was little reaction and very little interest.

It was only when his mother's face and voice were shown together in the way that he would normally see and hear them that the

This is probably what the new baby sees as he looks up at the human face: he sees the outline and not the detail, but eyebrows and eyes seem particularly important.

Inset left Gradually the face comes more into focus and is associated with a certain voice.

At four months – perhaps even earlier – he will distinguish nose and mouth. Familiar faces are greeted with squirms of delight.

The new baby's range of focus is limited to between six and twelve inches. He may keep his eyes open for up to an hour after birth.

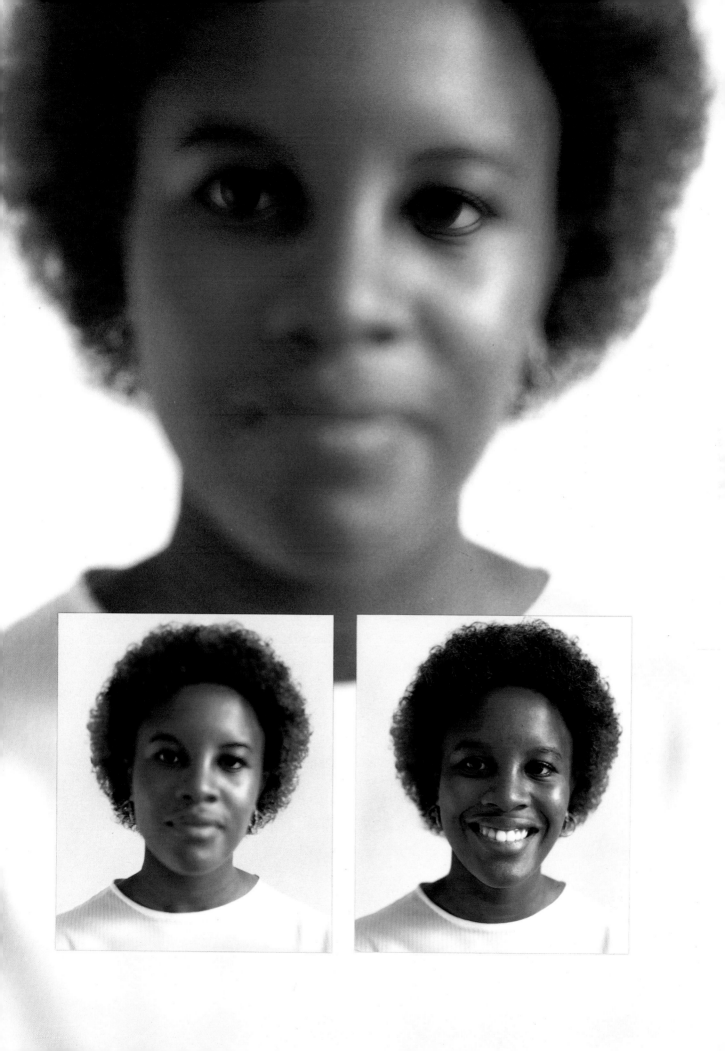

Memory is linked to sight as the baby stares at his mother's face. The epicanthic folds (see page 225) are clearly shown in this baby's eyes.

baby reacted with his usual enthusiasm.

So by three weeks of age your baby has learnt that it is only your face that goes with your voice. Naturally he has not got it quite sorted out yet – which is why the six-week-old baby, who prefers people to objects, can sometimes be seen smiling appreciatively at an object which has roughly the same detail

as the human face *and which nods at him* – in other words, seems to show some of the same reactions as the human face.

But not only can your baby sort out the first steps of associated sight and sound, he can also choose what he sees. Just as he cries to get your attention, so he will blank out anything he doesn't want to see. Either he'll go glassy-eyed or he'll turn his head away. 'Put the mobile away, Mummy,' he seems to be saying, 'I've had enough.' Another trick is to let his eyelids droop until a new distraction comes along that interests him – then the lids lift and a look of alertness comes back into his eyes.

And if, as a slow-learning adult, you don't take the hint that he is doing his best to give you, he will very quietly and dismissively go to sleep.

You know all this without a baby book to tell you. You know it by the daily care and contact with your baby – but it's only when they are recorded and analysed that the extraordinary abilities and rapid development of your baby are seen for the achievements they are. Within a few weeks of his emergence from the twilight world of pre-birth he can see, associate, choose, discriminate.

It is the gradual cross-association of the senses which leads to growth and awareness.

Much of what your baby sees will mean little to him for his mental ability is still limited. But as the weeks pass, ability and opportunity keep pace. As his eyes strengthen, he is able to withstand brighter lights. That means he can keep his eyes open for longer periods and so in turn he receives more stimulus. From two to three months your baby becomes more aware of his environment because he is more able to explore it.

Up to the age of about two months your baby will seem to prefer looking at pictures showing only eyes and eyebrows, rather than faces with only nose and mouth. That is only to be expected because eyes and eyebrows are what your baby sees most frequently as he lies in your arms looking up. But by showing that he *remembers* what he sees; memory is being linked with sight. The baby recognizes the 'picture' and responds to it.

Muscles around the eye are now becoming stronger and this means that both eyes are working together more efficiently. Previously your baby may have shown an occasional 'wandering eye' which can be alarming for as yet inexperienced parents. One eye may suddenly take off and wander in a different direction from the other, but this will right itself as the eye muscles strengthen. It shouldn't persist after three months however and if it seems to be doing so, you should consult your doctor.

Less and less now does your baby appear to stare straight through you. Up to two to three months his focus is still limited to about seven to twelve inches but by three to four months he will be able to focus at almost all distances. Earlier he had trouble keeping both eyes on an object for any length of time but now he will watch an object, follow it through movements and appear to study it.

By eight or nine weeks your baby is beginning to reach out and swipe at objects. He is beginning to realize that the world is three dimensional. At first he bats out and seems surprised if he happens accidentally to touch anything. He will swipe at little toys strung across the cot or pram, or a mobile within reach and it is an added interest if the thing he touches makes a pleasant noise. At first the movements are primitive but after a very short while he never misses – his hands locate accurately and purposefully the object his eyes have seen.

He has also discovered for himself two other wonderful toys. They are toys which seem always available, their appearances no longer dependent on the whim of an adult. At any moment these two objects can appear like magic before his eyes: his own hands.

Babies examine their hands for long periods at a time. At first, because the young baby keeps his hands fisted, he seems to study them as separate objects but as your baby learns to flex his fingers, to separate them and direct them to behave in the way he wants, he begins to use his hands to wave, to pluck and eventually to pick up objects. Babies spend a lot of time with their hands clasped in front of them: if you think about it, it is an achievement for a baby to direct two hands to meet.

By four months he is really taking off. His scope has broadened so that when he looks at faces, the eyes and eybrows are not enough: he'll want to see nose and mouth as well.

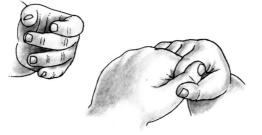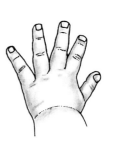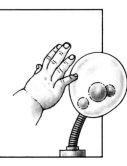

Hands have a particular fascination for the three month old as he moves and flexes his fingers and begins to swipe out at objects. His aim will be uncertain for some weeks.

Whereas before most objects have been either light or dark, they are now beginning to assume colours: he will probably by now be able to see red, yellow, green and blue. And he will also – from about six months – begin to perceive depth. Various researchers have tested this ability by using a device called a visual cliff. A clear glass covering is placed over what looks like a sudden drop; even when they are beckoned to come forward by their mothers the babies will not cross the apparent cliff.

Sight and memory are improving – favourite toys are remembered and welcomed; mother and father are greeted with smiles and squirms of delight. This 'reward' he gives so generously stimulates your own delighted reaction so that the mutual bonds of affection and response are constantly being strengthened. Baby's developing skills are nicely calculated to evoke the most reaction from his parents whose encouragement and pleasure will, in turn, help their baby to develop still further.

But life is not all sunny smiles. Because your baby now remembers familiar faces he will also recognize the unfamiliar. At about six to eight months the well-known 'stranger' anxiety may begin to appear: familiar means warmth and security, unfamiliar means uncertainty.

You will find a good example of how this develops on visits to the clinic or doctor for check-ups or immunizations. At two months your baby is unimpressed by this new face: at four months he inspects it a lot more closely but is still not too worried. At six months he prefers to hold tight to you and by nine months he will have nothing whatever to do with this white-coated stranger with her stethoscope and her prodding. But it is the right reaction – and the paediatrician is glad to see it.

By the end of the first year of life both your baby's eyes will work well together and will be able to focus close up and far away almost as well as the adult eye. Vision continues to improve through the second twelve months until 'perfect' vision is reached by about four or five years of age.

In his second year your child sees different colours, sizes, shapes, distances, depths and textures but of course he is not yet able to talk about them with ease. Being able to see red is a lot different from being able to tell you that it is red. He will see big, little, square, round, in, out and many more concepts – but he may not yet be able to vocalize them. During the second and third years his speech will catch up with what he sees and he will be able to tell you about it.

Physical skills are also improving so that sight is aiding movement. During his second

From about six months the baby seems able to perceive depth: he will hesitate to move across what seems to be a drop in height.

Babies are essentially fun-loving: they enter whole-heartedly into games and playing – and particularly into mimicry from the surprisingly early age of a few weeks.

year your baby will be able to direct most of the spoonful to his mouth; by the third year he will be feeding himself well. In the second year of his life he will begin to take things apart, examine detailed toys. Sight-memory is developing; your two year old can not only hide your car keys – a day later he will remember where they are.

He will enjoy looking at books and may recognize numbers or letters. He will recognize animals and begin to imitate the sounds you teach him that they make.

But although your two to three year old can see almost as well as an adult, he can't translate what he sees into speech or action. Properties like straight or curved may be totally ignored by young children so that letters like D and O are easily confused.

A classic example of the child's still immature visual skill is shown by what is

These shifting colours and movement delight the baby – but never leave a young child alone with a balloon. Burst, they can be sucked in and can suffocate.

Shapes moved round have different meanings. 'Which way it faces' becomes important as the toddler learns to recognize letters.

A mirror fastened securely to the cot side gives hours of amusement as the baby studies the moving reflections.

known as the 'property of rotation'. Until now it has not mattered to him whether teddy was facing right, left, upside down, forwards or backwards. It was still teddy bear. Now that you are beginning to look at letters of the alphabet with him it has become important to you that he should get things the right way up. You begin to want him to take the 'picture' *b* and make it a different 'picture' when it is turned the other way and becomes a *d*. Then you want him to turn it upside down and make it a *p* or inside and out and make it a *q*. At the age of two or three these things only become important to young children if an adult makes them important, but as they grow older, they understand for themselves that such things as 'which way it faces' are important. This realization is an enormous developmental step.

From their experience children come to understand that some things must face certain ways and changing their direction will either change the object or change the meaning of the object. It may sound even more complicated to explain this than it is to learn it – but it is one of the reasons why 'proper' school begins at about five years.

How can you help your baby?

Knowing as much as we now do about your young baby's ability to see means there are many ways you can help his development and enjoyment by providing the right kind of stimulus.

Mobiles are some of the first toys or decorations you probably thought of buying for your baby so now you know a baby's visual range you can make sure that you put them in just the right place.

Don't hang a mobile right above the cot, pram or wherever the baby is spending most of his waking hours. If you watch your baby you will see that he doesn't look straight up or straight ahead: he looks either to the right or left – he may show a preference for one or the other. So if you hang your mobile carefully dead centre, you will have made quite sure that he won't be able to see it.

Hang it where he's looking – right or left. Better still, hang one each side and position each at the right distance from his eyes – about ten to twelve inches. Mobiles should be simple, brightly coloured, curved and not have too many details. You could make your own – something like a kite face would be

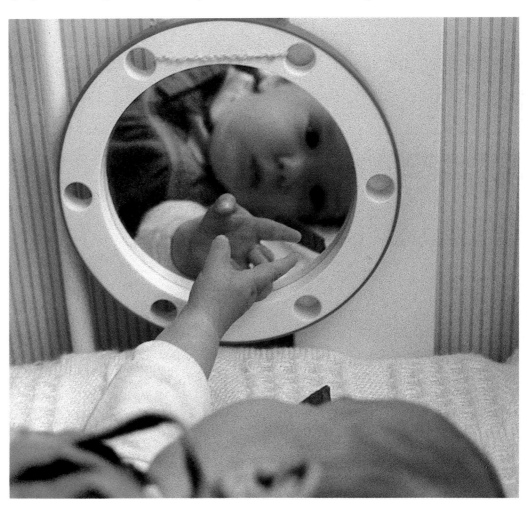

right, remembering to draw in the eyes and eyebrows in bold, bright colours (see page 114).

As your new baby will not yet be able to reach out and swipe them, the mobiles could be suspended on a string.

By the second or third month when he is beginning to reach and touch, you should replace the first mobiles with another type. (The first can still stay up on the ceiling or wherever, but the second one will be the one your baby is really interested in.)

This second mobile can have the same fairly simple outlines – not too much detail – but it should have a fixed base, so that when knocked it will return to its original position. A mobile which swings will, when knocked, disappear from the baby's sight range. Then it will reappear, disappear, reappear again – in fact behave in a totally confusing way. The toy with a fixed base will come back so that the baby can practise swiping at it again.

From about eight weeks on your baby will take great delight in being given a small mirror. Choose one about six inches across, unbreakable of course, and fix it out of his reach but still positioned within his sight range, and to his right.

By two to three months he will also enjoy company and he will enjoy being part of the family – perhaps propped up in a pram or bouncing cradle so that he can follow you around the room with his eyes. But if you use a bouncing cradle, make sure it is the kind that supports back and neck properly and that it is not acting as an efficient draught stopper. And *never* put it on a work top or table.

The outdoor world vies with the indoor in interest. There are clouds to watch (when his focus has developed), the pattern of leaves, the sudden miracle of a robin on the pram handle or a butterfly on a bush – for by now your baby is hauling himself up a little and

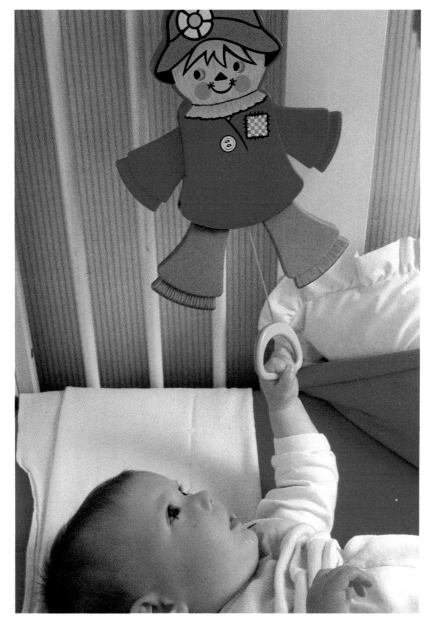

This toy – fixed by a firm base – allows the baby to swipe out without giving him the frustration of its disappearing as it moves.

Cause and effect! The baby soon learns that he can cause a happening: when he pulls on the ring, the puppet moves.

beginning to see what is over the side of the pram. By his size the child is much nearer the natural world than we are and a baby will examine for long sessions the marvellous intricacy of intertwining grasses, or a clump of leaves.

Soon – at about four months – he will stare at the place from which an object has disappeared and before long he will follow a falling object with his eyes. And the next stage will be that fascinating occupation – to the baby – the 'Where's it Gone?' game. The rattle thrown over the side of the pram, the teddy dropped ceaselessly from the high chair; what is more he won't only yell for you to pick it up, but as you bend to retrieve it, even before you have straightened up, dear old ted will hit you smartly on the head on his next downward flight. Take courage though – soon you'll be able to attach it to the chair or pram and he'll learn to haul it up when he wants it. And this endless game of throw and return does matter: your baby is learning that he can cause something to happen by his action; he is also learning that things that disappear also reappear, that out of sight does not mean out of existence. It is one of the ways he is learning that when you go out of the room you don't cease to exist: you will come back – and he really need not cry.

How much should you teach?
Stimulation is good: we are learning today that babies in the past may have suffered from too little. The danger nowadays could be that in our anxiety to make up for those lost opportunities we overdo the whole business. It is not necessarily true that the more you offer your baby, the quicker he will develop. He might indeed suffer from an overdose and take his own way out – blanking off experiences and stimuli he just

Swiping, reaching, stretching, the baby is endlessly amused by the routines of home. He is learning through involvement.

Tiring and frustrating it may be to the adult who has to pick up the toy, but the child is practising his ability to grasp and let go.

can't cope with. All learning must be leisurely with one stage leading on to the next and to try to force your baby at too early an age could well make him 'seize up'. There is certainly nothing wrong with beginning to expose your child quite early in life to all that the world has to offer but the brain is capable of understanding only so much at a given age. If we attempt to stretch the limits of a child's thought processes and understanding or even go beyond them we can run the risk of putting too much pressure on him. The child himself is often the best guide – showing when he's ready for new experiences, when he wants the time and privacy to explore on his own.

But don't worry either about underdoing the stimulus. It takes a mighty stark environment for a very long time to cause significant delays in development. In fact the normal, warm, caring home where the baby is from birth accepted as part of the family will provide enough natural stimulus for him to grow into a affectionate, alert child. To the baby all the world is playground and the home is his first schoolroom. Shapes, colours, sights, smells, noise – they are all there in the home. Later as the world extends we can spread before the child the riches of the wider opportunities – but the anxious parent so concerned to teach the academic skills at earlier and earlier ages will only communicate the anxiety to the child.

There is more about how and when to 'teach' a child in the chapter on becoming a person (page 168) and the feature on learning through play (page 158), but for the time being it is sensible to remember that babies need babyhood just as children need childhood – and that leading is nearly always more effective than pushing.

Reading with your child

'Story!' Your eighteen-month-old toddler dollops a book on your lap. Laboriously he hauls himself into a chair at your side, gathers his favourite toy or comfort blanket or whatever up after him, wriggles to make sure he has more than his fair share of the seat and taps the page imperiously. 'Story', he repeats. The tone brooks no delay – another storytelling session is in progress.

To give a child the love and freedom of books is to give him the key to life itself from reading the sports results to unlocking the humour, wisdom and mistakes of the past, present and future.

And you can begin all this almost from birth, for the first books are without pages – they are the rhymes and lullabies which have been passed down orally and which you can pass on in your turn. Later your voice will be translated into reading from a page and even

a young child recognizes this magic: a certain book produces the same story or the same pictures. So, from the earliest days, story-time and books are associated with the security of being cuddled, of togetherness, of the special privilege of individual attention.

If you have any doubt at all about the value of books for the tiniest babies, read *Cushla and Her Books* by Dorothy Butler. It is an account of how the author introduced her severely handicapped granddaughter to books almost from birth and the gradual and wonderful difference it made to her development. Dorothy Butler extends her theme in *Babies Need Books* which is solely concerned with books for children up to the age of four. Her immensely knowledgeable and practical approach lists titles and types of books suitable for babies from a few months.

The aim is enjoyment – not teaching. Of course the two should be inseparable but there's such pressure today on teaching younger and younger children the formal skills of writing and reading that it is easy for anxiety to force the pace. Don't let it. If you can think of the daily story-telling or reading sessions as enjoyment for *you*, then it will be enjoyment for both of you. There is after all no hardship in sitting comfortably and reading from one of the wonderful range of children's books being produced today. A baby of four or five months will sit happily propped at your side, chewing his rattle and occasionally swiping at the pages of the book you are holding. You may be *talking* about the pictures in the book – 'There's a lovely red apple; what a fat little baby' – it doesn't matter: your baby is enjoying the caring, the comfort, the proximity and the rhythms of your voice. And so, hopefully, are you. Once you have got over any initial self-consciousness it's a great ego-booster to be reading aloud, proclaiming like Olivier. Don't, however, feel aggrieved if your audience of one has fallen into sound slumber at your side, or even quietly dribbled over the text. He's meant to be enjoying it too! But make your reading a performance! Do it with style!

The best first books have one or perhaps two clear, simple pictures to a page, possibly with their names written underneath. The books illustrated by Dick Bruna are superb of this type. Laminated board pages make the book last longer, as your baby is bound to want to suck or chew them as soon as he gets hold of them. Important as books are, and precious, you have to allow for this type of handling and recognize that a young baby is not going to be 'careful' with books, however much you prize them. Later he will learn to hold books properly, to turn the pages carefully, to treasure them. But there is also

Security and involvement –
the baby enjoys the comfort
of being cuddled and
looking at the book while
the older child is being read to.

Magnetic letters stuck to the
refrigerator door can be one
of the earliest games to teach
that shape and position have
meaning.

always room for books that get into the back pocket of dungarees, squashed down the sides of armchairs and rolled on in bed. They are only being loved.

The big pictures and rhymes and verses will soon encourage you baby to join in, especially if the pictures make their own noises – 'miaouw', 'bow wow'. Certainly by twelve months he will recognize his favourite book and be able to imitate the sounds – and woe betide you if you try to dodge one of the pages: he'll know at once.

Later he will enjoy simple stories, perhaps associated with familiar situations – visiting

The pleasure of books can't be instilled too early. Fluency in reading is a lifetime's benefit.

grandma, going shopping. And he will also enjoy stories with a surprise or discover in them. *Where's Spot?* by Eric Hill is a lovely example. On each page the child looks for Spot the puppy – and finds him on the last. *But Where is the Green Parrot?* is another discovery book and so also is *Rosie's Walk* where a hen takes a walk, pursued by an unsuccessful fox.

Books for children of around two need not be concerned solely with familiar situations: pictures of animals and scenes they are unlikely to experience for years, if at all, extend knowledge and imagination. Have you ever seen a zebra in the wild? Yet doubtless you recognized it at first sight in the zoo – pictures made it familiar.

'Situation' books help a child to come to terms with real life. *Going to the Doctor, The New Baby* – titles such as these prepare your child for an event before it happens. Two and three year olds well understand the subtleties of meaning without being able to express themselves in words. Fairy tales

nearly always take into account the small child's physical disadvantage of living in a large world: how many times in those tales does the smallest win, the poor become rich, the third son (always the loser!) win the princess? Such tales reassure the young child; he can identify with the weakling turned conqueror because he lives in a world he is largely powerless to control. For the same reason children often delight in what to parents seem bloodthirsty deeds: it can be comforting to see, say, the devastating explosion of a volcano in pictures when you know there is just no chance of getting your own way in real life. 'Zap, powee and splat' have their uses.

What about 'reading'?

If you have instilled into your child a love of books and stories he will make the next step – wanting to read for himself – quite naturally. Learning to read is a complex business but you will know when he's poised on the brink of 'reading readiness' and it is not likely to be within the age scope of this book. But what you can do is show him the combination of shapes which spell out his name, so that he can recognize that when he sees it. And if he seems ready for it, then you can show him the shapes which make up simple words – 'teddy', 'cat' and so on. Always use the lower case (a, b, c) rather than capital letters (A, B, C). No more is really necessary at this age.

But what you can do is make him his very first own book.

Buy or make a scrapbook and on the front write his name and stick his photograph. Underneath you might write, 'This is me... John'. Inside you can write, draw or stick what you like – the bus ticket from when he went to see his aunt, the wrapper from the orange his cousin gave him, a drawing of his new shoes, sentence about what he did today, or ate for his dinner. It is *his* book, *his* life and it will be very precious to him.

What about television?

At today's stage of accessibility, television for children can't be ignored, nor should it be. Programmes on television for very young children are nearly always excellent, imaginative, humorous and employing some of the best illustrative and dramatic talent going. But what television for children demands is the involved presence of an adult to watch with the child. Monitor the menu first, then decide when the switch goes on. And when the programme is over, switch off. A TV set is not a babyminder.

You will also have to remember that your child can't always take things in as quickly as you can and this is why programmes for children are often at a slower pace, so the

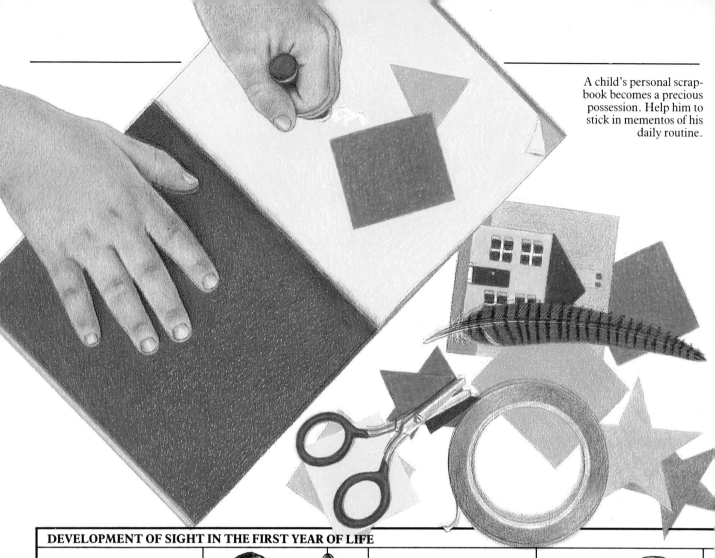

A child's personal scrap-book becomes a precious possession. Help him to stick in mementos of his daily routine.

DEVELOPMENT OF SIGHT IN THE FIRST YEAR OF LIFE

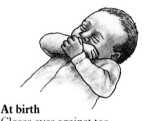

At birth
Closes eyes against too bright lights. Can focus from seven to twelve inches and turns towards sound. Recognizes his mother's voice.

First month
Stares at parent's eyes in eye-to-eye contact. Is relaxed when staring at her. Stares at objects but doesn't reach for them.

Second month
Prefers people to objects. Begins to swipe at objects. Becomes excited at familiar presence. Can watch moving objects. Explores hands.

Third month
Recognizes familiar people. Turns more definitely towards sound. Flexes and examines fingers.

Seventh month
Grasps with one hand and can hold different objects in each hand. Bangs them together. Claps. Anticipates actions.

Eighth month
Picks up small objects. Reaches with fingers extended. Points at objects. Follows pointer. Turns over and examines objects.

Ninth month
Approaches small objects with finger and thumb but large objects with both hands. Remembers likes and dislikes.

Tenth month
Fits things together. Posts shapes through correct holes in posting box toy. Searches for things. Imitates gestures, expressions.

child can understand what's going on. Not too noisy, not too quick, not too complicated or too frightening (and this varies with the child: what frightens one, another will revel in – but you are the expert here) – these are the criteria. And not too much and not alone: watching without an interested and involved and loving adult is a sterile business.

But don't make the television yet another battleground. If you really think your two to three year old is getting too interested for too long a time and wants everything on all day then distract rather than prohibit. Watching a fast-moving, bewildering cartoon might be fun but it will not compare in attraction with making jam tarts in the kitchen!

Television is not a childminder: young children need the enjoyment of watching with an adult though the youngest member seems supremely uninterested!

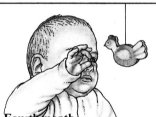

Fourth month
Stares at himself in mirror. Appears puzzled when object disappears from sight. Focuses well. Swipes more accurately.

Fifth month
Looks between hand and object. Recognizes familiar toys etc. Begins to look for a falling object.

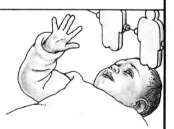

Sixth month
Eyes direct hand for reaching, pulling etc. Drops toys and begins to retrieve them.

Eleventh month
Begins to feed himself, guiding spoon to mouth with some accuracy. Searches for an object if out of sight.

Twelfth month
Reaches (accurately) for something while looking the other way. Enjoys stacking toys, hammering into pegboard etc.

All these stages are guidelines only. Each baby varies in his development and although the progression of development follows the same pattern, each baby is an individual and may achieve the milestones at a slightly different ages.

127

Moving

Your new baby lies where she's placed: on her back, on her front, on one side or the other; she's helpless to turn but not helpless to move. Placed on her back she can turn her head a little to one side: placed on her stomach she can lift her head a few inches and turn it to the side to breathe more easily. (But this ability is so limited that she can't indefinitely hold her head clear of obstruction: this is why pillows or a plastic sheet which can be sucked in could cause suffocation.)

If stroked on one cheek, the baby will turn her head towards the touch and she will also turn towards the nipple, possibly through her sense of smell. Put your finger in the palm of her hand and her fingers will close round it with a surprisingly strong grip. It's so strong, in fact, that the newborn baby can support her own weight from one hand and hang like a monkey from your hand. But don't try it – the ability disappears overnight and you may try her just as it has vanished.

She will put her hand to her mouth to suck and, supported under the arms with her feet on a firm surface, she'll make definite stepping movements one after the other. Put her down a little carelessly so that she feels you release your grip before another surface is ready to receive her and she'll throw out her arms in a movement of distress. She'll jerk and twitch in her sleep and she'll flinch away from the pain of a pin prick. Legs and arms flail and squirm if she is crying.

But your baby is not consciously directing all of these movements: many are reflex reactions that she can't help making. Her brain is not yet sufficiently developed for her to be in overall control.

And yet – within a few months – these random movements will be refined and perfected into skilful, subtle and coordinated actions and reactions. The previous chapter has shown how sight directs movements but the baby can't control her movements until her brain and body are sufficiently developed to do so.

All babies develop at their own pace. One will sit at six months, another at seven. One walks at eleven months, another at sixteen. The age that a baby achieves her first wobbly sit-up has little bearing on the age that she walks nor does the early walker indicate that she will be brighter than the baby who sits firmly on her seat and prefers to watch the world go by. Naturally the active baby who propels herself into movement is at the same time strengthening her muscles and explor-

Encourage your toddler as she practises walking and moving. Her success will become an enjoyment to be shared by all the family. Her foot grip on a carpet makes it safe but beware shiny floors and movable mats.

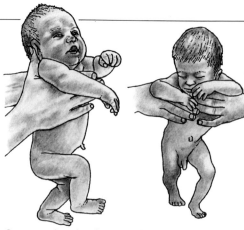

Supported under the arms the new baby attempts to stand and makes definite stepping movements.

Lying on his back, the new baby will stretch out his arm in the direction he is facing. This is known as the asymmetric tonic neck reflex and it will begin to disappear at about four months.

Supported by a hand and forearm, as his head droops back, arms are flung out in the 'startle' reflex.

Known as the 'prehensile grip', the new baby clings strongly to the supporting hands.

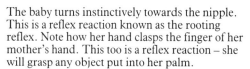

The baby turns instinctively towards the nipple. This is a reflex reaction known as the rooting reflex. Note how her hand clasps the finger of her mother's hand. This too is a reflex reaction – she will grasp any object put into her palm.

Some of your new baby's movements are those he cannot help making. A range of those reflex actions you can recognize for yourself are shown here.

Held in the position known as 'ventral suspension' the new baby's head droops, the limbs hang down and the hips are flexed.

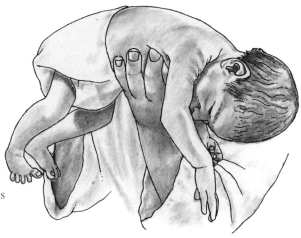

ing her ability to move and that may mean she walks sooner than her less active sister. At the same time her 'passive' sister may well be learning to use her hands more skilfully. You will no doubt know before she arrives which kind of baby you are having: the peaceful little thing who contemplates life with relative stillness or the mini-acrobat who has been practising somersaults for the last few months.

But although the pace of your baby's development of movement is individual, depending partly on environment, partly on heredity (and partly on the tendency for girls to develop rather more quickly than boys), the stages of development will always follow the same basic pattern – and knowing about it makes watching your baby much more interesting. It also means that you'll be able to provide the right kinds of stimulus at the appropriate times.

The first stage or rule is that the baby can only develop when her brain and her body are ready to develop.

The second rule is that the baby's muscles develop in a sequence beginning at the head and working down to the toes.

The third rule is that the baby first learns to control her major muscles and then learns the control of smaller or minor muscles.

So to think about the first rule – that the baby only develops when brain and body are ready to develop – you have to remember that at birth only the more primitive areas of the brain are fully developed and no amount of 'encouragement' will force your baby into an achievement her brain is not ready for. Without perhaps realizing it, that's something you already knew: it would never occur to you to expect your new baby to roll over, crawl or sit up in the first few weeks of life. All the same although many of her early movements are reflex actions, they are all the while strengthening her muscles. At the same time other parts of her brain are growing so that as the baby reflexes fade, the growing maturity of the brain takes over and allows the baby to control her actions.

It's like balancing a scale. On the one side is the reflex reaction, on the other voluntary control. As the reflexes diminish the other scale – that of voluntary control – moves down: eventually the scales are even but then gradually the voluntary control takes precedence and dictates actions; reflex actions all but vanish – often to lie dormant in some recess of the brain until some happening – illness perhaps, emotional upset, accident – triggers them into life. (You can see this in the 'startled' reaction of an adult to some unexpected incident.)

THE FIRST WEEKS OF LIFE AND MOVEMENT

There is not a great deal you can do to encourage movement in these first weeks nor is it necessary to do so. Your baby is learning to take stock of her surroundings and the feedback she gets from her random movements helps to organize and direct her next actions. Accidentally her hands may touch something soft: she enjoys the sensation and wants it repeated and so she may begin to pluck at the sheet or rub it tentatively. All babies learn very soon to fondle their mother's breast as they feed. Eventually the baby will be able to choose what to fondle and the first elementary exploration will refine into grasping, squeezing, rubbing as she learns to direct her movements and discovers for herself what is hard, what is soft, what is cold and what is warm.

Some young babies manage to squirm and wriggle along on their tummy or back, particularly when they're upset. It is automatic and not under their control but if they dig their heels into the mattress and then kick them straight they can manage to scoot quite a distance. You will need to watch out for this even before your baby is able to move voluntarily. If, for instance, you put the baby in the centre of your bed because you are called away to the telephone or to answer a knock, you must make sure she is adequately fenced in by firm pillows on either side.

Gradually in the first few weeks she will find it increasingly easy to lift her head. On her tummy she will just manage to clear her chin from the supporting surface, although her arms won't be sufficiently developed for her to push up. Some babies dislike being put on their tummy and it must be uncomfortable to try lifting that heavy head but a few minutes on the floor on her front is very beneficial. Lifting her head up will help to strengthen neck, back and arm muscles.

If your baby seems to dislike tummy lying, encourage her by singing or talking to her or showing her litle toys and don't let the session last too long: even two to three minutes about twice a day will do. As she gets stronger and can push up to see around her she will come to enjoy and even prefer front lying to back lying.

Floor play is invaluable because then your baby is getting a good view of the world and also has space to begin to explore. Don't leave her confined to cot or pram too long – she'll only get bored. Playpens have their use later for safety's sake when she becomes more mobile but in the early weeks they are hardly necessary. There is more information about playpens, swings, baby walkers in the chapter on play and equipment (page 164).

By about three months your baby will be

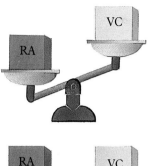
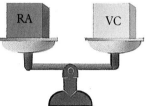
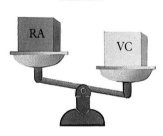

As the reflex reactions fade, voluntary control takes over and eventually dictates actions while reflex reactions lie dormant.

able to hold her head squarely in the centre of her body. More and more easily she will turn her head from side to side and her strengthening neck muscles mean she will be able, while lying on her tummy, to hoist head and chest up and take a good look around at the world.

At this stage you can put mobiles directly overhead as she is now able to look straight up when she is lying on her back. She won't be able to swipe straight ahead just yet though.

She is also learning to circle her arms and kick her legs and gradually she'll begin to reach out and grasp small objects. Don't always hand your baby the object she's reaching for: let her grasp it for herself because she needs practice. Simple, bright toys or pictures at the side of cot or pram or within reach will encourage her to stretch out and grasp. She is mastering a complicated set of skills: seeing an object, controlling hand and arm to stretch toward it, making contact, opening her fingers and then closing them again. When she has mastered that she will begin the next development – bringing the toy in triumph to that great explorer, her mouth. Soon everything will go into her mouth and although it may distress you to see just about everything being tasted or sucked, this is a natural instinct – the best thing is to try and limit her orbit to reasonably clean objects.

In the meantime if you see your baby repeatedly trying to reach an object and not quite making it, do help her out. Learning to live is a very tiring business.

Grasping is still very strong and instinctive – but opening her hand voluntarily is something she won't learn for some months. You will find yourself prizing her hands open to release something she is grasping. When she does learn the release mechanism, then the fun begins, because at about seven or eight months the game of 'Pick it up, Mummy' begins in earnest. It is a tiring stage all right – for parents that is – and more than a bit exasperating but it helps to remember she is not being wilfully 'naughty'. She is not only experimenting with an object, she is learning that out of sight does not mean out of existence, that some things make a noise when they hit the ground and that some things don't. She's also finding out about gravity – and she has never yet heard of Isaac Newton.

FROM FOUR TO SIX MONTHS

Your baby's development of movement is gradually progressing according to plan; head, shoulders, arms, hands are now in use and movement ... and now another delightful object appears – or rather two objects. Her feet.

Lying on her back, she makes a grab for them, misses and gets her knees instead. Practice helps to strengthen the muscles and also make them more flexible; before long her toes are in her mouth. (Doing this, her back may become so rounded she will topple over to one side.)

Supporting herself on her arms – now aligned directly underneath her shoulders and not, as previously, tucked to her chest – she'll watch your movements. Cautiously she will support herself on one arm only – which means she can grab sideways at any toy she fancies. You can help her by putting rattles or other graspable items within reach but rememeber small items, toys that break into tiny pieces, anything sharp or toxic must be kept away. Things travel from hand to mouth at the rate of knots.

Accidentally now – about five months –

Everything now goes in her mouth to be sucked, explored, bitten and generally tested.

Opposite With her toes in her mouth her back may be so rounded that she will topple over to one side

Opposite left and right At about five months a baby learns to 'airplane'. Head lifted, back arched, and legs lifted straight behind her, she bounces gently on her tummy. Supporting herself on one forearm she can lift the other arm off the floor.

Opposite Balancing a cup and bringing it to her mouth is easier if the cup is two handled.

she'll roll over on to her back. Mostly that happens when she reaches out for something at her side, loses her balance and turns turtle. You might spend a few hours turning her back but within a week or two she will have learnt how to do it herself – or perhaps she will begin the other way and turn first from back to tummy.

At this age don't put your baby on high surfaces. Every day there's a new development of movement: she will suddenly get herself a purchase with her feet against something firm and could easily shoot herself off into space. She will also learn to 'swim' or 'airplane' about this time. Lying on her tummy she will arch her back, lift her arms with elbows behind her, straighten and lift her legs and bounce up and down on her tummy. Exhausted, she collapses, rests, then begins the whole business again.

By her sixth month she can push herself

up from her tummy on straight arms. She's doing push-ups. When you hold her on your lap her head is well-balanced and her legs are balanced sturdily and straight. When put sitting up, her back is not quite straight – she'll need to be supported or she'll pitch to one side. She needs help to practise sitting. A few times a day let her sit between your legs on the floor or sit her facing you on your knee while you sing or bounce her gently up and down. She can sit on the couch next to you, propped with pillows while you read a book together – she won't stand it for long but the time span will soon improve.

If you give her a toy in one hand she will bring the other to join it – her hands are no longer fisted and anything within arm's reach is in danger of her swiping fingers. Discard anything flimsy – it will only end in pieces and probably in her mouth.

SEVEN, EIGHT, NINE MONTHS
Wobbly at first, still with a rounded back and only for a few seconds at a time, she will

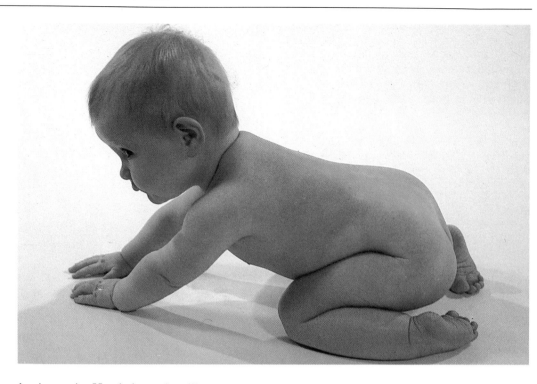

One of the early stages of crawling: she pushes herself up on extended arms and looks around.

She supports herself on the furniture and pulls herself up to a standing position – often in a favourite spot.

begin to sit. Her balance is still precarious and she may fall quite heavily sideways, so pad the area round her with rugs. Soon she will begin to creep and crawl. Sometimes babies push themselves backwards, gracefully backing into furniture to their own surprise (and sometimes to their annoyance as they find themselves retreating from, instead of advancing towards, their toys). Sometimes they push their bottom right up into the air, then they'll go into a knees-bend routine, or rock backwards and forwards. The engine is running but the brakes are still on. Sometimes your baby will pivot on her stomach, pull herself by her arms across the floor, then the legs begin to help to push. However she may choose to begin, one thing is certain: baby is on the move.

And one day you'll go into her room and find her standing calmly in her cot holding on to the rail.

This is really when the fun begins and the home, not just the baby, begins to move.

Take away any cot mobiles that could twist round her neck as she begins to stand. Pad any corners of sharp furniture which can't be moved. Move coffee tables – they can be lethal: they have sharp corners, are just the right height to grab objects from and mostly they'll tip over if your baby hangs on to one end.

She will probably have favourite standing spots so you may have to pad the furniture round them. Watch doors: she is bound to love to get behind the door just as you open it. Or else she will close it for you, shutting herself in and you out, then probably yell to come out, so remember she'll be directly in the line of the reopening door and her head could get a nasty knock.

Remove breakables. She'll reach higher than you think. Watch out for tablecloths or hanging curtains. There's more about child-proofing the home on pages 32 to 35 but increasing mobility brings back increasing dangers. With babies it is nearly always later than you think.

TEN, ELEVEN, TWELVE MONTHS

She sits and gets herself around on the floor, perhaps by creeping, or crawling, or pulling herself along, or scooting. She'll move easily from sitting to all fours and back again. She'll get herself over to the cupboard and if the door is open, disappear inside and have a riotous time with the contents, so watch what you keep there. She'll eye the stairs – or do more than eye them. She'll practise standing and she's skilful enough to pull herself up with one arm while holding a toy in the other. She'll rock on to one foot and then back on to the other, testing the water before she takes the plunge. She may practise walking by holding on to furniture, attempt to stand for a few seconds alone before collapsing.

She may use a supportive toy – like a baby walker – to hang on to and push forward with staggering steps. Make sure the walker doesn't run away with her if the wheels move too freely. She will probably try walking with her arms held up and her legs well apart to help her balance. She will fall, pull herself up, try again.

And it's not only walking that she's learning. She can point, use her index finger, put index finger to thumb to pick up small objects. She can drop objects into larger containers, poke, prod and explore crannies you didn't know existed.

THIRTEEN TO EIGHTEEN MONTHS

She'll stroll down the room now although if she's in a hurry she will drop down on her knees to get there more quickly. And she'll climb. Beware of silence – it means she's limbering up on chairs, tables or stairs. Babies have even been known to scale bookshelves . . . You will need to supervise her stair-climbing – safety gates are discussed in the previous section on childproofing the home (page 30) – but with supervision she may safely crawl upstairs, though she won't be able to get down. Show her how to come down backwards. Eventually when she climbs the stairs instead of crawling up them she will use one foot first always, pausing on each step to change over her weight and start again with (usually) her right foot.

The daily walk will last for hours. Not only does she want to walk, she wants to explore – examining every leaf, every crack in the pavement, front gate and animal on the way. But all the time she is learning to balance on a variety of surfaces – gravel, grass and paving stones.

She loves playing ball although she will

Climbing obsesses her – when there's silence, watch out. The chances are she'll be up to mischief.

The daily walk may take hours as she studies every inch of the route – but she is learning to balance on different surfaces.

send it off in a variety of directions – sometimes straight in the air, sometimes dribbling at her feet, sometimes, to her suprise, over her head.

She will scribble and draw with a crayon – at first making light strokes only, then learning to make them more heavily. She will enjoy watching you draw or helping her to scribble, using different bright colours. Don't leave them within her reach though, or she will begin decorating the walls. It is not easy to provide freedom for her to explore while still keeping control over safety – and sanity – but it can be done.

This summary shows how three children may progress through the first three years of developing movement. It demonstrates that different individuals will reach the milestones of learning – how to reach out, how to sit, how to crawl, how to walk, how to run and how to jump – at different times. The upper child may be running and jumping earlier than the middle child, but the lower child won't be far behind either of them.

First crawling

Moves easily from sitting to all fours

Just lifting head

Needs support when sitting up

Tries to get on all fours

Strengthening neck and back muscles

Pulling on furniture to stand

Still squirming and wriggling on back

Creeping and crawling

| 0-3 months | 4-6 months | 7-9 months | 10-12 months | 13-18 months |

A sturdy climbing frame on a soft surface to cushion falls will encourage not only skills of coordination and balance, but also a sense of adventure.

Runs steadily

Plays ball with confidence

Step jumps with one foot

Jumps confidently with both feet

Uses supportive toy to move around

19-24 months

25-36 months

NINETEEN TO TWENTY-FOUR MONTHS

She walks smoothly and steadily and learns to run. Once she learns this you will think she'll never walk again – she runs everywhere. She rearranges the furniture, pushes things around. Later she will *pull* them into place. (Watch out for chairs pulled over to windows.) She can't quite jump with both feet at once but she soon will. She can kick a ball and play ball with an adult or older child.

She will begin to switch on lights, unscrew bottle tops and turn doorhandles. Be prepared. She's not so keen on dressing herself but she loves undressing. Again – beware of silence. A quiet hush while she is out of sight may mean she will soon be prancing round the garden with no clothes on.

By two years of age she may attempt to copy the lines or circles you draw for her with her crayon.

By her third year your daughter walks, runs, jumps. She can turn sharp corners and manoeuvre quickly to avoid obstacles. She can walk fairly well along a straight line and balance on one foot for several seconds. She may come downstairs using alternate feet but must still hold on to a rail. She can pedal her tricycle, turn and twist it with amazing agility. She can dress and undress herself with much trouble although you may have to put her clothes out in order for her. Large buttons and zips she can manage, smaller ones may still defeat her. She can build a tower, balance bricks on top of each other, construct 'edifices' and catch a ball with comparative ease. Natural zest for living and curiosity have propelled her through the first three years of developing movement. She has progressed through the stages – learning to reach out, to sit, to crawl, to walk, to run: to control the major muscles and then to refine control to the smaller muscles. Developing mind has kept pace with a developing body. She is ready to reach out and conquer the world.

Shoes and Socks

You don't need to worry about shoes until your baby begins to walk. Pram shoes are a waste of money: tights, stretch suits, sleeping bags, will keep your baby's feet warm.

When your baby begins to walk let her go barefoot as much as possible: her grip on the ground will help her balance more easily. Don't let her wear just socks or tights as they are slippery (though there are some slipper socks/tights on the market with rubber on the soles which would help her grip).

When she needs shoes – for warmth and protection – make sure they fit properly and are measured by a fitter in a reputable shop. It is tempting to pass shoes on from one child to another but this could be a mistake if the shoes have moulded to their first wearer's feet.

It is also tempting to keep one pair of shoes for 'best' but children too soon grow out of them for that to be sensible. Check constantly that her shoes are big enough.

And check constantly that your baby is not growing out of her stretch suits – curled-up toes could result if the feet are cramped. You can always cut the feet out of the outgrown ones and put socks separately over the top – like wellies – to keep her feet warm.

Nylon socks may not stretch enough: wool or cotton mixture may be better but there again check after washing to make sure they haven't shrunk. And make sure they are not

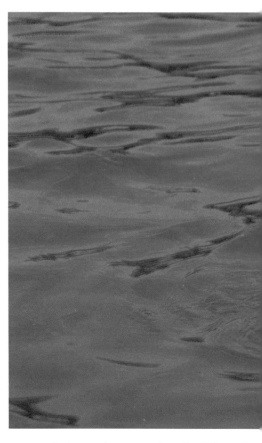

too restrictive at the top so they don't impede circulation.

Swimming

Most young babies love water – they have been used to the feel of liquid around them before birth. They can learn to swim or keep themselves afloat very early and it is not too soon to take your baby to the pool when she is a few months old. But the operative word is 'take' her: an indoor swimming pool is full of reflected lights, echoing noises and could be very frightening, so hold the baby very securely in your arms and go gently down into the water with her, holding her so that she enters the water very gradually. The water must be warm and you shouldn't stay in more than about ten minutes. All you need to do is let the baby play with the water while you support her. She may enjoy being dunked – she will hold her breath automatically. Demonstrate by putting your own face under the water, then repeat the performance with your baby.

Many pools now have Dolphin Clubs where special instructors will teach mothers and babies to swim. Ask at your local pool whether they have such a service and if not where it can be found. If there is not one locally, write to the address for the ASA on page 230 for details of your nearest, or how such a service may be set up.

A SUMMARY OF THE STAGES IN THE DEVELOPMENT OF MOVEMENT

About one month
Holds head up for a few seconds. Turns head and eyes to light or familiar voice. Eye-to-eye contact begins to strengthen.

About three months
Holds head up from tummy: supports weight on arms. Watches people and hands etc. Swipes at objects.

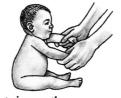

About six months
Holds arms up to be lifted. Turns and twists. Kicks very strongly. Bounces up and down with alternating legs. Will 'stand' if supported. Turns turtle.

About ten months
Sits unsupported for some minutes. Can get from lying to sitting. May crawl, squirm or otherwise self-propel. Reaches, picks up small objects, holds rusk.

One year to fifteen months
Sits, crawls, stands. May walk alone or with walker to aid balance. Climbs stairs. Reaches out for one toy while holding another in the other hand.

15 months on
Walks, feeds herself. Climbs obsessively and seems to get into everything. Becomes adept at playing ball. Starts to scribble and draw.

Doing things together is the best way of learning. A young child can learn to swim, or at least be unafraid of water, if there's an adult within reach.

All these outline stages are guidelines only. Your baby may achieve some earlier and some later. Girls often reach various milestones sooner than boys, but don't worry if she does not exactly match the blueprint! Don't try to hurry her on.

Communicating

'I'm here! I've arrived! But I'm not sure I like it!'

The baby slides head first into a world of lights, noise, chill and change and signals his arrival with a cry. With the cord still pulsating he is lifted and given to his mother, to be greeted with embraces and sounds, if not words, of comfort and welcome. The baby stops crying.

Communication through the voice has begun.

But of course communication has begun long before that moment when father, mother and child first meet face to face. It has grown steadily with the child in the womb – in his increasing awareness of the warm comfort of the liquid that surrounds him, of the rhythm of his mother's life, of the muffled sound of her heartbeat and the distant sound of her voice. For we communicate through all our senses and the baby more so than most.

So communication to a baby is touch – soft bedding, the security of familiar arms; it is taste – the warm milk which gives him life; it is smell – the smell of mother, father, milk and home; it is sight – the gradual clearing focus of a familiar face.

And it is sound. Within a very few weeks it will be the sounds of home that become increasingly important to the baby – the bark of a dog, the whirring of the washing machine, the lullaby of a lawnmower heard on sleepy summer evenings. But for now the sound that the new baby associates with comfort is the voice – until with the months 'sound' turns into 'speech' and takes precedence over those earlier and more primitive means of contact.

Learning to speak is the everyday miracle. In the first few years of life the small child masters a subject that for complexity and subtlety he will probably never surpass in the rest of his life. It is the skill which separates humans from animals and it is at once the most commonplace and the most mysterious of achievements.

So this chapter is about how 'voice sound' turns into speech and what happens in that rainbow of achievement that spans the baby's first cry to the time when he has exploded into the flow of talk, chatter, monologue, commentary and questions with which the typical three year old greets each day – and, alas, occasionally the night.

The basic tools necessary for the miracle called communication to occur are language and speech. Language is what the baby

Communication is a two-way business but it does not always need words. We 'talk' with expressions, gestures, eye contact, touch and even by just being within sight of others.

thinks ('I want some more milk!') and speech is how he verbally lets you know he wants that milk. Of course this communication of a thought may and usually does involve more than 'speech' as the baby wriggles, points, and cries to help you understand what he is thinking.

But language must come before speech as the baby must 'think' of something to say before he 'says' it.

There is a case for thinking that a baby arrives with an inborn instinct to speak. He doesn't need to be taught to hear, or see, or taste, or smell, and just as in time he will, unaided, achieve that first wobbly sit-up and progress through crawling to walking to running a marathon, so he will learn to speak through some instinctive drive to communicate. Of course he will only learn to speak if he hears speech around him, and yet the child – completely untaught – will still construct and apply his own rules of language. He applies them wrongly but this is inexperience – what matters is that somehow he realizes there *are* rules.

'What has?' asks the two year old, looking towards his mother's cup of tea.

That's incorrect but it isn't nonsense. The sense is quite plain: 'What are you drinking? What's in the cup?'

No adult has taught the child to ask, 'What has?' He has never heard that expression – like Topsy, it has just growed. Later these rules will be straightened out. Word is joined to word, words become phrases, will be extended into sentences: then he will be in the deep end – questions, statements, suppositions pour forth – while grammar and syntax lie in wait.

The baby surrounded by speech will pick up for himself the skills of speech, but he will learn those skills much more easily and quickly and fluently if he is encouraged and helped by those who care for him. And mostly that means parents.

No-one can overestimate the part that parents – or whoever cares full-time for the baby – play in helping a child into speech. Children who are deprived of this early loving stage of learning – pre-verbal communication, to give it its formal name – may never catch up on verbal skills in after life. Of course they will learn to speak and to express themselves but they seldom achieve the fluency and flow of those who, from birth, have been surrounded by the to and fro of loving dialogue.

Ideally the baby learns the mystery of speech in the merry-go-round of home and family, long before he is ensnared by the more formal teaching of school. And yet – the mystery deepens here – he will be taught these complicated rules by parents who have never themselves been taught to teach – and yet who all seem to teach in the same way. So are parents programmed to teach as instinctively as babies are programmed to learn?

Instinct or imitation? We're back where we started – that first cry. The baby is using the only tool he possesses: his voice. Is it an utterance of distress or greeting? A cry for help or a vocal visiting card proffered to the world?

Sounds before birth

The child in the womb doesn't live in silence. He hears his mother's heartbeat, the noises of her digestion. He will start at a sudden loud noise and may seem to quieten if the mother sings a lullaby. In London's Natural History Museum there is a much enlarged model of a womb. Step inside the small dark room in which it is kept and you'll hear the sounds a baby hears in the womb. If you watch children and adults listening to this sound you will often see a withdrawn, absorbed look creep over their faces as though they were being taken back into some peaceful prebirth memory. Nowadays you

Communication begins in the womb – in the warm comfort of the liquid that surrounds the fetus and the sound of its mother's heartbeat.

can buy recordings of 'womb music', music, that is, composed to reproduce as closely as possible the sounds the baby hears before birth. Such recordings, played to fretful babies after birth, have had remarkably soothing effects. So from birth, sound is not a new experience for a baby, nor is it a new means of communication for as far as we know, it has already been associated with comfort and security.

Communication is a two-way business. It needs both speaker and listener. At first it is the parent who listens and learns to interpret the meaning of the baby's cry. The development of the eventual dialogue which will take place between the baby and his parents progresses in a series of steps, each one of which has to be negotiated before the next can be tackled. It is like climbing a ladder – and just as one child may take longer to

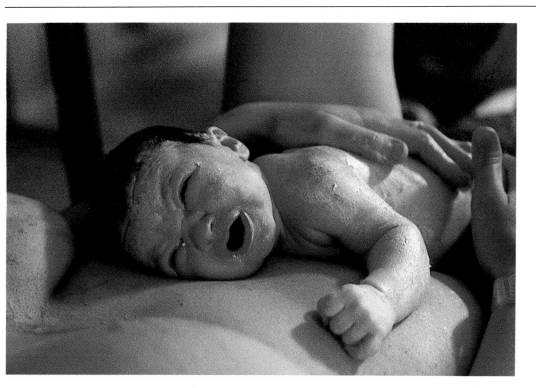

The baby's first cry signals
his arrival in the world. But
is it distress or greeting – a
vocal visiting card proffered
to the world?

A baby learns the mystery of
speech in the merry-go-
round of home and family,
long before he is ensnared
by formal learning.

climb than another, so each child's development proceeds at his own individual pace. Try to hurry the child along and he'll miss a step, falter and be hindered. It will make him worried, tense, unable to move forward. Half the art of parenting is knowing when to follow and when to lead a child.

Children frequently progress at a different pace within each stage of development. The child who speaks early may be slower in walking. While you have a crawling little chatterbox on your hands, there is a walking – but not talking – tornado of energy next door. It is as though nature sometimes directs energy into one channel at a time. Other children plod steadily onwards, each skill keeping pace with the other.

Comparing children's achievements – which sometimes seems to be a parental obsession – is quite useless and could cause both you and your child a lot of distress. And it won't speed up any processes – only delay them.

Parents listen – but baby hears

To a stranger all babies' crying may sound the same: not so to the parent who spends a lot of time with the baby. Within a day or two of birth a mother will pick out her baby's cry from a nursery full of decibels. She will also rapidly learn to distinguish between the different kinds of cry: pain, hunger, fear, boredom. Instinctively she reacts in the same way to all the cries – she will speak to the baby, but her tone will vary according to the signal which prompted her response. If it is a whining, grumbling, getting-off-to-sleep sort of noise she will probably be just a bit matter-of-fact: a cry of pain or real distress will be met with a much softened and more sympathetic tone. The remarkable duet between caregiver and cared-for has begun: the baby cries, a parent responds, the crying stops. The crying has achieved its object: it has brought action.

And within a very few days of birth comes the first voluntary action on the part of the baby: he reacts to a familiar voice. He is perhaps whimpering a little in his cot and the telephone rings. He may stop for a moment or two but then he will begin again. But – as you go past him to answer the phone – try reassuring him. 'All right, I'm coming. I won't be long.'

He stops crying. The baby is listening. He recognizes your voice and what is more he has learnt that your voice means attention is coming. He would not be so soothed if, for example, you turned on the television or the vacuum cleaner, or if the dog barked. It is your voice that matters. Your voice – not anyone else's. Experiments have proved this sound and sight association (see page 114).

The tone of your voice is what matters. If, for instance, you pricked yourself with the nappy pin while you were holding the baby and let out a little cry of pain, the baby would almost certainly begin to cry also. If you shout at a cat while you're holding the baby, then again the baby will react to the anger in your voice.

Before very long you will find that if the baby is lying in his pram and you go near and talk to him, he will begin to wriggle and throw his arms about in excitement at the sound of your voice. If he already happens to be wriggling then he will freeze: either way he will respond to your voice.

So the baby has already taken several steps up the ladder of language. He's listening and learning: he has sorted out that voices have meaning. The next important step that comes along is when looking and listening are coordinated. Previously he may have reacted to your voice but not turned towards you but now comes the ability to match sight (an object) to sound. It is the moment you have been waiting for when, having carefully scanned your face in his usual considering way, he will look you in the eyes – and make his tentative gesture of friendship to the world. The first smile.

So how many steps up the ladder are we now?
1 Sound has meaning
2 Voices have meaning
3 One voice has more meaning than the others
4 That voice belongs to only one face
5 That voice and that face make things happen
6 *This* is the voice and the face – so I shall acknowledge it
And he's still under six weeks old.

Smile awhile

Now, smiling comes easily. You smile, he smiles back. He smiles first and you reward him by smiling, picking him up, cuddling him, telling him how lovely he is … talking to him.

And a week or two later he 'talks' back. Small experimental sounds come from him – not those early reflex sounds of hunger, pain, boredom, but small overtures of sound – a bit like an orchestra tuning up, which of course is just what it is. He's playing with his voice, getting the right notes, trying out new sounds. He does this in two different situations: he practises on his own and will practise with you. This baby plays solos and duets.

On his own the baby 'talks' to himself a great deal. You will hear him repeating the same sound over and over again and, listening to him, you'll notice that he will make a sound, pause as though he's thinking about it, then make the same sound again. If you join in he'll stop as though he's a little surprised to find himself overheard and interrupted. But then after a moment he will join in with you quite amicably.

The baby uses these sounds for his own amusement and as a two-way sharing of pleasure and content with you. He is not trying to *tell* you anything; he is just interacting, being friendly. And what's more he seems very polite. He makes a few remarks and you join in. When you have finished he will start again. He already knows all about the to and fro of conversation.

These first sounds – from about two and a half to three months – are some of the most delightful and endearing of childhood experiences for the new parents. For the baby invariably begins to make the vowel sounds first – aah, eeh, ooo – and he sounds just like a small dove, cooing away with contentment. Soon they will be joined by the consonants but for that brief time while just the vowels are being vocalized, the sounds he makes are pure joy.

And now he moves on to the the next rung of the ladder: the consonants, or at least those which are easily produced at the front of the mouth – p, b, t, d – to be followed swiftly by the nasal sounds of m and n. At this stage, quite accidentally, the baby may produce a sound very like 'mama' or 'dada'. And no doubt you'll pick him up joyfully, tell him how clever he is and go on repeating 'Mama, Dada' to him several times hoping he'll say it again. The chances are he will regard you with a confused stare and eventually smile tolerantly as by now he knows smiling is a good thing and always met with approval. You will now possibly call his father and announce that you have a genius on your hands.

Don't be misled. The sound was accidental: he was not 'naming' you. At the same time that your baby was bringing joy to your heart by the accidental combination of sounds, little Russian babies in painted wooden cots and little Eskimo babies slung on their mother's backs were probably producing the same sound. For all over the world babies begin by making the same sounds and only later discard the sounds that they don't hear around them all day, retaining the ones they do. In that way your baby will speak English and the Russian baby will speak Russian – and also in that way not only languages but regional accents will be passed on and kept alive.

Talkative parents make talkative babies ... but not if the talking goes on above their heads, if the conversation is too quick, too adult. And certainly not if you never give your baby a chance to join in. It is by patience and by praising that your baby will be encouraged to try out his voice still more. It's the old psychological trick – praise the 'good' behaviour or, in this case, the behaviour you want to encourage. And partly because the baby values your approval and partly because it is in his nature to experiment with his voice he'll go on progressing.

Although the baby who is talked to and is encouraged to join in will babble more fluently and in later life will be more easily articulate, the neglected baby will also babble although to a lesser extent. And so will the deaf baby. The deaf baby can't help babbling – it is built into his system. It will be only later when he can't reinforce his babbling with the sound of other voices that he'll fall silent. So under six months you can't assume that a baby's hearing is normal simply because he's making the usual baby

Sounds before words – to a baby the sounds of home and his parents' voice give comfort and security and encourage him to join in.

sounds. It is only in the second half of his first year that it's possible to suspect by his behaviour that there may be a hearing difficulty. But of course the caring and informed parents will by then have noticed if his reactions to phones ringing, dogs barking and the other everyday noises are not normal (see page 149).

But now the noises coming from the baby seat, the playpen or the cot begin to take on a different quality. Inflections and tones are creeping in: up to now he has seemed to be practising a five finger exercise – now he is on to the scales. His voice will question, harangue, express disgust, cajole, sympathize, scold ... and all without a single word. And he will understand your variations of tones too. Ask a baby a question and he will begin to look surprised. 'Where's the dog?' 'Now, what did I do with my shoes?' Of course he doesn't know what you're talking about but your *tone* is asking a question. Gradually by the association of sounds and objects he will come to understand that sounds have particular meanings. Sounds, in fact, are words.

And just as he knows that his voice can control you, you'll find that your voice can control him.

'Oh, look what you've done,' you exclaim in despair as a bowl of sticky cereal trickles steadily on to the carpet. His face crumples, his eyes fill with tears ... clearly he's done something wrong ... but then –

'It's all right – you couldn't help it. There, it's soon cleared up.'

Miraculously the face straightens, the eyes beam. All, it seems, is well. The crescendo of noise, action and interaction continues.

At the same time it has to be admitted that babies are not always the most stimulating of companions, particularly if you don't have much adult company either. And sometimes the prospect of weeks of 'prattle' seems very bleak indeed. But be reassured, this time in a baby's life is pure gold. Not only is the amount of stimulation vital but also the time of the baby's life that he is given it will have a profound effect on his later ability to communicate – and thus make relationships. Up to the age of two the foundations of his future are being laid. Listen to this:

'Live language directed to the child is the most consistently favourable kind of educational experience an infant can have during the eleven to sixteen month period. Neither language from a television set nor language engaged in by nearby people and overheard by an infant seem to play a substantial role in the process of acquisition of intellectual or linguistic skill.'

That is a quotation from thirteen years of research into the development of the child in his own home during the first years of life. The research – known as the Harvard Preschool Project – is by far the most intensive examination of the development of the child yet undertaken.

A noisy, communicative baby is a contented baby. Unhappy babies don't 'talk'. You may be able to cajole him out of his mood by your voice or your antics and hopefully the sounds will begin again but the rule is – while he's chatting, he's happy.

Words have meaning but sounds will have meaning before words. The previous months of chatter have taught the baby (or rather allowed him to find out) that sounds have meaning – 'Grr ... yum yum ... yuk ...' They are not words in the adult sense but they have a very definite meaning.

Many parents worry because their baby is not saying recognizable words ... 'He's nearly one and hasn't said anything yet. The baby next door is only ten months and he says a lot of words ...' This does not matter at all if the baby proves that he understands words, if he reacts to simple commands: 'Peek-a-boo. Wave bye-bye.' Can he imitate some of your sounds? Miaouw with the cat, bark with the dog? If so, speech as you and I know it is all there, ready to burst the banks – and when it does, the flood will soon follow.

The first word may come at about one year or so, sometimes earlier, and when it does, it's usually followed by others quite quickly. By his first birthday the baby may know from one to ten words, although the brightest children are not always in the forefront of the early to speak.

As the baby turns into a toddler and his world expands, so he understands more and needs more. Quite naturally he's propelled into learning more words to communicate his growing needs and experience. He explores the house – looks, touches, pulls, pushes – and the adult with him will naturally find himself naming the objects the baby is touching. 'Chair. Stool. Ball. Car.'

If you listen to yourself speaking to a baby or young child then you will hear yourself speaking slowly, distinctly and with pauses between the word which you will also probably repeat several times. 'Car: car: car.'

You will also quite naturally extend and elaborate on the words the baby uses. 'Car,' he will say. 'Yes,' you will reply. 'It is a nice car, isn't it? A lovely red car.'

Talk to, not *at*. Overheard language is not as helpful to a child as the direct involvement of a caring adult.

You will also put his thoughts into words.
A dog barks. 'Spot is hungry,' you say.
You give him food. 'Now he's happy.'
'Good dog, Spot',
The door slams, 'There's Daddy,' you say.
(There will come the day of course when you will have to be careful. An acquaintance blessed with the ability to make furniture, accidentally hit her finger with a hammer, 'Oh damn', she says – a phrase joyfully repeated by the two year old to the astonished grandparents.)

The chances are that mother or childminder is also interpreter-in-chief because those first words, so lovingly welcomed and heralded by you, could very well not be understood by anyone else.

'What's he saying?' friends ask and you will spring into translation. No wonder the baby is so bonded with the adult who looks after him most. At times it must seem like him and you against the world.

Baby talk

Baby talk is very endearing – when it's the baby who's talking. It is not altogether so riveting when a six-foot-four father erupts into a stream of gibberish among which only the sounds 'bikky' and 'nicey picey' may be understandable.

It is very tempting to prolong baby talk by encouraging and imitating it. But it's not very wise because sooner or later your baby will need to use the right words which others will understand. The best solution is to use the right words yourself but at the same time let your baby know that you understand what he means by his version of the word. Sometimes you'll have to settle for his simpler version and mark time a little until he is able to cope with the adult pronunciation. Words do not come fully formed and baby talk may be the order of things for several months.

Pronunciation is a very complex skill. It depends on a combination of hearing, intellectual and emotional development, and the ability to use tongue, lips, teeth and jaw in the correct coordination. A tall order for a rising two year old.

Here's an example to explain the processes. Slowly make the sound 'bay' as it appears in 'baby'. Now try to analyse what has happened as you made that sound.

First   your vocal mechanism had to be alerted to produce a sound.

Second   your lips had to come together to form a seal.

Third   your tongue had to be on the floor of your mouth.

Fourth   air pressure had to be built up behind your closed lips.

Fifth   at the right moment, your lips had to open for the small explosion to come through (which is in effect the 'bay' sound).

If you want to test this out, put your hand in front of your mouth as you say the word and you'll feel what's happening.

Try some other sounds – the 'ca' in cat, the 'da' in dad, the 'mmm' sound in mum. Making each one of these sounds often requires vast and complicated movements of the tongue, lips, teeth, jaw and voice. To say each sound separately is difficult enough – to put them all together in the right order for a word may be impossible at first for a child.

Fortunately a lot of these sounds can also be seen. As well as hearing what you say the baby can watch you saying it – and this is why he will be most successful in pronouncing correctly the words he can most easily see e.g. 'bay' in baby and 'mmm' in mum.

Some sounds are very difficult to 'see' – the 's' in soup for instance and the 'z' in zebra and although pronunciation will gradually improve, some of the more difficult sounds may not be mastered until about the age of five.

What is certain is that if you try to force correct pronunciation by holding on to the biscuit until he says 'biscuit' and not 'bikky', you will end up with tears of frustration. Correct pronunciation doesn't matter – it will come naturally if you don't deter either by reinforcing the incorrect by repeating it or by not realizing that the child may just be incapable of saying the word 'properly'. He is *trying* to sound like you and what matters now is that you should understand each other and accept and reward his effort – because that's the purpose of communication.

Your child knows a great many words before he says them. Suppose you have a cat called Ralph. All day long the chances are that your child is hearing the word 'Ralph'. 'Where's Ralph?' 'Ralph, come and eat your dinner.' 'Good pussy, Ralph.' So the sound Ralph goes into his computer. Suddenly something happens to press the 'print out' button – and, hey presto, the child throws his arms round the cat's neck and says … 'Ralph!'

There is also a chance that he might call the cat 'bed' if that's a word he has often heard. It really doesn't matter in the slightest. He's not slow, or retarded – he'll get it all sorted out in time if you don't start fussing and over-correcting him.

These months between the first and second birthdays are days of wonder. He is an explorer and the whole world is a marvel – under the bed, at the back of furniture, inside kitchen cupboards – the days are not

Don't worry if your child's early words are not fully formed. Pronunciation is a complex skill to acquire and an important part is for the child to watch your lips speaking a word correctly. Here is a baby's eye view of mother (*top to bottom*). Saying 'baybee'. The text explains the coordinated movements of jaw, lips and tongue to produce just the first syllable 'bay'.

Success comes when the child uses words to make friends and communicate needs and feelings to those around him.

Finger games and rhymes, singing and talking, all help the baby's vocabulary to grow as he listens. He will in time imitate.

thinks. They make things happen.

He is more than half way up the ladder to acceptable communication. Between two and three the single words are turned into doubles. 'Mummy go. More drink.' It is rather as though the child is sending telegrams where every word has to be paid for. But soon he's way past this stage. Complicated concepts are beginning to be learned. 'On the table' means something: 'in the cupboard', 'outside the door'. Small joining words are developed ... 'and', 'but' ... and the possessive assumes enormous importance: 'Mummy's hat. Daddy's shoes'. The verb ending 'ing' is sprinkling the phrases now ... 'Mummy singing ... Daddy working ... Daddy sleeping ... Mummy laughing ...'

Pictures in books are correctly named: not every animal with four legs is a dog.

From now on the steps up the ladder are sure and swift. There are tricky moments still to be negotiated but the rise is rapid and perhaps the final triumph comes when the child uses words to express his needs, wants and feelings in a way understandable to those around him.

With luck from now on all will be plain sailing. The top of the ladder has been reached and perched up there on the heights the child can see the landscape spread out for the conquering. Giants there may be still to overcome but there are glimpses of glory all right. They key has turned in the lock of language and the door is opening to a future of conquest, friendship, learning and love.

Delayed speech development

Every child grows up in different circumstances. Position in the family, parents' disposition, heredity – all these play a part in

long enough. Shopping, housework, gardening, driving – everything is new and stupendously exciting. With the security of parents as base he can make little forays into the unknown. It may exhaust you but for him all this is the chance to learn new words, Finger games, rhyming games, singing, talking, looking at books – his vocabulary is growing by leaps and bounds. 'Ba' somehow ensures that a ball is given to him: 'din' produces food ... 'dink' produces drink. Words are useful and wonderful things, he his development. The youngest child in a family is often a rapid learner, pulled on and encouraged by much attention and the stimulation of always having other children around. This can also have the opposite effect. An older child can 'interpret' so successfully for the younger that he makes no effort at all to speak for himself. The caring parent will soon know if the speech is there and just lying dormant or question if there is some other underlying cause for the lack of speech. The chart below may help.

The main point worth remembering is that if by the age of one your child does not understand you and by one and a half is not 'speaking' a few words so that you – or whoever is with him most – can understand him, then it would be wise to ask for medical advice.

One cause of a child not speaking properly when it is reasonable to assume he might be doing so could be impaired hearing (see page 213). Severe deafness will almost certainly be picked up very rapidly but it is more difficult to pinpoint a slight hearing loss. A child could be thought stubborn, miserable, inattentive when all the time the trouble might be that he can't hear properly.

If you think your child may be slightly deaf, try out some simple tests of your own. Doesn't he hear the sound of a knock on the door? Has he ever startled at a loud sound? Does he want the television turned up or not hear you when you call from one room to the other?

These are elementary steps but they are pointers to a possible difficulty. Nowadays there are sophisticated methods of testing

Use this chart to follow the development of your child's speech and hearing ability. If at any age all your answers are *yes*, your child is developing hearing, speech and language normally. If, however, you score between one and three in the *no* column your child may be developing more slowly, and if you score more than three in the *no* column it would be as well to seek medical advice.

FIND YOUR CHILD'S SPEECH AND HEARING AGE

CHILD'S AGE	HEARING AND UNDERSTANDING	YES	NO	TALKING	YES	NO
BIRTH	Does your child listen to speech? Does your child startle or cry at noise? Does your child awaken at loud sounds?			Does your child coo or gurgle?		
3 MONTHS	Does your child try to turn toward the speaker? Does your child smile when spoken to? Does your child stop playing and appear to listen to sounds or speech? Does your child seem to recognize mother's voice?			Does your child babble? Does your child cry differently for different needs? Does your child repeat the same sounds a lot?		
6 MONTHS	Does your child respond to no and her/his name? Does your child notice and look around for the source of new sounds? Does your child turn her/his head toward the side where the sound is coming from?			Does your child's babbling sound like the parent's speech, only not clear? Does your child make lots of different sounds?		
9 MONTHS-1 YEAR	Has your child begun to respond to requests ('come here;' 'do you want more')? Does your child turn or look up when you call? Does your child search or look around when hearing new sounds? Does your child listen to people talking?			Does your child say words (8-10 words at age 1½; 2-3 words at age 1)? (Words may not be clear). Does your child enjoy imitating sounds? Does your child use jargon (babbling that sounds like real speech)? Does your child use voice to get attention?		
1½-2 YEARS	Can your child follow two requests ('get the ball and put it on the table')?			Does your child have 10-15 words (by age 2)? Does your child sometimes repeat requests? Does your child ask 1-2 word questions? (where kitty? go bye-bye? more?)? Does your child put 2 words together (more drink)?		
2½-4 YEARS	Does your child understand differences in meaning ('go-stop;' 'the car pushed the truck – the truck pushed the car')? Can your child point to pictures in a book upon hearing them named? Does your child notice sounds (dog barking, telephone ringing, television sound, knocking at door and so on)? Does your child understand conversation easily? Does your child hear you when you call from another room? Does your child hear television or radio at the same loudness level as other members of the family?			Does your child say most sounds, except perhaps *r*, *s*, *th*, and *l*? Does your child sometimes repeat words in a sentence? Does your child use 200-300 words? Does your child use 2-3 word sentences? Does your child ask lots of why and what questions? Has your child's jargon and repeating disappeared? Does your child like to name things?		
	TOTAL			TOTAL		

Visual aids now help a child who is hard of hearing to pronounce correctly. This computer translates sound into a trace on a screen so that a child can match his pronunciation with that already displayed for a word as a correct example.

case their child suffers emotionally through being teased by other children or through the impatience of other adults. Interestingly enough, other children rarely notice or are critical about the speech efforts of themselves or others. As long as one child is able to understand another, they seem satisfied.

It is often the parents who aren't able to accept less than perfect speech in their children. Try asking yourself some questions to see how you measure up in this respect. Are you embarrassed when your child speaks at home or in public? Do you correct him, or try to accept him as he is? Do you try to talk for him so that he isn't embarrassed (or are you protecting yourself from embarrassment)?

The way you react to your child's speech efforts will significantly influence the way others will react. Begin by looking at the disorder as a whole. If the problem is such that, after reading this chapter, you don't think your child will outgrow it, then you should seek help.

A speech therapist however can only do part of the job. She will point the way and show you how to help your child to better speech and it will help you if you think of the problem as being temporary – one that will be improved through the combined efforts of your child, yourself and the therapist. It is helpful to remember that most, if not all, communication problems can be lessened and the majority entirely cured.

Stammering

Most children as they are learning to communicate, hesitate, search for words, go back and repeat sentences. This could be because the child is thinking out what he's trying to say, or is being distracted by something else, or else is trying to formulate the right words. Boys seem to be more liable to stammer than girls and if they're going to show signs of it then it probably won't occur before the ages of two to five. It can take the form of sudden long silences in the middle of a conversation or of drawing out one of the sounds in a word. It can come on very suddenly and sometimes the child doesn't seem aware of what's happening.

So far this is a normal phase and if properly treated it will disappear as rapidly as it came. If you become anxious, try to correct the hesitations, draw attention to them and generally set up tension in the child, the problems could move on to the second and more serious stage where correction is more difficult, if not imposssible.

In this secondary stage the child struggles to correct his impediment. His face grimaces, he may wriggle with distress – he has now become aware of the problem.

which don't need the baby's cooperation and such tests are readily available.

Often there could be a slight hearing loss after a cold or an ear infection, which is one reason why either should always be taken seriously and a doctor consulted. Such a loss is nearly always temporary but it is in the early years that children catch a great many of these infections.

If by any chance a hearing impairment is confirmed then a great deal can be done to help. Children with quite extreme problems of deafness are being helped towards acceptable and 'normal' pronunciation. A game which translates sound into sight has recently been introduced to help deaf children to correct their own pronunciation by way of a screen on which they can 'see' how their own speech differs from that of hearing speakers.

Emotional aspects of slowness in speaking

Parents of the slow-to-speak child or the child with a speech disorder often worry in

The child in the first stage of stammering should not be made aware that he's doing anything unusual. Just ignore it. Reward his efforts and the symptoms should subside. If they do not and the child becomes upset, ask for professional help.

One language or two

Paul is nearly six months old. His mother is Spanish, his father is English although he speaks Spanish fluently. They live in England and when they are at home Paul's parents speak to each other in a mixture of both Spanish and English, mostly quite unaware of which they are using. Paul's father is out at work most of the day while his mother stays at home: she speaks English easily but with an accent and her endearments to her baby come naturally in her native Spanish.

Should they teach Paul to speak Spanish or English: or both languages simultaneously?

It's a difficult question. Some children seem able to manage to acquire two languages without much trouble: others slow down in both – and unfortunately there doesn't seem any way of finding out in advance which type of child you are dealing with.

One way to avoid any possible confusion is to teach the child one language only and then, when he is reasonably fluent, introduce the second. When parents do this they usually teach first the language of the country they are not living in – perhaps reasoning that when the child grows and mixes more he will have every opportunity of learning the language he is hearing spoken around him every day. So in this case Paul would be taught to speak Spanish first and then English.

One possible hazard of this method is that it may, in the early years, limit the child's ability to mix easily since he would have to rely – in Paul's case – on being understood only by adults and other children who spoke Spanish. He could easily become isolated, unable to have those special 'chats' with the shopkeeper, or the woman next door, which are a small child's invaluable steps into a social world. You could of course think that until he is two to two and a half Paul would not be making many of his own contacts anyway since he would not be mixing on his own without an attendant adult – who presumably in his case would be both caretaker and interpreter.

As with most things to do with children, the answer may well be 'take the pace from the child'. If he seems confused, worried and not making headway in either language, then it's time to think again. What is certain is that it is much easier to become fluent in a second

language if you learn it during childhood or adolescence rather than wait until you are adult. And if there is the rich choice of two languages in one family it seems unfortunate to waste that opportunity.

Speech pronunciation disorders

Parents often become concerned that their child's pronunciation is not 'normal'. Even though you've followed the advice about not overcorrecting your baby he may still not seem to be learning exact pronunciation as rapidly as you think he should. Lisping and other substitutions (wabbit for rabbit) sometimes seem they will never go away. But remember pronunciation is very difficult and a real struggle for a child. Lips, tongue and teeth all have to work together but if your child is able to suck, swallow and chew accurately (which is the primary function of the muscles and mechanisms we use to pronounce words) and is able to understand you and follow directions appropriate

Children today can experience another language without necessarily leaving the country. Even your local café can display both French and English so that the languages are blended.

pronunciation will probably occur.

It is best to look forward to the result of treatment rather than question why this has happened to your child. You'll find that – as middleman between expert and layman – family and friends will look to you for understanding your child's problem. A positive approach will help towards your acceptance of the child's disability and this will be the most necessary emotional aspect of the relationship between you.

Always give the child *time* to speak. Don't appear impatient or unwilling to wait for him to complete his thought. Don't fill in the word for him or complete the thought – let him finish himself. Look at your child when he is communicating. This may be difficult, especially if he is having problems with stammering, but it is necessary. Relax while he is speaking so that you show him that he has time and so do you. And unless specifically requested to do so by the therapist, never correct his speech efforts or allow anyone else to do so.

Even if you think your child will outgrow his disorder without the need for special help, following these rules will lessen the emotional tension you may feel.

Very often a great many worries and fears are based on myth rather than fact so take every opportunity to ask professionals about the particular type of problem your child has. Each problem has many different aspects and your understanding of these will go a long way towards alleviating your worries and concerns – and, most importantly – towards helping your child.

How can you help?

Talk *to* your child not *at* him. 'Did you like your dinner then?' 'Look at the rain. We'll get wet.' If there's too much talk going on above his head he won't be able to sort things out. As he becomes more able at communicating and using words, try not to answer your own questions: give him the chance to reply.

● Keep your speech simple and short. Don't use long, involved sentences. Repeat a word several times but slowly and distinctly.

● Make sure your child can see your face as well as hear you. He needs to 'see' the sound you're making.

● A new baby with a couple of older children already in the family may be bewildered by their expertise in language – half phrases, interruptions and so on. Try to see that the baby has some time with an adult for his own 'talk'. But even quite young children, left alone with a baby, will instinctively modiify their language to suit him: they will use simple words, repeat them, say them slowly ... just in the same way that an adult will.

● Talk, play, chat, read, point – but don't drown the baby in too much sound. Match your pace to his.

● Use every opportunity that the day presents to help with sounds and – later – vocabulary. But talk about things he can see. At first, the abstract of 'yesterday' will mean nothing. Talk about what is happening *now*.

● Talk about things he likes to hear about. Going shopping, what he's done today, what he had for dinner. Children love to have the story of what they have been doing during the day told back to them at night. It seems to fix the order of things more securely – gives them a pattern to their days.

● Never mock or laugh at mispronunciation. It's not necessary for you to repeat your child's mistake and don't hurt his feelings by turning it into a joke and telling everyone about it in his hearing. If he has taken a stab at a really difficult word, it could be best to praise him for attempting it, at the same time, bringing the word – correctly pronounced – into your own sentence. 'What funny chibleys,' he may say. 'Yes, they are funny chimneys, aren't they?'

● Don't compare his progress with other children.

● Use everyday words frequently so that he learns them as he goes along. 'Where's the duster?' rather than 'Where is it?' 'Is that the bell?' rather than 'What's that?'

● Never frustrate him by withholding something he wants just because he's not using the correct word.

● Be prepared for regressions into baby talk, sounds and noises if he's tired or not very well.

● Make words fun. Singing, looking at books together. For a baby the best books have one picture on the page and one word.

● Expand his own words and interpret his needs. When he lifts his arms to be picked up and says 'Up! Up!' say, 'Up comes John' as you lift him. (If of course his name is John.) He won't understand 'me', 'you', 'they' and all that for some time yet.

● When he's at the 'Why' stage, try to answer questions simply: 'Why is pussy mewing?' 'Because she's thirsty.'

● Be careful about correcting too much. If your child has struggled to express something and you correct the pronunciation he may easily think you're questioning the statement not the word.

● Help your child to mix. Young children don't play together so much as play side by side but they are learning to enjoy company and becoming used to others. Later this will help them learn to share and learn new words.

When the key has turned in the lock of language, the door opens to friendship, love and learning and understanding.

THE STAGES OF LANGUAGE

From birth to four weeks	**From four to eight weeks**	**From eight weeks to six months**
One-way distress calls – crying, wriggling. Recognizes his mother's voice: puts voice to face.	Smiles, gurgles. Coordinates sight and sound – will turn towards some source of sound. Acknowledges parents' face and voice.	'Talks' to parents with tones, coos, grunts. Makes separate sounds – may say 'Mama . . . Dada'.
From six to ten months	**From ten months onwards**	**About three years**
May begin to say single words.	Single words become two words. Simple phrases, sentences, growing articulation.	Proper sentences with more than one clause. All these stages and ages are approximate: your child may be quicker or slower.

Thinking

Your baby is an explorer. She looks around, sucks, licks, listens, reaches, touches, grasps, examines. Her senses feed her information and her developing abilities, both mental and physical, begin to interpret that information. She learns to draw conclusions, she learns to think and she begins to understand the world she lives in.

Remember the drop-the-teddy game and the amazing number of things your young Sherlock Holmes was discovering through that obsessively repetitive action? The baby of seven or eight months, flinging a teddy over the side of her high chair, may, after a few trial runs, flinch at the exact moment the teddy is due to hit the ground. Memory and judgment are being added to the skills of opening her fingers, releasing the contents of her hand, flinging away, causing something to happen. Tie that teddy to a ribbon to her chair and your baby will not only learn that the teddy doesn't make a noise (because it doesn't strike the floor) but that by hauling on the ribbon she can bring the teddy back.

So your baby is not only assessing and storing information, she is solving problems, reasoning: later she will begin to understand concepts and categories. You are teaching your baby a concept when you hold out her empty dinner dish and say triumphantly, 'All gone.' Within a short time she too will gaze at her empty plate and echo your phrase – probably only the tune of the phrase, not yet the words: they have still to come. And you are teaching your baby to categorize when she learns from you that your cat (a black one), the cat next door (a tabby) and the cat in the picture book (a Siamese) are all cats, even if they look a little different.

Of course your baby doesn't understand that she's learning concepts, or to differentiate, to reason, to categorize, to solve problems but you will know through your affectionate and informed observation. Later, when speech is added to your baby's other skills, she will be able to express in words what she is thinking and doing. Speech is one of the skills which divides humans from animals but so also do thought, judgment and the ability to understand abstract ideas ... and the growth of this is called cognitive development.

During the first few years of life your baby's brain grows at an amazing rate and its growth is paralleled by the rapid development of these cognitive abilities. By the time you first wave au revoir to your five year old at the school gate she will have developed

The baby is an explorer. Senses feed her information and her developing abilities begin to interpret that information. She draws conclusions.

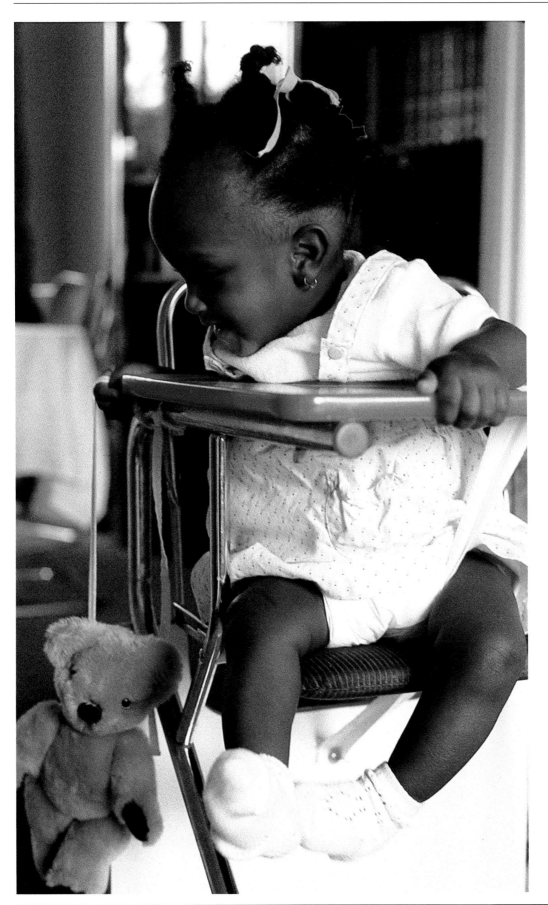

For the umpteenth time the teddy bear goes over the side: she is learning concepts – cause and effect, grasping and letting go.

She explores with touch, sight, smell. She touches when she should taste, tastes when she should look – but she is learning.

She makes social contacts in the casual friendliness of home: window cleaner, milkman, woman next door – all feed her experiences.

most of the basic thinking skills.

Which doesn't mean – and you can't remember it too often – that all children develop at exactly the same rate. Some children will take a while to understand something, others grasp it straight away. Yet they may both have similar intellectual abilities. Other children keep pace with each other then one will surge forward, so if your baby is really quick on the uptake, don't get too elated ... there may be shallows ahead. The opposite is also true: the slower developer will almost certainly catch up so don't worry if your baby doesn't quite match the blueprint. If you notice, however, that her development seems unduly delayed (and you will be able to see the outlines of the time scale from the development charts on pages 160 and 162), ask for professional advice. (The chances are that – like the toothache in the dentist's waiting room – the cause of your anxiety will disappear as soon as you do something about it. But it is important not to fuss or force – your baby is sensitive to the moods of the house and stress is infectious.

What influences cognitive development – the ability to think and reason?

A child's abilities are determined in part by her genetic make-up but dozens of other factors can impede or encourage progress. Your child will perceive, adapt and react to her world in her own special way. Environment is of paramount importance – whether the world stimulates, bores or merely confuses her with too much activity and noise. Tiredness, illness, emotional strain may all effect a child's rate of cognitive development, so obviously will physical deficiencies of hearing, sight, or an underdeveloped sense such as taste or smell. Physical activity may also affect the rate of development: the physically active baby will explore her surroundings earlier than the passive child who – nevertheless – may be learning through observation rather than participation. We all know the three year old who sits mute in a corner in company yet later launches into a detailed account of what was said, done and worn which would be the envy of a gossip columnist.

Which brings us to socializing – not just mummy and daddy but grandparents, aunts, the children next door, the postman, the milkman and the man who cleans the windows – for the *involving* world of human contact is the sun and rain which make a baby grow.

The pattern of cognitive development

Just as your baby grows physically in an orderly sequence – sitting, crawling, walking, running – so her thinking and reasoning powers progress in a pattern which is common to all children, although the speed at which the child advances from step to step differs widely and has no bearing on the eventual intelligence of the child.

Mental growth depends on the organization of received and perceived information. As your child encounters new experiences she has to try and fit them into her existing knowledge and image of the world. An example is that of a two year old who sees a bird picking up seeds from a windowsill and then flying away. Through watching that happening she formulates an idea of what a bird is. A few months later she is taken to a zoo and sees an ostrich – also a bird but a bird which doesn't fly. So her idea of a 'bird' must be broadened to include birds that don't fly. Later your child may ask, 'Why doesn't the ostrich fly if it has wings?' and you will probably answer, 'Well, birds fly so that they can get out of danger quickly but an ostrich has such long legs that it can run fast and doesn't need to fly. And because it hasn't used its wings for so long they've probably grown stiff.' More layers of knowledge are being added to your child's existing store. Later she may think further and ask, 'If I didn't use my legs would I stop being able to walk?' And your answer would be, 'If you did it for long enough.' Further thought may lead her to the conclusion that as she has legs to run she doesn't need wings – and later still she may well put all this theory into practice by sitting still and asking you to wait on her, 'Because my legs won't work because I haven't been using them!' She's not being artful – she's playing out being a bird that can't fly.

In this way the child gathers in knowledge, fills in the cracks, organizes – and one of the ways she consolidates her learning is through play.

Learning is play: play is learning
No-one works harder than a child at play but then a child sees no difference between the two. It is only as adults that we learn to separate the two. Try playing a game with your baby: roll an orange across the floor. It is an easy direction to write *'Roll an orange across the floor'* but if you divide the implied action you will find it has, like the orange, many segments.

The orange is brightly coloured and your baby can follow its progress with her eyes. If she can crawl she will probably try to follow it and then grasp it. (Already sight, move-

No-one works harder than the child at play but then children see no difference between work and play. Only adults learn to differentiate.

ment and grasp have been involved.) She will probably try to bite it and discover that the skin is sour. So she will also be learning one of the basic tastes. She may try to roll it as you have done, she may retrieve it and give it back to you to roll again. Physical skills, mental skills and reasoning are all being used. But what you have also done is teach your baby a physical law: a round thing rolls because it's round. (It was understanding that which led to the invention of the wheel.)

Fortunately the process is not as complicated as the words it takes to describe what is going on and fortunately too you do not have to think about all this whenever you play with your baby: your main thought is that you and your baby are enjoying a game together – but beyond that she is learning with leisure, and in a relaxed and enjoyable atmosphere, and you are helping her to learn.

Physical influences on development

Among the physical causes which may affect intelligence are glandular (thyroid) problems, nutritional deficiencies, certain prenatal infections – if the mother had German measles (rubella) for instance in early pregnancy – or prebirth exposure to smoking or alcohol. Birth injuries or abnormal brain or body structure could also retard development. Depending on the particular deficiency these may affect either the inborn capacity to develop or the acquired knowledge. In today's atmosphere of knowledge and resources such problems are happily less frequent than in previous years. Immunization prevents rubella in the mother (see page 66), malnutrition is not common in the western world (see page 59) and enormous strides in prenatal and postnatal care have alerted professionals to potential concern and eliminated many former hazards.

Because babies learn through the input from their senses, the growth of reasoning and thinking is influenced by the maturity of the senses and inevitably one area of growth overlaps with another. Babies also grow continually, not in periods of set time, so it's no good trying to set your watch by your baby's ascent up a chart. Certain developmental stages it is true take place during certain time intervals and so we can make a rough timetable of ways to help development in your baby at different stages. They are not 'lessons', they are ways of enjoying and discovering different experiences and of growing together.

A round thing rolls, a square thing won't, neither will a triangle or a rectangle. Without words or explanations, she has learnt that a round thing can roll. Rolling is a property of round things.

She loves mucky play and learns the different properties of mud, water, sand through touch – and sometimes, alas, through taste as well.

BIRTH TO THREE MONTHS

She knows and is learning how to see, hear, touch, smell, taste – what milk tastes like, what a blanket feels like, mother smells like, looks like, sounds like. How to control muscles (see page 131).

How to help:

Chose the right kind of mobiles (see page 120).

Move a colourful ball slowly across your baby's field of vision. She will turn her head to follow to mid-point of her body then stop. Up to five or six weeks when the hands are still fisted, put your finger into her hand so that she learns to grasp it, and to exercise her muscles by grasping. Put different objects into her hand – the handle of a rattle for instance, so that she begins to understand about different textures. Let her clutch her blanket. When she puts her hands into her mouth don't pull them away – you will be stopping natural exploration. Her mouth is her most effective and available tool. Constantly keeping a pacifier in her mouth will prevent her exploring other objects. But keep pins, pencils, small bottle tops very well away. When she begins to swipe at things, change the mobile. Provide pram or cot toys, rattles, especially ones which make a gentle noise when moved. Talk and play with her. Sing to her and rock her. Let her kick freely and look around.

At three months she is interested in everything, she watches her world and her improved ability to focus allows her to see and then reach out with more accuracy.

FROM THREE TO SIX MONTHS

Senses are becoming integrated, focus improved to nearly all distances. Sound stimulates movement. She will look for the source of sound. Follows well with eyes. Is interested in everything. Is learning to coordinate hands and eyes. Watches her world, focuses on an object and reaches for it. Repeats activities. Looks at hands. Grasps and reaches. Rolls over. Plays with toes. Reaches and grasps a toy without first looking from toy back to hand. Very nearly manages the first wobbly sit-up.

How to help:

Prop her up so that she can see what's going on. She will still need to be supported but will enjoy watching you moving about. When she's on a rug on the floor put toys at different distances from her so she can stretch out and try to grasp. If she gets frustrated, help her, but don't always hand everything to her. Sing, listen, talk, imitate sounds. She will probably enjoy smacking the surface of the water in her bath so cover up! She will still need supporting in her bath but will enjoy water play with toys that float, sink, squirt and bubble.

SIX TO TWELVE MONTHS

Aware of strangers and may be frightened but still going out to meet the world instead of letting it come to her (see home proofing, page 30). She will be into everything and increasingly mobile. Crawls, shuffles and grasps. Is learning to do everything. Often concentrates on one area of development – speech or movement – at a time. Shows when she's cross but on the whole is too busy, most of the time, to be angry. Wriggles like mad when you're dressing her (keep a toy or mobile handy to distract). Begins to feed herself, holds rusk, waves spoon.

How to help:

Don't fence her in but make the home safe (see page 30). Use the playpen only for safety's sake. Make her a textured ball to play with. Let her go barefoot when it is safe and feel the difference between boards (watch splinters), carpets, grass, sand. Likes water and mucky play. She will eat sponges in the bath so watch her. Offer her small, safe objects to pick up and practise grasping reflexes e.g. seedless raisins or sultanas. Have endless patience with the drop-the teddy game. Involve her with what is happening. She will love to watch the washing machine going round. Talk to her about things that are happening. Make the daily walk enjoyable with chats. She will love to crumple paper, shake rattles, wave from the wrist. But allow her privacy, time to explore without fussing.

At six months she can just manage to sit up and try to grasp an object without hesitation.

At one year she can hold and grasp and, becoming increasingly mobile crawls into everything. Allow her time to herself to explore.

TWELVE TO EIGHTEEN MONTHS

Is much more mobile and probably has her own favourite toy. Knows where things are when she can't see them – e.g. her dinner in the fridge. She will wait outside for opening time. Actions are more meaningful – might hand you her plate at dinner time. Is learning to learn, explore, arrange. Fits things inside each other. Pulls along a toy on a string. Begins to climb – takes books from shelves etc. Becomes a real companion and joins in all you are doing.

How to help:

Let her explore cupboards (if safe), arrange your pots and pans. Ask her to hand you named things – lid, spoon, pan. Show her what to do with cleaner, duster – she will follow you around doing the same. Let her 'help'. Play the game of 'Where's it gone?' by hiding something under cloth then finding. Likes her posting box.

EIGHTEEN TO TWENTY-FOUR MONTHS

Knows her own mind. Says no. Knows the difference between you and herself. Shows likes and dislikes. Is learning to think ahead – she will trip over the same steps every day to begin with but will later learn to step over without tripping. Lives in the present. Knows objects from different angles. Recognizes voices. Knows animals, names. Not bored – too busy. Likes to look at books. Can handle and manipulate well.

How to help:

Play the guessing game – shut eyes and feel what toy it is. Play hide and seek. Teach her to crawl downstairs backwards. Give her space and time. She likes mucky play – clay, dough – so provide it. Knows a lot of words. Looks out of window. Show her flowers, birds, leaves. Show her shapes and imitate more sounds. Look at books together and talk about them (more about this in Play, Toys and Books, pages 164, 166, 123). Point out her reflection in a puddle. Talk about the daily walk: listen to the wind, play in piles of leaves. Is learning about differences and similarities i.e. two plastic rings look alike but are different size and colour, so play with these. Knows several words and baby talk turns into phrases so help to teach new ones. Likes supermarket shopping – red apples, shiny lemons, green peppers. Is learning about concepts – circles are round, square bricks will stack. Can sort, match and classify. Puts all reds in one pile, white in another. Praise this and let her sort out plastic forks and spoons. Make her a simple jigsaw puzzle. Improved hand control means she will like to scribble and 'draw'. Ask her to put the missing nose in the face you draw for her. Matches pictures. Let her tidy away her toys, sorting out into different coloured boxes.

By eighteen months she will be walking, pushing, pulling, loading up trucks, stacking bricks. She knows things exist even when she can't see them.

At two years she works things out for herself. She can solve simple problems – like latching these two carts together. Too busy to be bored, she can handle and manipulate well.

TWENTY-FOUR TO THIRTY-SIX MONTHS

Asks questions continuously, speech improves. Watches a great deal with attention – the cat playing, the baby eating. The first two years have been exploring and discovering, now she is reflecting and weighing things up. More and more interested in new circumstances, objects and people but doesn't always put her thoughts into words. Learns about emotions (possibly from books): sad boy, happy puppy. Plays with friends rather than alongside them. Is learning to share – this comes more easily if she is not an only child. Can use crayons with more control. Increasingly interested in books and stories. Her play is sophisticated and imaginative: she pretends to be something or somebody: when she listens to teddy's heartbeat she really is the doctor. Can draw vertical lines, almost complete circles. Plays out happenings, going shopping, taking car ride. Has a better understanding of time – 'soon', 'later', 'this morning' – but not always understanding about 'tomorrow' and 'yesterday'.

How to help:

Encourage independence by letting her stay overnight if possible with aunt, grandparents, cousin. At three will be ready for playgroup (page 230). Help her to understand about quantity – a small pile of sand added to another small pile makes a bigger pile. Show her one car, two cars. She begins to learn opposites: hot/cold, sad/happy. Help with her understanding of time – 'After you've had one bedtime' is a way of explaining tomorrow.

By rising three your child will be ready for playgroup and all the delights of friends and new experiences.

36 MONTHS

For two years she has explored and discovered, now she reflects, tries things for herself, is inventive and begins to learn about emotions.

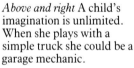
Above and right A child's imagination is unlimited. When she plays with a simple truck she could be a garage mechanic.

Boxes and drums on heads turn children into space men. The best toys are often the least expensive.

LEARNING THROUGH PLAY

Through play a child learns, explores, grows, rids herself of fears, copes with emotions, makes friends.

Toys are the tools of play but toys are not only objects you can buy in a toyshop. A toy is anything your child chooses to play with and her first toy is your face – its texture, warmth, smell and reaction. A child will turn into a toy anything she wishes to play with, from the third tread of the stairs which, she says, is a magic carpet not to be trodden on in case it whisks you away, to a battered wooden spoon which – as one two year old put it – was her 'own dear love'.

Play has no rules: when it has it becomes a game. If you try to turn playing into 'learning' then you will have destroyed the spontaneity of play and with it some part of childhood. This is why it is useless to worry too much about 'educational' toys: every object your child meets is educational; sorting spoons from forks is educational and so is sorting out the colours to go in the washing machine. You may be working when you do this: your child is playing.

All the same there are toys which may meet your child's needs at particular times: soft toys for comfort and caring, bashing-about toys to get rid of aggression, hypnotic toys (like snowscenes where the white flakes drift down inside a glass ball) which allow your child to withdraw and meditate about something or sort out a problem in her mind:

there are toys of imagination – like dolls' houses or farms or garages with lots of people about – and there are toys which teach skills, like stretching muscles, or helping with coordination. At different times a cardboard box can be a boat on a carpet-sea seething with sharks or a castle with a princess to be rescued. Play comes from inside us and it is one of the ways we deal with stress.

Play can be used for letting off steam: 'Stop that, teddy! At once – do you hear?' 'Another cup of tea, my dear?' (role play) or power play: 'Mm, we'll have to cut that leg off!' On occasions, you will learn as much from your child's play as she will.

Don't interfere with your child's play. At times she may need help or she may want you to join in but don't try to make her play a different way from the way she has chosen, unless she has got out of her depth.

Brenda Crowe, in *Play is a Feeling*, writes of acquaintances who have remembered play or experiences when they were only six months old. How powerful must be those influences on their later life.

Playing with safety

The manufacture of toys in Britain is governed by the Toy Safety Regulations of 1974 but in practice British toymakers apply even more rigid standards and it is likely that these standards will become law for Europe in 1985.

The regulations cover the materials used

and the construction. Toys produced by well-known firms are invariably subjected to the most stringent tests but the danger comes from toys imported from foreign countries where such regulations are not applicable. In general cheap toys from a market stall may be suspect, so look out for nails instead of screws, plastic that could splinter, the wrong filling in soft toys (home-made toys have been filled with termite-infested wood shavings), eyes which can be pulled off, small pieces which can be swallowed, paint you think might have too high a level of lead – although that is a danger you can only guess at.

Manufacturers are now required by law to state the age of suitability of their toys. Look here for the *lowest* specified age because an older child might play with safety with a toy designed for a younger age but a younger child can't always cope with a toy meant for a more developed child. On the other hand an older child could wind, say, a mobile string round her neck while a baby could not.

However much toy manufacturers try to produce safe toys, in the end it is your responsibility to see that your child is not given unsafe toys or misuses them in a way which makes them dangerous. Children can twist cords around their necks, get too near a swing ball, or drown in a few inches of water.

What to watch out for in toys

Wood or plastic that might splinter; toys that might break when dropped; sharp edges; too many small, swallowable parts; stuffing or granules which are sharp and protrude through their casing (there should be an inner casing anyway); toys that might tip over if a child sits on them; wheels that run away too fast on baby walkers; machinery or clockwork insufficiently cased; inflammmable material or material giving off toxic fumes. Soft toys' eyes that are inadequately attached or have dangerous pins.

Regulations in America differ from European standards but at present (1984) efforts are being made to bring the two into line.

One of the points you have to remember when you're choosing toys for your baby or young child is that very often he will be playing with them alone. Naturally there will be an adult within earshot and keeping an eye on things but it isn't unreasonable to assume that the baby is out of harm's way if he's occupied with his own possessions. Accidents can happen even with the most carefully chosen toys and so shown opposite are some dangers to look out for.

WHAT ABOUT A PET?

Sooner or later most children want a pet and, if you agree, the question is then to decide which animal is most suitable, and that decision will inevitably depend on your lifestyle and your personal preferences.

It is worth thinking about why children always seem to want pets, and whether or not they are a good idea. Children need to love as well as be loved and a pet in the house releases love and a sense of protection and responsibility. Obviously a young child can't take full responsibility for an animal, but she will learn that a pet has to be fed regularly, exercised, kept clean and provided for when the family goes away. It may also give lessons on mating and birth.

A 'cuddly' pet releases tension in a child and its loyalty is reassuring when everything else in the world seems to be going wrong.

The death of a pet will inevitably cause suffering to the child but a period of mourning is necessary and natural. Don't immediately rush out and buy another to replace the first. If in time the first is replaced, don't think of the second as the first 'coming back again': each will have its separate place in the family's affections.

If you already have a dog or cat before the baby arrives, take care that the animal does not become jealous of the newcomer. Don't leave the baby alone with the pet and do continue to make a fuss of it as before, so that it does not feel displaced. (The need for a cat net is mentioned on page 29.)

What about diseases?

● Dogs, cats, hamsters and several other domestic pets can all bite and scratch, and a child must be taught not to tease or put her face too near.

● Animal fleas and mites can cause skin rashes. The rashes can be treated with creams but care should also be taken to get rid of the fleas (ask your chemist for treatment).

● Cage birds can cause psittacosis but they can be bought already vaccinated against the disease.

● Teach your child the extra hygiene necessary when there's a pet in the house: animal dishes should never be washed with the family's: hands should always be washed before meals after touching the pet.

● Toxocara can be spread from dogs to children (see page 226): rabies is not at present a threat in this country provided the laws of quarantine are observed.

DANGER POINTS TO WATCH OUT FOR

Soft toys with eyes that are insecurely fastened

Metal toys with sections that easily come apart

Wooden toys with sharp nails easily exposed

Bright and colourful toys with paint likely to contain lead

Toys made from plastic which can split with age

Small toys in shapes that can block the windpipe

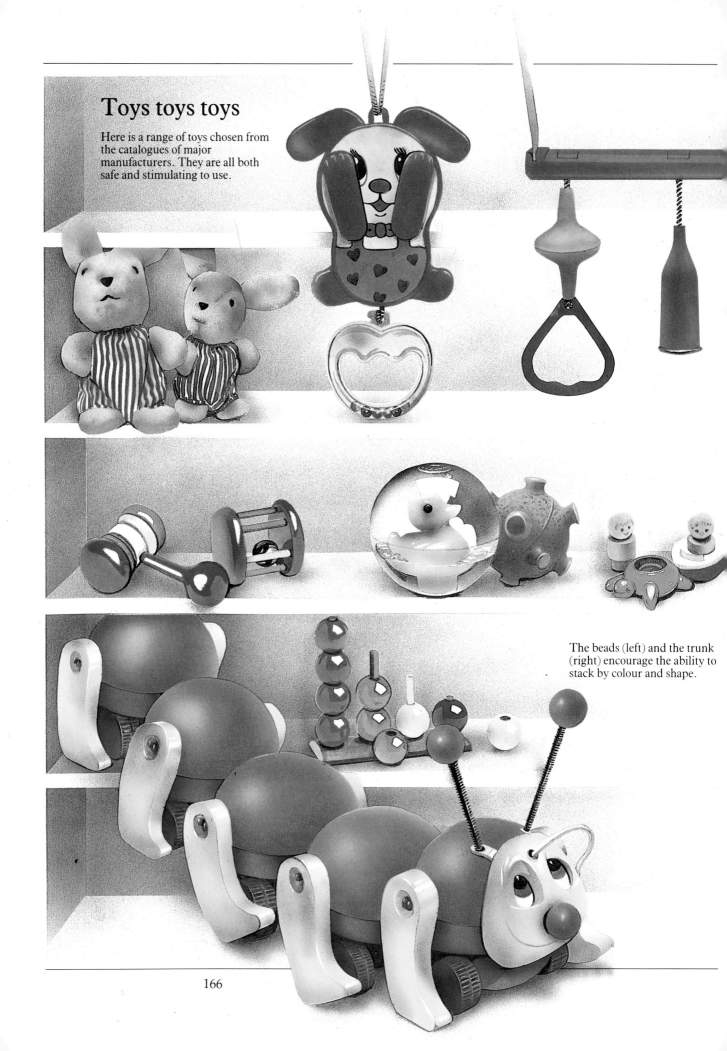

Toys toys toys

Here is a range of toys chosen from the catalogues of major manufacturers. They are all both safe and stimulating to use.

The beads (left) and the trunk (right) encourage the ability to stack by colour and shape.

Toys to suspend over the cot (left) encourage baby to watch and reach out. The musical activity house (right) provides noise and movement – at first with an adult's help and later through the baby's own involvement.

Soft cuddlies, like the bunnies at far left, can provide comfort and security. If they squeak on squeezing, so much the better. The push-along train rattle (left) will encourage finger manipulation and two-handed coordination.

From left to right are rattles creating sound and movement, floor toys and bath toys. The posting box (right) will encourage an appreciation of shape and space in a child of about twelve months.

Pull-alongs (left) and push-alongs (right) give confidence to the just-walking toddler. Stacking (far right) develops logic and order.

Becoming a person

'What colour eyes will he have?' 'Suppose he has Grandpa's nose or Uncle Willie's feet?' 'I hope he has your nature ... my mother's commonsense ... your father's wit ... my father's practicality ...' 'Do you think?' 'Suppose ...'

The questions have lasted for nine months and have now been answered. Or at least some of them have. 'It' has become 'our son, our daughter': birth-blue eyes are settling to their permanent colour, you've checked the nose in profile against Grandpa's and breathed a sigh of relief, though you're not too sure about the size of the feet.

Some of the questions have been answered but only the future will answer the others – 'What character, temperament, personality will he have?'

Yet the future is being made in the present. So far it has been easy to observe physical progress. Book in hand, you have checked reflex, and grasp, or applauded the first smile: on Monday you thought you had a genius, on Tuesday you weren't so sure. But understanding the development of personality, the characteristics that make your child uniquely himself and different from anyone else can seem more complicated, particularly as you know that his personality is being partly formed by your handling. Character, temperament, personality – call it what you will – is formed by a combination of the traits your child was born with and the influence you bring to bear. Given a basic temperament, your job will be able to help him master his environment, to be aware of him as a person and to judge and assess the moments when he's ready to be helped on to the next stage of development.

Because 'readiness' is a familiar word it would be easy to overlook its particular importance when it is applied to learning. 'Readiness' means the stage just before learning a particular skill and it demands from the child a level of motivation, competence and maturity: he must want to be able to do it. It could be likened to the moment in mid-air when you have left the side of the swimming pool but have not yet hit the water. It is your sensitive ability to recognize this stage of readiness which will most help your child's formation of a healthy personality. You can provide the essentials for a healthy personality whether you are a single parent, married, divorced or part of an extended family. The cornerstones are a loving, steady relationship, continuity of care and affection, adequate stimulation and

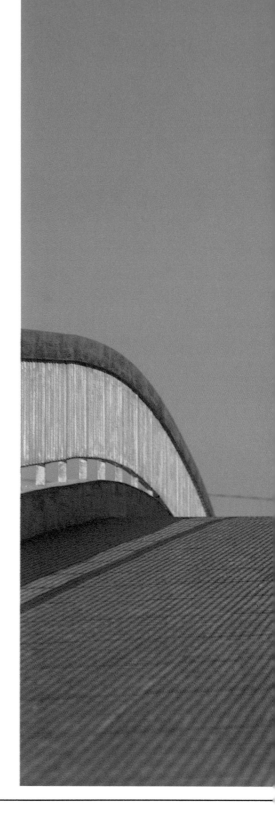

The future is being made in the present but still the question remains: 'What temperament and character will he have?'

The interaction between you and your child is important to the formation of personality. Even a young child will try to attract attention and will visibly respond if he succeeds.

opportunity for attachment initially to one person, later to others.

Watching a child come to terms with his body and his world is to see an almost frightening single-mindedness at work. At four months he tries over and over again to roll from tummy to back or vice versa. He tries, fails, attempts again – and to be able to turn from back to front your four month old must:

'have the ability to selectively push off with one arm and leg while holding the other against the body while at the same time suppressing the asymmetric tonic neck reflex.'

It sounds a tall order for a four month old – and yet they all do it, and watching those frantic scrabblings on the rug you know that though your baby is not quite there, he is at the stage of 'readiness'. Just as his physical progress takes place in a logical and orderly fashion – sitting, crawling, walking – so will the developmental steps towards personality.

Even before birth you know your baby to be a unique individual. Birth deepens that knowledge in the first amazing face-to-face confrontation with a new human being. Awe often overrides love in those first moments of encounter. There may be too many emotions for love to be an immediate reaction . . . weariness, apprehension, fear of inadequacy may be densely jumbled, but with a properly managed pregnancy and birth love grows rapidly (see page 43).

And with love grows sensitivity. Within hours of his birth you'll know what his particular cry means and you will learn his individual likes and dislikes. Dedication and commitment deepen so that you respond automatically through your own weariness to his daily and nightly demands . . . He has

caused changes in your life and you have responded by modifying your own behaviour to meet his needs and tempo. The baby's welfare takes precedence over your own: in such a way the cornerstones of personality are being laid as, within his limits, the baby learns that he is loved.

And he meets you half way: the more intensely he reacts to you, the stronger you become attached to him; the stronger your attachment to him, the more he becomes attached to you.

He listens to your voice, responds to your face, snuggles into your arms. Your baby makes deliberate efforts to hold your attention and this interaction between you and your child is the beginning of a process important to the formation of personality. A three-month-old baby will wriggle, smile, make efforts to attract a parent. One study of a three month old's efforts to attract his father's attention showed that if the father sat impassively and unresponsive the baby after a while cried or else became quiet and looked away, sucking his fingers for comfort. The father had blocked interaction. When he responded with smiling and talking to his son, the baby's movements became stronger and more rhythmic and he was obviously pleased. When your baby 'flirts' with you in this way you will have an opportunity to see this in action. What you are doing is showing him that he is of interest to you and that you value him as a person. You are helping him towards the beginnings of self respect.

But you are still allowed to be human. On the off days the foundation may show hair cracks but the structure will survive. Other demands and inclinations will occasionally dictate that he has to wait a little longer for his feed or for his rattle to be picked up. This won't leave a permanent scar on his personality. Babies are surprisingly resilient and unless a baby is subjected to very severe deprivation or outright injury he can tolerate a fair amount of stress for short periods.

Examples of severe deprivation would include being left alone in a cot without stimulation for most of the day and night for several months, or being fed for days or weeks with a propped-up bottle instead of being cuddled. A temporary upset or family stress would not leave lasting damage; some stress is needed to build a healthy personality and we all experience it to a degree. A life without stress could lead to a vulnerable blandness. It is when the stress is prolonged – if for instance a parent is seriously depressed or ill for some time – that you might be concerned about the effect on your baby, and it would then be the time to ask your doctor, health visitor or clinic for advice.

There is no one style of parenting, family

pattern or surroundings that would be right for all children. If there were we might be raising near-clones instead of individuals. The parents' goal is to provide the best environment and support system they can for their baby and simply being themselves will provide the right background. You can't force your baby to develop, only provide the conditions in which he will be encouraged to develop.

Sugar, spice or a little of both?
Within days of birth – perhaps even before birth – you may know what sort of baby you've got. Placid, irritable, uncertain – at times some of these characteristics will change, but some researchers have identified three main temperamental styles – the easy child, the difficult child and the slow-to-warm child.

Sixty-five per cent of the babies studied from birth to the age of seven showed the same temperament for the whole time: the remaining thirty-five per cent varied over the same period.

Then the research was taken further. Results suggested that one particular characteristic in a child remained stable over the whole time: timidity.

The timid or fearful child will tend to withdraw from new experiences. The difficult and slow-to-warm children may each have elements of timidity to which each responds differently: the difficult child becomes awkward and irritable: the slow-to-warm child becomes passive and withdrawn.

From research of this type we learned that difficult and slow-to-warm children will benefit most from being treated with a balanced mixture of firmness and affection.

Part of the difference between a difficult and a slow-to-warm child is in the intensity of their reactions. The difficult child tends to react intensely, throw a tantrum when confronted with a new situation, fight being held by a stranger, spit out unaccustomed food, clamp his jaws shut. The slow-to-warm child will shrink back from new situations, may whine and not snuggle rather than fight if embraced by a stranger, be more passive. He may turn up his nose at new food and push the dish away but he may not actively resist if he is offered a taste. He may not like it but he may in time suffer taking it. The difficult child takes more time and effort.

Any child in any category may switch from one to another quite suddenly. Once again firmness and affection will see them through. And will see you through too.

There are general principles which can help you deal with each of these stages and will also help your child to assimilate new experiences and move on to further development. These principles apply to all types of children and have much to do with your own interaction with others and between partners. Here are some of the goals to aim for:

Agreement Make sure as parents you discuss together your approach and then act together.
Example: Junior throws his dinner at the wall. Father wants to send him out of the room: you would prefer to ignore it. Don't discuss it in front of him: support each other. Don't undo the discipline by hugging and kissing afterwards along the lines of 'Daddy/Mummy didn't mean it.'

Consistency Try to keep to settled methods of dealing with a situation e.g. if your toddler wakes for a night drink, don't turn it into a

Below left The 'difficult' child leaves you in no doubt about his wishes: reactions are quite clear.

The 'passive' child is less violent in his reactions and may be persuaded against his inclinations.

social occasion with chats and talks.

Tolerance Your toddler is almost potty trained and demonstrates his accomplishment in public. Do not make an issue of it, or shame or spank the child. This will give the message that there's something shameful in his action and will set him back.

Tact – think ahead A two year old does not willingly share his toys. If you take him to mix with older children who do, expect a hassle. Don't project him into situations he is not ready for and which will provoke a tantrum. Avoid and/or distract or help him to cope.

Divert – or cut and run When shopping, your toddler puts all the things he can grab into your trolley. Don't yell or scold . . . divert him by asking him to find something he is familiar with – cornflakes packet, cocoa tin. If he can't be diverted peacefully and you are not prepared for a tantrum in public, give up, go home and try to come again on your own. He'll learn in time.

Taking it gently He does not like carrots/new people/new situations. Not liking strangers can be a sign of intelligence and also of self preservation (strangers could mean threat and danger). Take the carrots/people away and try them again a few days later. Introduce them both gradually and from the safety of your lap if necessary. Would you like to be made to kiss auntie, stroke pussy and play nicely with strange children?

Prepare verbally Tell him what's going to happen. Let him 'play it out'. He's going for a first visit to the dentist. Tell him about the chair that goes up, the special toothpaste, the whirring brush and that the dentist will look in his mouth with a lighted pencil.

Substitute He is juggling with your best china. Give a gasp of horror and he'll drop it. Remove to safety before he can reach it. Giving him brightly coloured plastic replicas or providing his very own miniatures might help . . . cup, teapot and so on.

Don't be ashamed of him He wants to take his comforter with him when meeting your classy friends. The 'comforter' is a bit of torn blanket – let him take it. You might even be able to suggest a 'best' one (i.e. cleaner and more respectable) for special occasions!

No-one denies that children at times are frustrating and infuriating. Try to keep your sense of humour, to remember that most stages pass. Look after yourself too, physical-ly and mentally (see Self-help groups, page 230). A tired, off-colour parent won't be able to cope and you can easily get into a vicious spiral of depression. If you feel you are losing your sense of balance, ask for professional help.

You can't think about your child's development of personality without taking into account how he is developing with moving, speaking, understanding. Physical and mental development may also lie behind your child's change in temperament. An eight month old baby may suddenly begin to cry at the sight of his father if he has been used to being all day at home with his mother. It is a stage which may only last a few weeks. Don't try to rush him – he will probably come out of it as unexpectedly as he went into it.

The Swiss psychologist, Jean Piaget, defined guidelines to the stages of development through his observation of children. Many of his theories have since been extended or modified but they still remain interesting and valuable (see panel opposite).

'Readiness' to tackle a new step or skill depends on maturity (the natural physical and mental growth), previous training (the experience the parents provided) and motivation (children are naturally curious and want to learn).

The support and praise of parents is vital to the growing child since a child may all too easily become sensitive to failure and then lose the wish to learn. This assessment of readiness by the parent is not as difficult as it may sound on paper. The parent is already the expert on his or her own child and is able to assess the child as an individual. Just as you have to think for a young baby ('When he crawls I must watch out for danger in the home.') so you will assess the more subtle requirements of the growing child. The young child is not able to assess cause and effect. He doesn't know that the teapot fell on him because he pulled the tablecloth: or that his hand was burnt because the radiator was hot. He can't make decisions about his movements in his own surroundings. But by two years of age basic reasoning has developed. Your two year old will know that he can only push teddy through the bars of the cot if he turns him first in a certain way: he will no longer need to experiment.

It's a toddler's job to become independent and a parent's job to let him be. He may stagger off on his own but keep turning back for reassurance. Sensible praise and support will encourage him all the way. Even as a baby of a few months he will, before he can feed himself, put his hand on yours as you take the spoon to his mouth in a charming gesture of companionship. When he first feeds himself he will make a mess, but he

SOME OF PIAGET'S BASIC DIVISIONS:

Between five and eight months
The baby still lives in the present but acts on his environment instead of the environment coming to him. He shakes his cot bars, reaches out for something he wants.

Approaching one
He knows objects exist even when he can't see them. He can discriminate sounds but not use them – he will know what objects are and may recognize 'shoe', 'walk', but not be able to say those words. In the same way he knows what objects are for but can't use them. The family car at the door may mean an outing and he will become excited.

Eighteen months to two years
Makes use of things that aren't there by making 'pretend' games. Speaks in more complex sentences and can translate what he is doing into telling you about it. Knows when to go for a walk, shop, storytime, but doesn't understand hours, minutes, weeks, months. Can only see things from his own point of view. Attributes feelings and actions to inanimate objects: 'The bike threw me off', 'The floor hit me'.

must be allowed to do so: when he dresses himself he'll get both legs through one side of his pants (the first time he does it and you see him lurching along you will fear he has developed some terrible injury to one leg). When he's about fifteen months you may find you have to set limits. 'No' is more effective in the opposite ratio to the frequency of its use: say it twenty times a day and it will mean nothing: reserve it for when you must have control and obedience and it will produce them. 'No' can save a life if you see a danger that the child does not.

It might at times be necessary to provide a distraction or an alternative activity. Toddlers like pets but have to be stopped from hurting them. Your child might pull the cat's tail but he can learn from you how to stroke gently: he has to learn not only not to hurt the cat (which might in turn hurt him) but

Be interested in what your child is doing and enter into her successes: praise her efforts.

Left Dressing is an arduous process and vest and pants difficult things to sort out! Try to encourage these important early steps towards independence.

also to relate properly to an animal.

All this may seem obvious but we live in a very fast-moving and demanding society and often this means we have trouble with basic relationships – there seems no time to establish these interactions. Many parents find it really difficult not to spank or yell at their children or to slow down their lives to the child's pace. Inconsistency bewilders a child – laughing one day when he throws sand about in his play bin and then spanking him the next day because he has done it again and some sand has gone in another child's eye. So don't yell across the garden at him, go to him: speak calmly but not hesitantly. All this takes time and self-discipline but don't be misled into thinking that you are being liberal minded if you let your child get away with everything. 'Not wanting to curb his spirit' can often be a cover-up for the parents' laziness or indifference.

By about eighteen months the child who has been handled consistently is able to exercise the beginning of self control and will be able to respond to simple directions. And he will also be able to make the connection between the statement and the event. 'Oh dear, the truck's broken. Put it aside and we must try to mend it after our walk.'

By about two to two and a half your child is forming attitudes towards the people in his world. 'No' and 'I won't' come into his vocabulary and you, as the setter of limits,

will probably be on the end of it. It's annoying, but you can cope. What is important is that one parent should not provide the discipline ('Just wait till your father gets home') and the other the comfort. Easy comfortable communication between all family members helps him to become a happy, congenial person. Occasionally, too, 'No' may be right – but be reasonable: if he's really tired he just won't be able to pick up his toys before bedtime.

Aggressiveness needs to be channelled. Frequent 'No's,' aggression and anxiety about being separated are all natural to the two to three year old. It is best to offer alternative solutions rather than head-on battle. Not all conflicts need be avoided, however. Suppose your two and a half year old was under the weather last week so you stayed with him until he went to sleep. Now he won't go off without you and threatens a tantrum – so offer an alternative; a few minutes' cuddle, a story, or a drink (just one).

If you possibly can, ignore tantrums because shouting, spanking, punishment are all ways of paying attention. It is the lack of attention that is most punishing and this is why good behaviour and effort should always be rewarded with praise. Giving your child a choice is also giving a measure of control – 'You may take my hand or auntie Mary's when we cross the road.'

Smacking is not usually effective as a

Setting limits is important. The child who does not hear the word 'no' too often will respect it when he does.

Tantrums in public can be embarrassing. Keep as calm as you can, and if possible, ignore him. No attention often means no tantrum.

deterrent. It may make you feel better but it doesn't offer your child an alternative way to act and it may teach him that physical violence is an acceptable way to control others. Too frequent smacking can become something the child expects and he can come to think that the smacking means he doesn't have to take responsibility for his own action – it has let him off the hook, so to speak. A child who is not being given sufficient attention and support from parents may provoke smacking by misdeeds because it means the parent is at last taking notice of him. You can sometimes see this in the mutinous expression on some children's faces. 'Well, I'll show her,' they're saying – but it is a sad reflection on their environment that they have to be naughty to be noticed.

So smacking, if at all, should be reserved for very, very special occasions – when perhaps the child is doing something dangerous to himself or others: running into the road, or going near an unattended swimming pool. Remember that when you are worried and frightened it's easy to lose control and harm the child.

In some ways tantrums are expressing the stage of readiness to greater independence. Very often they are the expressions of frustration – when the child can't physically or mentally cope with a situation, and the sense of inadequacy erupts into yells and screams. So anticipate if you can, divert if you can, 'punish' only if it is absolutely necessary, avoid battles unless you intend to win (and then not by force) – and all the time praise when you can.

'Stars' for achievements are very much appreciated by a young child. If he's trying to do something or learn something, put a chart up on the refrigerator door with his name and the days of the week. Buy a packet of sticky stars and give him a star every day he picks up his toys. At the end of a good week he could have a bigger star and when he's had several good weeks the behaviour pattern will have become fairly well established so he will probably forget about the stars.

What you are doing is using a 'positive reinforcement' system, not negative punishment. If you promise a reward, give it but it need only be small. You're not buying good behaviour, but rewarding it.

The word 'discipline' has come to mean 'punishment' or 'restriction' but what you are teaching your child is self-discipline – internalizing reasonable external standards of behaviour. Parents should be models of what they teach and this is not always easy, partly because as adults we often let self-discipliine slip, and partly because we are also the products of our own childhood. If our own upbringing has been harsh, or perhaps too lax, then we too may need to change our own behaviour in order to pass on acceptable standards to our children. On the whole adults learn to cover up their less attractive traits when they want to. At times we all probably have tantrums but we learn to excuse them or disguise them. Sometimes we have to face that we have unpleasant traits, or that we had wrong handling as children, in order not to make the same mistakes.

Grandparents

They can be the parents' greatest resource. Usually they are as delighted to be grandparents as you are to be parents and will sometimes be willing to baby-sit (for short periods) or to provide regular care if you are working out of the home.

The birth of a baby often brings greatly deepened relationships between parents and grandparents and is sometimes an opportunity to sort out some of your own unresolved conflicts. You may still have hangovers of dependency or inadequacy but you are now entering a new role and your own parents will often come to recognize this.

You should sort out as early as possible your ideas about your baby, recognizing at the same time that you will wish to respect an older person's experience and concerns. Your mother's experience, for instance, of weaning may be different from the method you intend to follow so you will have to make the differences clear from the beginning, although without rancour. If a difference in treatment still persists, you may have to arrange for your baby to be cared for between feeds so that the possible conflict is avoided. On the other hand grandparents are miraculous at comforting children and at distracting them before a tantrum erupts.

Grandparents also have their rights. Don't overburden them with too much baby-sitting. They have their own lives to lead and young children can be tiring or meddlesome in an older person's home which may not be equipped for them.

Grandparents have a very special relationship with young children. Often they have more time and patience to give and small children can learn a great deal from them. A warm and enduring relationship between grandparents and grandchildren also gives to the young child an image of older people – the sense of security to be gained from them and also some of their needs, for a young child can take great pleasure in 'helping' them. Grandparents too are usually adept at finding ways for children to amuse themselves and are past masters at reading stories and telling them of their own childhood. For a small child grandparents can be both a loving presence and a window of the world.

Grandparents are very special people. Often they have more time and patience than parents and 'helping' them can be a special treat.

Helping your child to become a person is the outcome of a series of complex interactions between the physical charateristics of the child and the world around him. It can't be remembered too often that a child has to develop one set of skills before being able to learn the next, and that children differ from each other in the time they take to progress, but that the order of development is usually the same.

When the baby is young, he is totally dependent. Once mobile he seeks independence, becomes aware of his separateness and begins to experiment on the road to self-control. Give and take is crucial now: children need to have limits, so they feel safe, and freedom, so they can explore. Providing this balance is one of the most rewarding and difficult tasks of parenthood: it is also one of the most necessary.

A child reflects his surroundings but is not a large mirror image: a doormat parent can produce a selfish child. The parents' job is to build the foundation of trust so that the child learns self-respect, and values himself while recognizing that he is part of a larger social structure whose members have their own rights and needs. The child who knows himself loved knows he is worthy of love.

Observing the interaction of parents and of parents with others is the child's hourly lesson in becoming a person. For a child to grow courteous he must see courtesy in action: for him to give care to others he must see care being given to others. He needs to see the daily give and take of difficulties and disappointments overcome, of challenges being met, of good humour and humour.

A young child will cry if his mother cries: he's not crying because his mother is sad, he's crying because somehow the atmosphere makes *him* feel bad. Later if he sees his mother crying, he'll be sad *for* his mother. This is where another adult can help. 'What can we do to make Mummy/Daddy happier? Let's make her/him a special meal.' You don't have to give a present: giving a service, something of yourself, can be much more valuable.

Love is not dependent on good behaviour: give a child enough supportive love and you'll be giving him the gift of loving. Having children may be a life sentence but their actual childhood doesn't last for long. Parenting is not easy but the rewards far exceed the effort.

Children need limits to feel safe, but also freedom so they can explore. Once a child becomes aware that he is a separate person he begins to experiment on the road to self control.

FAMILY MATTERS

'They must go free
As fishes in the sea
While we remain the shore
Where hopefully they come again'

That more or less puts it in a nutshell – the relationship between parents and children.

From the moment the cord is severed your child is learning to 'go free', and for you not to anticipate the inevitable coming separation could mean you are sowing for yourself the seeds of loneliness in later life.

It's all too easy to become immersed in parenthood and in the very early days that is almost inevitable because the young baby needs continual care and protection. But children grow up. Babies turn into toddlers who need to explore a wider world than the home: they go next door to play, they stay with relations and friends. Other gods will threaten your infallibility. . . 'But teacher says. . .' 'But Bobby's father can. . .' Mummy and Daddy are being edged into a back seat and in a surprisingly short time you may see in your child's eyes that same faint boredom they feel with you that, years before, you had felt with them.

Separation is an intrinsic part of growing up but it is a growth that seems to last a lifetime as we continually reassess needs and make new decisions both for ourselves and for our children. Getting the timing right – knowing when your child needs support, and when he needs to fend for himself – is part of the alchemy of parenthood through which a baby becomes a child and a child becomes an adult.

Learning to separate comes more easily when it comes gradually and in the stages of 'readiness' – when both baby and parents are ready to anticipate the pull apart. For the baby this will be governed by his natural physical and mental development: first he explores but looks back to check that the friendly adult is still there if he needs a quick retreat to base. After a few forays he looks back less, and thinks more of the goal ahead. Finally he appears not to look back at all – but it is the heritage of security given him in those early supportive days which has strengthened him into independence.

So this section is about the growth of independence and how parents can gradually help their child to learn to separate.

Mothers who work outside the home are naturally concerned that their child shall not suffer from their absence. They take trouble to provide the best possible substitute care, but may still wonder if they are spending enough time with their child. The axiom to remember is that 'it isn't the quantity of time you give to a child that counts: it is the quality'. But separation between parents and child is not only physical – it may be mental or emotional. An abstracted, cold and distant parent who is nevertheless always physically present is much less valuable to a baby's development than an involved parent who may spend less time with her child. The parent who is caring, interested, listening *when she is there* is laying the foundations of a lifetime's security.

Weaning your child into greater independence often entails asserting your own rights and preferences. Parents not only owe it to themselves to preserve their own individuality, they owe it to their children. Life may seem to have conspired to turn you into a function rather than a person – provider, supporter mopper-up – but by defining territories of time, space and privacy for yourself you are teaching your child that others have rights apart from his needs. The boundaries and definitions must obviously be moveable and elastic but by two years of age, rising three, your toddler will not only have recognized your rights to your own preferences, but he will also within his limits take pleasure in helping you achieve them and be encouraged by your appreciation.

But to become loving and caring, your child will need to be loved and cared for. He will need to have his own preferences respected: it is through being respected that a child learns self-respect. If you have freed him into a mutual tolerance of respect for others in a world where he is sure of his own worth, he will be on the road to separation without anxiety.

Separation is part of growth but growth implies having a goal to which to aspire. For a child the goal is the adults he takes for his model: his parents. To a child they hold out the promise and privilege of independent adulthood.

The working mother

To return to work outside or remain at home? That is the question many new mothers face. Mothers usually return to paid work outside the home because:

- they need the money;
- they miss the imposed discipline of work outside the home;
- they are lonely;
- they believe they should exercise their talents or training.

Some of these needs can be partly met without going out to work, although not always easily nor satisfactorily. You may find it possible to earn money from home although the work is likely to be poorly paid. You can impose your own discipline of work at home, which may seem pointless and will certainly be difficult with a baby in the house. You can make local friends in similar circumstances, probably through clinics or Mother and Toddler Clubs (see page 20) and arrange mutual help with their children. Or you may find your new lifestyle encourages you to develop a skill you have been unable to follow previously, or to study for a different career when your family is older.

With certain exceptions, a woman in paid employment has the legal right to return to work within twenty-nine weeks of the birth of her baby.

Even if you have already made the decision, before the birth, that you will return to work, putting it into practice will not be without pain. Mothers sometimes miss their babies more than babies miss their mothers. Apart from the practical considerations – coping with a new routine of a home with a baby and work – you may well have feelings of guilt. And the guilt will not be eased if the attitude of those around you is critical. 'Do you really *need* two salaries? Isn't the baby *enough*?' It is somehow implied that not only should you stay at home, but you should be happy to do so – and if you aren't, you must be failing as a mother.

It is a particularly difficult situation to cope with, particularly at a time when you have mixed feelings yourself, but is it a good idea to try to be a twenty-four hour mother? Many mothers of two or three generations back were supported in their role as full-time mothers by larger, closer-living families where one of a galaxy of mothers, grannies, aunts, cousins could 'keep an eye on baby' while the mother was freed to be herself for a few hours, although not necessarily in paid employment. Richer families employed nannies and there were, moreover, many 'sur-

For many mothers, working from home with a young child is preferable to leaving her to be cared for by someone else. Even with a cooperative child it will take a lot of organization, however, and be warned – home workers are usually notoriously underpaid.

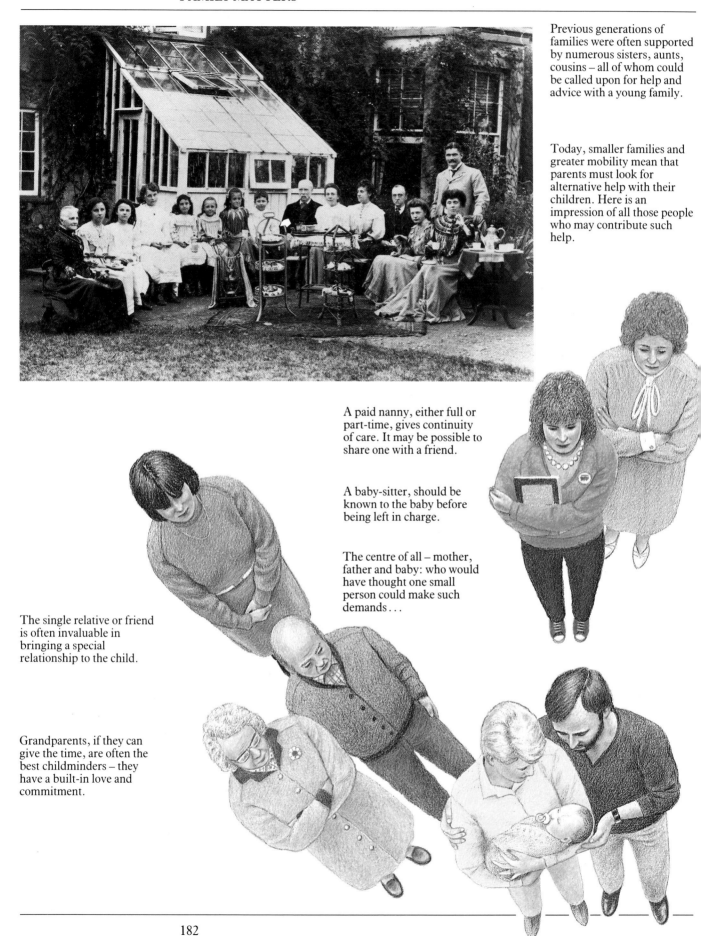

Previous generations of families were often supported by numerous sisters, aunts, cousins – all of whom could be called upon for help and advice with a young family.

Today, smaller families and greater mobility mean that parents must look for alternative help with their children. Here is an impression of all those people who may contribute such help.

A paid nanny, either full or part-time, gives continuity of care. It may be possible to share one with a friend.

A baby-sitter, should be known to the baby before being left in charge.

The centre of all – mother, father and baby: who would have thought one small person could make such demands...

The single relative or friend is often invaluable in bringing a special relationship to the child.

Grandparents, if they can give the time, are often the best childminders – they have a built-in love and commitment.

plus' women – owing to wars and the earlier death-rate among men – who couldn't find employment anywhere but in domestic service. This meant that even far from affluent parents often had an extra pair of hands to help with the family.

Equality of education between the sexes means that many more women now have the ability and the incentive to pursue a career outside the home. It has also led both men and women to a greater expectation of fulfilment and companionship within marriage that the homebound mother may find difficult to maintain without outside stimulus.

So, some of our nostalgic vision of twenty-four hour motherhood rocking the cradle may be illusory, and questioning it may help to allay guilt.

If you are a single parent, you may have no choice but to return to work and your priorities and needs may be different from those in a stable relationship (see page 192). But if you are one of a pair, the first essential is to make sure you are agreed on what you're doing. Adding conflict to all the other

emotions at this time will be destructive, and an atmosphere of resentment or begrudging martyrdom is not the healthiest atmosphere in which to bring up your baby. To work or not to work is something that may have to be discussed at some length between you both, and if your wishes don't coincide, you'd better concentrate on reaching a workable compromise. However efficient your baby-minding arrangements are, there are still likely to be concessions to be made on either side: there will be domestic responsibilities to be shared, perhaps at weekends or during the evenings, or baby routines to be reallocated. It is best if the framework is laid down at the beginning: rules are always easier to break if there are rules to break in the first place.

If you decide to go back to work whole or part time, it may come as a shock when your baby develops a special relationship with whoever looks after him while you are away. You may possibly feel aggrieved that you've been usurped in his affections – even though this is only partial. But then what is the alternative? That he cries every time you

A childminder will care for your child along with others and will be registered with the local authority.

The family doctor's specialized knowledge of the family can be invaluable when it comes to advice on health and immunizations.

Friends and neighbours with children of their own are often the best solution to baby – and childminding. It is often possible to work out reciprocal schemes of help, and baby-sitting circles where babyminding is taken in turns, usually prove very succesful.

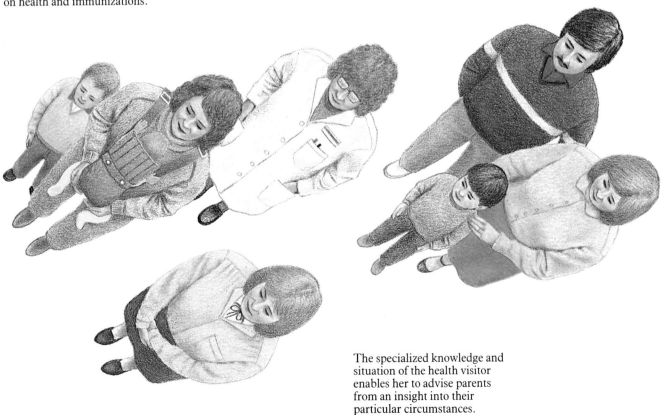

The specialized knowledge and situation of the health visitor enables her to advise parents from an insight into their particular circumstances.

If you want to...	You may be...	And may react by...
. . . stay at home but can't.	. . . resentful, begrudging, martryed at home, and slapdash at work.	. . . irritation with partner; indulgence with child; belittling partner to child and others.
. . . work but stay home because 'it's best for the children'.	. . . withdrawn from children; physically present but mentally absent; a high-powered, wearying mother cramming 'good mothering' down their throats – and your husband's.	. . . telling the world about your 'sacrifice', letting the children know they are obstructions to your 'real' life.
. . . work and do so but feel guilty.	. . . unhappy; defensive; aggressive.	. . . indulging and spoiling the children or being more severe with them because you are aware of being too indulgent.
. . . go to work, do so and enjoy it without guilt.	. . . stimulated, fulfilled, without resentment.	. . . enjoying both roles – motherhood and working wife – much more and being an easier person to live with!

To the above could almost be added the mother who wants to stay at home and does so, with perfect content, but is questioned about being 'just a housewife' to such an extent that she begins to feel guilty about being happy!

hand him over? Do you want him to be unhappy during the time you are away? If your baby has formed a special relationship with his minder, welcome it: you have a good minder. One trap you must not fall in to, however, is undermining her authority – that's why the choice of minder is so important (see page 186).

But the mother's health and contentment in her role, whatever that might be, is vital to the happiness of children and indeed the whole family relationship.

One of the alternatives to working full time may be to work part time or to share a job. The former largely depends on what's available but there are still occasional Saturday jobs or evening work to be had or as temporary staff at holiday times. Very often it is a case of asking rather than waiting to be asked. Job-sharing – where two people share one job, working either mornings or afternoons, or for half the week in turn – is now officially encouraged. Ask at your local Job Centre for opportunities in your area. There are benefits for employers in the idea of job-sharing, once they have become convinced of its practicability, since it is alleged they get more than one day's work from the two half days they employ their job-sharers. Even if there are no vacancies advertised it is worth writing to firms stating your qualifications and experience and suggesting the idea. Another way of tackling it is to offer yourself and a friend for the one job: that could mean that you could not only share a responsible job but also share caring for each other's families.

Will the baby suffer?
In the babycare jargon a baby 'bonds with his primary caregiver' – that is the adult who looks after him most. Usually in the first few weeks that's the mother, but it needn't be. If father or granny copes that's fine by baby. The most famous example of imprinting to the first object the baby sees is that of the naturalist Konrad Lorenz who acted as nursemaid to a clutch of baby goslings, having first removed their mother. The goslings thereafter waddled after him, thinking he was 'mother'. What applies to animals need not be applied to humans. Two human mothers, whose babies were mixed at birth in hospital, took home the 'wrong' babies. When the mistake was discovered, both mothers refused to give up the baby they had nurtured as their own – although the fathers were willing to do so. This special relationship and affinity now known as bonding is believed by many to be essential to a baby's development but the degree of dependency changes with age and it goes like this:
Up to six months: will smile more readily at mother and father or the adult he knows best, but won't object to strangers. Doesn't see himself separate from the adult giving him care.
From six to twelve months: he begins to separate. Often shows fear of strangers and may cling to the familiar adult. He begins to crawl away from you but looks back to see if you're still there – and if danger threatens he's back to base quicker than a ball on elastic.
From twelve to eighteen months: knows he's a separate person but still needs to be looked after. Walking brings greater independence although he still needs the comfort of his base. He may take a substitute comforter with him – blanket, toy – for when

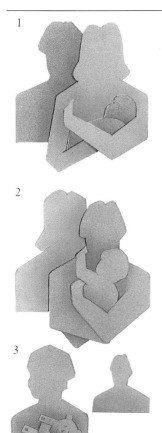

The dependency of your child on you changes as he gets older. Up to six months (1) he doesn't see himself as separate from his caregiver and will not object to strangers. For the next six months (2) he begins to separate but he may show fear of strangers. From twelve to eighteen months (3) he knows he's separate but he needs a comforter when alone. After a period of love/hate with you and intense shyness, separation will become more tolerable at around two years (4) and he will start to function as an individual with trust in others.

mother is not there – at night, for instance. The comforter serves as a support until he can bear separation – but the movement is going outwards away from you.

From eighteen to twenty-four months: brings things back to you – words, objects, experiences. He feels close to you but separate from you, and this leads to frustrations, temper, tantrums. Love and hate battle as he both needs you and resents needing you. He may be intensely shy and feel threatened by strangers – which doesn't mean you can't leave him: at times you'll have to, to go into a shop, see friends, and so on. Through this he begins to learn and to recognize that you will return, that you have a separate interest and life from him.

From twenty-four months on: separation is far more tolerable. Nurturing has been supportive enough for him now to feel confidence and trust in others. The image of you as parents has become part of him and he will incorporate your rules of behaviour and conscience. He is attached to you, his parents, with an attachment which will last for life, but he has also begun to function as a separate individual, and is able to tolerate some separation.

These are some of the ways by which you can help him to develop this sturdiness of growth:

Your. . .	teaches him . . .
love	to return love to you and others.
regularity and reliability	trust.
ability to tolerate his anger	to accept limits and still love.
allowing him freedom to learn and explore while still supporting him	confidence to move outwards to a world beyond the family.

If attachment between parents and babies is so vital a reaction, destined to affect the child for the rest of his life, how will its disruption, whether partial (through the adult closest to the baby working away from home), or entire (through separation, divorce), affect the baby? It's a good question – you can't have it both ways: or can you?

Listen to this: '*it is an excellent plan to accustom babies and small children to being cared for now and then by someone else*'. That was written in 1969 by John Bowlby whose writings and research into maternal deprivation have been the most influential on the subject. Because he was a pioneer into research about the closeness of the bond

between mother and baby, his views were sometimes misinterpreted but he never claimed that 'proper' mothering could only be twenty-four hours a day mothering. What has emerged through all the subsequent research is that there are perhaps six necessities for 'good enough' mothering: these are a *loving* relationship, *attachment*, *security of that attachment*, enough *stimulation*, the *constancy of one person* which, if possible, is in the *surroundings of the family home*. This last does not mean that you can never take your baby to someone else's home to be looked after (see page 189), but that a very young child may be less disturbed by staying in familiar surroundings until he has formed a relationship with his new caregiver, so that his security rests with her and not with his surroundings.

Separation is not automatically bad for a baby, but the quality of the substitute care provided must be right. Research indicates that although mothers are no less important, well-planned creative substitute care may well have some advantages (see page 189). Children of full-time mothers have been noted to be more timid, less exploring and more diffident about entering new situations than those in part-time day care. Children who have experienced such care seem to have fewer stereotyped ideas of a 'woman's place' – which could be useful in view of the world they will probably live in. They appear to learn new skills as well or better than those at home, and they also seem to show little difference in their emotional stability, intellectual performance and social skills. It's also worth remembering that a child who is cared for every weekday for three hours each morning spends fifteen hours away from home and 153 hours at home each week.

Who will care for your baby?

There may be several alternatives – or none. In theory these are what may exist.

Father: he may well be the best alternative if his employment is suitable and you are both agreed, either because he has not a job outside the home, his job is less well paid than yours, or he can carry on his work from home. Some parents work a shift system, but this could mean you have very little family life together.

Friends, relations, neighbours or granny: again could be excellent provided the points of reference are agreed before you begin. How many hours a week? Is it being done as a 'favour'? Or grudgingly? Do your ideas on feeding, 'spoiling', cuddling, discipline, coincide, and if not, are you both prepared to make compromises? And is the minder likely to become possessive and undermine your place in your baby's affections? Grannies are

Father may well be the best alternative caregiver to mother if this is agreeable and feasible to both.

usually the unsung saints because they already have a built-in commitment and affection for the baby even before he arrives. The older generation may have different ideas on feeding and discipline so you must talk about this before you begin the arrangement.

Day nursery: there are very few of these about and places are usually reserved for children of single parents, or where social conditions make it impossible for the baby to be cared for during the day at home. They will be run by the local authorities and will be staffed by a qualified nurse with assistants. If one exists at all in your neighbourhood it will probably be open from something like eight in the morning until six at night. The care given will necessarily concentrate on keeping babies fed and clean, and there is probably not much time for stimulation or education. They will cater for children up to three years of age. One of the drawbacks is that because of changing staff, holidays and so on, there is seldom much continuity of care, and this is bewildering for a baby or young child. Attention is unlikely to be individual. Charges will be made

according to your means.

Crèche: there may be a crèche attached to your place of work or college, or one in the neighbourhood where your employers have arranged a number of places for their employees. Standards vary very much according to the firm and the locality. The advantage is that they are likely to be near – or attached to – your place of work so you may be able to visit and/or feed at lunchtime (although this may be disruptive to the baby). One disadvantage may be that if you leave the job you have to find alternative care. Sometimes the crèches are provided free by the employer – if you have to pay, charges may be as high as £40 – £50 a week (1984 rates).

Childminder: very often childminders provide the best alternative care, particularly since they are now required by law to be registered with their local authority which will lay down certain standards as to hygiene, the number of children being cared for, space available, suitability of the home and the personality of the minder. By employing a registered childminder you are automatically sure of certain standards. Your local

Grandmothers are often the
unsung saints of a family but
may have different ideas on
discipline and feeding.

The number of children for whom a childminder is permitted to care is controlled by the local authority, who will also ensure that she has adequate room at home, and is of suitable temperament for this demanding job.

council offices will have a list of those registered with them, and will also tell you what the charges are likely to be, though this is a matter of personal arrangement. Childminders are not permitted to care for more children than the authority stipulates, bearing in mind not only safety but also the minder's ability to give individual care. It is essential that you find a childminder who suits your own personality and agrees with you on flexibility, feeding and so on. Very often you can find a suitable childminder through the personal recommendation of friends. Childminding is tiring and requires a particular personality. Some mothers undertake it because they want to stay at home with their own children, and see childminding as a way to do this and to earn money at the same time.

Full-time or part-time nanny: these tend to be expensive but it is often possible to share a nanny with a friend and cut down the cost that way, although it still won't be cheap. You will naturally look for a qualified and/or experienced nanny – possibly through nursing agencies or through personal recommendation. Since the nanny will be in your home it is even more essential to make sure you agree on all the fundamentals of baby care and upbringing and attitudes. You won't have to provide a room or meals for a part-time nanny other than when she is on duty. Payment is likely to be around £70 a week (1984) but this can be reduced if you share with another family. Full-time will mean a lower salary – about £50 – £60 – but you will have to provide accommodation and all meals. You may also be liable for National Insurance contributions and for deducting income tax. (Your local Inland Revenue Office will advise you.) Nannies don't expect to do any housework other than that directly connected with their charges. Agencies exist to arrange part-time nannying and to put families in touch with each other for the service (see page 231).

Baby-sitter – see page 97

Au pair: not so easy to come by as previously, possibly because many were exploited or, conversely, because they were not prepared to work as required, and the news has travelled back home. It could be that an *au pair* proves an entirely satisfactory arrangement. A girl from a large family could cope quite naturally with looking after a baby or toddler; on the other hand she's likely to be young, will need to lead some of her own life, learn the language and can become an added responsibility rather than a built-in support system. Home Office regulations stipulate that an *au pair* should only work for five hours a day and should be paid not less than £15 pocket money a week (1984). She should not be employed by full-time working parents.

There may be no way of telling in advance whether your personalities will suit – and some *au pairs* come determined to do very little work while others are exploited. Your *au pair*'s stay in Britain is likely to come to an end when your child has become fond of her – which will mean yet another disruption.

It is sometimes possible to find an older woman whose family has moved away and who will come into your home for a few hours daily or occasionally and care for the baby. If your personalities match, the arrangement can be of great mutual benefit. You have the advantage of employing someone who has experience in looking after children, and she has the enjoyment of entering into the life of a young family while earning money. As with all these arrangements, it's essential to make sure you agree about feeding, 'discipline', routines and so on, as well as making sure that her health will be equal to the energy needed to cope with a baby. It could be that an older woman would not be able to cope with a lively toddler.

Whatever choice you make, the characteristics to look for in the caregiver are the same: interest, involvement in your child for his own sake, ability to give individual care, flexibility and tolerance and a familiarity with the ways of young children – their fears, dislikes, and the mess they make. He or she should have a warm personality and be prepared at all times to discuss your child with you, pass on triumphs and setbacks, and work with you to the best benefit of your child.

Before you make your decision pay several visits to the childminder or to whoever will be caring for your child. At first go alone if possible and then, having made your choice, either take your child with you for short visits or – in the case of a childminder – ask if it is possible for her to visit you in your own home, so that your child can get used to her in your own surroundings. You may also find it possible to leave the baby with her in her home for short periods until he doesn't miss you: this will make the longer stay more normal and acceptable to him.

It is best not to leave a child under three for more than four to six hours a day if possible. Leave him a 'love-token' to care for while you are away: a small toy he can feel in his pocket, or something belonging to you to reassure him that you will be returning. Plan something you will do together when you come to fetch him. 'It's Tuesday – shall we have scrambled eggs for tea? It's Thursday – your favourite programme's on! It's Wednesday, Granny will be coming,' and so on.

One of the rituals all children love and find consoling is a kind of 'de-briefing' session where they tell you what they have been doing during the day. It fixes the day and the experiences in their mind and allows you both to share and talk about them. Bathtime and bedtime can be good times for this (see page 95) but sometimes on the walk home will seem right. Don't force it though – being left without mother means your child has expended a lot of energy and he may be tired and want to take stock before he begins to share with you. Some children of course flatly refuse to 'give' on demand. 'What have you been doing today?' 'Nothing.' 'What did you have for lunch?' 'Nothing'. 'Who did you play with?' 'Nobody.' But then you're older and ought to be more artful: silence is a great way of getting people to confide in you.

There is no certain way of anticipating what effect separation will have on a baby or young child. It could take the form of tears, extra clinging, apathy, aggressive or regressive behaviour – bed-wetting, tantrums, thumb sucking. Handled with affection and sensitivity and, above all, patience, these are temporary setbacks. But the transition may not be easy for both of you: babies do grow up very quickly, although it won't seem so to you when you're coping with the endless uncertainties of a new life and a new lifestyle: no-one could pretend that it may all be plain sailing.

But anxiety is an inevitable fact of life. It's up to the adult who cares for the child to monitor the level of anxiety the child can tolerate, and to support the child as he learns to grow. If your child is not being cared for at home and he's spending some part of the day in someone else's home, he may worry that your home will somehow have changed while he's away. Children are also sometimes alarmed by a radical change of hairstyle in mother, or by unfamiliar clothes. Mention any changes before they take place if you are able.

Other separations

Children experience separation through other ways than physical distance. Divorce, the separation of parents, death, child abuse – all these may lead to emotional separation when there is a danger of a child withdrawing into herself. Much as you would wish to protect your child from any of these happenings, it may not always be possible. So a period of sorrow and adjustment may be inevitable in your child's life, but hopefully you will be her support system during that time. What affects the child will also affect you – and this may make giving support doubly difficult for you when you are yourself suffering. Yet parents who have experienced such times inevitably say that the child has supported them (see page 231 for associations who give advice on counselling).

A death in the family or of a close family friend is a traumatic experience for adults and may be more or less so for a child, depending on the closeness of the relationship, the circumstances of the home, the age and character of the child.

The death of a parent is certain to affect a child – more so if it's the mother who dies, if she has been the closest figure to the child previously. To the child's bewilderment and grief is added the practical difficulty of arranging who will care for the child. A baby or young child may be cared for by several relatives or friends for short periods while a permanent solution is being sought so that the child may learn to trust no-one – feeling that if she allows herself to love and become attached she will only lose that person.

A baby or young child also has no idea of time: she may mourn and sorrow for much longer than could be expected. The stages of grief in children most often follow the same pattern: anger, sadness and finally indifference as though she has forgotten her loss. Anger and sadness must be worked through and it is only when she has worked through to the third stage that she will be able to make a new relationship, hopefully with someone who will provide her with lasting care.

If a substitute is to be provided, look for kindness in preference to hygiene. Of course it may be possible to get both but a natural parent is interested in his child's development and a child, deprived of one parent, needs to find that half of the support and interest elsewhere. Lack of interest in speech development, for instance, can lead to slowing down in later intellectual development.

The loss of a father may not affect a child so much unless the father has cared for the child while the mother has been absent for various reasons – perhaps working or through illness. In all cases of loss the child may regress to bed-wetting or aggressive and difficult behaviour. A child at about the age of three or four reacts more to the loss of a parent of her own sex because that's the age when the child is beginning to model him or herself on the father or mother. A relative or older friend or sister or brother can help in this instance.

Happy families can often cope better with the loss of a parent than families which are unhappy: the surviving members are able to 'close ranks' and support and care for each other: whereas the partner left from an unhappy marriage often feels guilt and remorse which limits the quality of the attention being given to the children.

A child's questions about death must be properly answered: it's useless to imply that the dead parent will be coming back. A child often feels guilt for the death, as though she were in some way responsible: she may also fear that she too will die. Preoccupied with his own grief, the surviving parent may find it difficult to be aware of all these undercurrents or to cope with them. Meeting people in like circumstances and the support of professionals and expert counselling will help to sustain through what can only be distressing periods.

Stillbirth, miscarriage or the birth of a handicapped child are also bereavements because the parents, the family and relations have been deprived of the child they expected. With all bereavements, a period of grief and mourning must be experienced – shutting oneself away from grief is to stunt its progress and make the effects last longer. In these cases, however, the support of partners should be of mutual comfort.

It is also essential that a widow or widower maintains outside interests so that the children do not become too dependent on this one-parent relationship nor the adult too dependent on the children, which will make the inevitable and necessary later separation more difficult.

In Britain today one in three marriages ends in divorce, and of that number sixty per cent involve at least one child under sixteen. One family in seven is headed by a lone parent. Unless a different agreement has been reached before the divorce, custody of the children is usually given to one parent with varying degrees of right of access to the

Children experience loss through divorce, illness, death – and in all these situations a period of sorrow may be inevitable.

other parent. The father of the children is normally made responsible for financial maintenance. Usually custody of the children, when decided by the court, is given to the mother, although in increasing frequency in recent years fathers have assumed responsibility.

Divorce and the children

Divorce must change children even if it doesn't harm them – but if the actual divorce has been preceded by a period of quarrelling, fighting and discord in the home, then the final separation may come as a relief to the children. If the child loves the parent who is no longer living with her, that child is suffering bereavement, and everything should be done to help her over her inevitable sorrow.

Divorce is seldom entirely amicable and in the heightened emotions at this time it would not be difficult for the parents to use the children as weapons against each other. Instead of being able to vent anger on each other, it's vented on the nearest object to hand . . . the child. At such a time professional counselling may be imperative (see page 231). The reaction of children to divorce may well be a mirror image of how the parents react. Relief, spite, anger, sense of guilt, sense of failure, loneliness and bewilderment. Children, however, need to be protected, while adults don't often have such a luxury. With a conscious effort on the part of one or both parents to continue to provide stability, warmth and consistency, the long-term effects can be overcome. But it can take years for a child to accept divorce, or to give up the idea that her parents will unite again.

If the divorce is the culmination of a period of dissension, quarrelling and even physical violence, then during those preceding months the child may exhibit all the symptoms of strain – bed-wetting, aggression, reversion to younger behaviour. If the mother, or whoever is caring most for the child, is depressed and withdrawn, she's likely to be unable to give the child warmth and attention. The child will be either ignored or treated harshly. If the mother is apathetic she may indulge the child too much, ignoring 'bad' behaviour.

Asking the child to 'side' with one or other of her parents is to take a terrible revenge on the child for something which is not her fault. A parent who does this has in effect split the child in half: where do her loyalties lie? It would be no wonder if the toddler did not then retaliate by playing off one parent against the other.

Here are several particularly criminal and dangerous sentences that could be easily used in the turmoil of breaking up a home:

'It's all right for *him/her*' (implying the one with the child is martyred: making the child feel guilty, apologising for her existence).

'*Your* father/mother' (Nothing to do with me: he/she belongs to you – guilt again).

'If it weren't for *you* I could . . .' (blaming the child's existence for all the trouble. You should not be living, you say).

'You're just like your father/mother' (always pointing out something bad – and so saying that the child is half bad too).

All this may seem a one-sided view: what of the parents' suffering and difficulties at this time? No-one would wish to minimize that hardship but because they are unable to look after themselves and pursue their own lives, children are frighteningly vulnerable to the stress and difficulties of their elders. Once again the adult may have to come to terms with his or her own sufferings in order to explain *in terms the child can understand* just what is happening. The withdrawal of love is an experience which can mar a lifetime: the apparent withdrawal of love without the maturity to understand some of its reasons could be a watershed which changes the course of the child's life. And yet it's worth remembering that 'broken homes' have been shown to result in less subsequent delinquency in the children than unbroken homes in which there was neglect and disharmony. But the aim should be to keep the bitterness away from the child. 'No: we are not living together any more because Daddy/Mummy like to do different things . . . live in different places . . . have to work somewhere else . . . but we both still love you.'

Children often skilfully hide their feelings, waiting to express them when a familiar situation makes them feel safe and to a certain extent, masked. Of twenty five year olds being given individual reading tuition, five confided to the teacher, 'Daddy doesn't live with us any more', while apparently absorbed by the task in hand.

But supposing the parent who has left the home does not, manifestly, care about the child? Suppose he/she never writes, visits, takes responsibilty? The ideal of two adults agreeing to part but still nobly maintaining an interest in their child may be far from reality. The two- or three-year-old child understands sadness and can cope with seeing it in an adult, but its intensity needs to be diluted so that the child still feels protected, wanted and worthy of love. To pass on the ability to love may be the greatest achievement to which most of us can aspire: it begins with valuing oneself as a person, the seeds of which are planted in childhood.

Coping on your own

A single parent can provide the emotional

stability in which a child can grow and thrive, but this will undoubtedly take more courage and commitment than if the parent is supported by a partner.

A single parent, and it is usually the mother, needs support: if she's fortunate she may receive it from friends and family and she should at all times welcome this, not only for the practical and emotional benefits to her, but also to enable the child to develop wider social relationships than she can provide in the home.

Single parents are not always lone parents – that is to say if the parent is bringing up a child alone through divorce or bereavement, then the other parent has been more or less a presence in the child's life. In that case his/her memory needs to be kept alive or his/her occasional presence acknowledged.

If the mother is single because the father has drifted away before the birth of the child, or very soon after, her loneliness and financial worries may be extreme. She may decide to stay at home, supporting herself on Social Security payments, which will not give her much above survival existence, or she may decide to go out to work. If her baby is well cared for, this may be the best solution as it will give her companionship and stimulation. To stay at home with a baby but without the support of a partner can lead to feelings of aimlessness through sheer boredom – babies are very boring quite a lot of the time. Babies also grow up: they become ready for a wider world, and when they begin playgroup or school the parent may miss their companionship more keenly if the child has been 'all' to her.

This is not to say that one course is better than the other: it depends almost entirely on circumstances and the nature of the parent; whatever is decided the parent must not add guilt to her/his other emotions because she/he hasn't chosen to do the opposite.

If the lone parent decides to stay at home, local friendships and clubs – such as Mother and Toddler Clubs, Gingerbread, One o'clock clubs etc. (see page 231) are available These not only provide companionship but also give the mother the invaluable chance to discuss her child's development and behaviour in a relaxed and friendly atmosphere, and to compare experiences with other mothers. The responsibility of bringing up a child alone is very demanding, and the inevitable setbacks regarding discipline,

A father can miss his child as much as the child misses him: his involvement may be important to the family well-being.

behaviour, and all the other stages a child passes through, can assume an importance out of all proportion to the problems if there is no-one to discuss them with. Discovering that her child is only going through a stage which other children also go through is reassuring, and will help the lone mother to keep things in perspective.

For a single working parent the daycare of the child is naturally of paramount importance. Not only must the qualities of the child-minder previously mentioned (page 189) be met but warmth and reliability must be priorities. Through these the child will not only learn trust and how to make continuing attachments, but the parents will also have support and peace of mind.

One difficulty the lone mother may experience is that her child has little opportunity to make relationships with men. If possible an uncle, grandfather or brother could be asked to take an active interest in the child. This is particularly important for a boy about the age of three when the child is beginning to identify himself with an adult. Another aspect of isolation applies to a father bringing up a child alone: single fathers have said one of their difficulties has been that they lack easy companionship with mothers who in daily conversation are always passing on examples of experience with their own children. Lone fathers have no access to the to-and-fro of childlore. This is where associations such as Gingerbread help.

A succession of boy or girl-friends is no answer. Even though they may have affection and involvement with the child, the temporary nature of their presence may add to a child's uncertainty and distrust of any permanent relationship. Because this lack of involvement with men in the children of single mothers is being acknowledged, more men are becoming active in playgroups, nursery schools and even as nursery nurses, though at the moment they are still fairly few and far between.

So although single parents should never hesitate to take advantage of any help offered, and should seek professional counselling when needed, they may still feel confident that with steady commitment they will be able to rear their child successfully.

Step-parents

One of the worst reasons for remarrying could be because the child says, 'I would like a daddy/mummy'. Marriage is between two people to which the family is added: it need not work the other way around.

If, however, you choose to marry a partner who already has a child or children then at least you know what you're in for – in theory. Many step-parents say they married the man or woman and realized only later that they had married the child as well.

If the child or children in question are under three they will probably have little difficulty in accepting the new parent, provided the parent inspires their trust by continuing care and involvement. They may well feel jealous, however, at having to share the attention of their own long-term parent. It is a natural reaction and needs to be watched for. It is very hard to appear to be displaced in another's affections. The step-parent may find that the child resents 'discipline' if it comes from him/her while accepting it quite happily from the natural parent: it is sometimes the case though that step-parents are so determined to make a relationship with the child that they become over-indulgent. Particularly bewildering would be a step-parent who is over-indulgent before the marriage and strict afterwards.

For the natural parent remarriage is also a time for adjustment: he or she is becoming used to the new relationships. It is best to take things slowly, allowing the step-parent to take on some of the routine (bathing, feeding for instance) gradually if the child seems willing. In time it is a good idea if some routines become 'Daddy's time' and some 'Mummy's time', so that the child can feel he has his own special period of attention and the sole interest of the adult.

One of the difficulties in remarriage is that the step-parent may not previously have had experience of being tied by a young child, and realizing that there will be limited time to spend alone with the new partner could be something of a shock. This is where it is of value if there has always been a time that the child is cared for by others – childminder, baby-sitter, granny, aunts – so that she realizes the parent has a right to some time on his/her own, and does not resent being excluded from some activites.

Step-parents do make enormous successes of their new role; they are often spoken of with the greatest affection in later life by their stepchildren, but it may not be easy initially. To all the stresses of bringing up a child is added the difference of an added responsibility and unfamiliar experiences. A child can run through all the gamut of 'stress signals' (page 189) and behave in a manner calculated to drive both parents away, if not crazy, and endless patience may be called for.

It is doubly important that the parents talk about discipline, rewards and general treatment of the child before they marry so that they present a united front, and it's probably best if the step-parent for a time adopts the habits of the natural parent so that change is not too abrupt. Compromise ought to be reached later if needed and adjustments made mutually. A time for extra wariness could be needed if the new husband and wife have children of their own. Another baby in the family is quite disturbing enough anyway (see page 196) and to be coping with both a new parent and a new baby is a heavy undertaking for a toddler. If possible, it would be kinder to wait until the older child is settled into the new situation before embarking on a second family.

Joining two families needs the patience of a saint and the wisdom of Solomon. It will probably be easier if the children of the families are of different ages so that they do not rival each other. Each child needs to be given privacy and also different privileges and responsibilities. And if either parent cannot really love one of the children then at least that child must be given respect.

Think carefully before changing a child's surname. Names are very personal and to change a name could make the child feel she is losing part of herself. Unless you have adopted a stepchild you will have to get both parents' agreement to the change.

It is not an easy time for the parents either. Don't let the family be split down the middle – if a new baby arrives don't let the step-parent regard her as 'special' while the natural parent of the first favours that child as 'special'. A child old enough to remember a time when she was the only one in her parent's life could well develop an early taste for nostalgia.

How it's done may be a matter of day-to-day developments, but the aim must always be to make the first child realize she has a secure place in the family and is valued as a person in her own right. She has her own privileges, her own responsibilities and she ought also to have some time alone with both parents individually. If the child has become used to a certain routine – Saturday morning walks with father: bedtime story with mother – then do your best to see the routines don't change. If they have to, then anticipate them and try to change them before a squalling baby makes it imperative.

Joining two families is never easy. When there's a wide difference in the ages it's important that the older children have time and attention to themselves and are not expected to help too much.

Adding to the family

To have a second or third child when the nearest is only a year or eighteen months old imposes a physical strain on the mother. Not only is she coping with lifting a heavy toddler when she is pregnant, she will find after the birth that the demands of the two can't help but coincide. The older child may not be mature enough to wait patiently while the baby is attended to: what a toddler wants he wants *now* – food, attention, or to be hauled down from the wobbly stool he's managed to climb while you're trying to change the new baby. If the older child is about two years old when the next arrives he is usually able to understand that he has to take his turn at times, and he is also old enough to be interested in what's going on with the baby.

On the other hand, some parents believe that children born close together are more companionable. It also means the parents are released from baby caring in a shorter time. What they gain in earlier independence they probably make up for in greater concentration of care and work for a shorter time. Children born close together do grow up to be close emotionally, however, and usually develop a self-sufficient companionship – if the parents have been able to give adequate emotional support to each.

A very young child will not be able to understand that a new baby is on the way: a toddler can with limits. If a second child is on the way while the first is too young to understand what's in store, it could be a good idea for the parents to 'borrow' a young baby occasionally so that their baby sees another in the place he has always thought of as his own – his mother's or father's lap. It may only be a gesture but it could help a little.

A gap of about two years or more is thought to be adequate for the mother to recover from the pregnancy and birth of the first, and for the first child to have been given sufficient attention and sense of security to carry him through the squalls ahead.

The toddler and the new baby
However well you prepare your child for the arrival of a new brother or sister he is going to have a surprise when the promise becomes reality. The third or fourth child they usually take in their stride, with a kind of resigned stoicism – but the second is a different matter. It has been compared to a husband bringing home a second wife and allowing her to use the home as her own. . .

On the whole, second and subsequent babies do seem easier to manage than the

A toddler may be surprised at the helplessness of a young baby. It is a time of adjustment – and not always easy for the older child.

Opposite Involve the older child in as much responsibility as she can cope with – while still remembering she may feel supplanted.

A second or third child when the nearer is still very young may impose a physical strain on the mother. She is coping with pregnancy and the demands of a still-dependent toddler.

first and fit more easily into the family routine. But for the first few months at least they are going to need as much attention as any new baby.

The older child first has to cope with the surprise of his mother disappearing for a few days (if she's having the baby in hospital), and then reappearing with this new creature. Moreover, the new creature doesn't disappear: it's there all day and all night. And at times it interferes in the pleasant routine he has been used to.

So how do you prepare him? Don't talk too soon about the coming baby. A toddler who can't yet cope with 'today, tomorrow and yesterday' is not going to understand 'nine months'. About the seventh month you could begin to drop a few hints, let him feel your tummy, listen to the baby and feel her movements. You can begin to collect baby clothes and take notice of babies in prams you meet on your walks.

If any changes are going to be needed to

the toddler's routine then make them well in advance. If, for instance, he is to be moved out of his cot or room, make sure he's happy with the new arrangement as soon as you can. If the toddler sleeps in your room and you are thinking of moving him into another when the baby comes, it is most important to do that well in advance: if he seems very distressed at this you could consider putting the new baby into the other room, and keeping the older child in with you. The chances are that after a few weeks he will ask to have the other room as he is now the 'older' child.

Occasionally the older child can become very possessive if he sees some of his outgrown clothes being prepared for the new arrival. If that happens then give them up to him, or ask if you could borrow one or two as a favour to you. Never appropriate a toy or piece of favourite equipment for the new baby without the child's permission – and give it back if he changes his mind.

find it strange when you are home all day on maternity leave. If he has been going regularly to a childminder, you may find it better to let him stay at home sometimes with you and the new baby, so that he feels more relaxed about this stranger in the house. For a while he may only feel safe if he can be near enough to keep an eye on the baby – once he relaxes a little he may ask to go back to the childminder for some sessions – or you can suggest it.

Give him things and times which are entirely his. If you can, feed the baby while he has his nap, then he can have an uninterrupted story later. Or talk to him or watch a programme together while you give baby a feed. Involve him in responsibility – as much as he can cope with – fetching towels, testing the bath water. Most toddlers can't wait to soap the baby's back in the bath, although the baby never seems so keen. Let him help with tasks which are clearly superior to the baby's abilities. A toddler is usually very surprised at how helpless a baby is, and this brings out his protectiveness. Helplessness has its advantages too – as one three year old said, watching his new sister being put into her pram, 'Well, there you go and there you stay: you with your stupid bendy legs.'

Don't expect the child to share his toys with the new baby: later, when she crawls she may infuriate him – knocking over his bricks, squashing his drawings, tearing his books. You have to be watchdog there: explaining that the baby can't really help it. Remove potential trouble before it happens: the child's reaction of sorrow is only the same as your own if your precious ornament is smashed while the toddler is attempting to use it as a scoop in the sandpit.

Do

Ask grannies, friends and neighbours not to *coo* over the object in the pram and ignore the older child. Or bring the new baby presents and none for him.

Explain to him that he is older, has more privileges, special times.

Let him join in all the routine of babycare: imitating it with teddy if he wants.

Do not

Worry if he regresses to baby habits – bed-wetting, thumb sucking, bottle-feeding – give him a special new feeding plate and spoon so that he feels grown up. Take him to the shop and let him choose them for himself.

And don't forget that mother's best friend is father when it comes to taking some of the heat off the work. . .

By the time the third has arrived in the family, the others are able to be of great help – even if they find it rather a bore!

If so far your child has not spent much time away from home then plan a few occasions when he remains for a few hours without you at granny's, or with a childminder, baby-sitter or friend. He will get used to the fact that when you go away you also come back. If you plan to send him to a childminder or playgroup when the new baby arrives then again, begin this well in advance so that he doesn't feel he has been sent there to get him out of the way while the baby has taken his place.

For a mother working outside the home it is rather different: your child will be used to a childminder or other company and he may

Having twins?

If father is mother's best friend for one baby, he is twice as valuable with twins.

Most prospective parents of twins know they are having them: it is diagnosed before birth in eighty per cent of cases. That still leaves twenty per cent amazed at the last moment. Twins often run in families and they occur in about one in every eighty births.

There are tremendous advantages in being a twin – for the twin. Mutual support and the sense of security can help each through many difficult situations. At the same time each child has to struggle to maintain his individuality in a family and a world that tends to treat him as part of another person. Twins have to learn not only to separate from their parents, but eventually to separate emotionally from each other. That is why, right from the beginning, they must be treated as separate babies, not two editions of the same baby. As they grow older don't compare them or expect them to develop simultaneously – one may walk sooner, the other speak earlier. Dressing twins – or more than twins – alike is quite usual, and when they are small it saves a lot of work as you won't have to keep matching things up, but as they grow let them be different if they choose not to have identical clothes. Sometimes the same clothes in different colours is the answer but the basic thought remains the same: they are two different children.

The idea of coping with twins may seem daunting; some parents, however, take the attitude that they are getting two for the price of one pregnancy. Fortunately the arrival of two usually excites a great deal of interest among family and friends – take advantage of it and accept whatever help is offered, or even orchestrate it a bit yourself. The most valuable help is the firm commitment: 'on Thursday I'll do your ironing', 'on Wednesday I'll take them out for a walk'.

Twins are often premature and it is not uncommon for the mother to be asked to spend the last few weeks of her pregnancy resting in hospital (hospital deliveries are usual for twins). The uterus reaches full-term size earlier and frequently the babies are born about the thirty-seventh week.

Expecting two need not mean that you have to buy two of everything so, for instance, buying five stretch suits instead of six, or seven instead of eight could help with both space and money.

Plan furniture and routine to save the number of steps you'll have to take. If, for instance, one baby proves restless during the day or evening then put one baby upstairs and have an extra crib downstairs to save constant trips up to the nursery. (Laundry baskets are cheap, portable and practical for the first few months.) A small store of nappies, gowns, and so on, downstairs could also save your feet – but don't let the babies' equipment spread everywhere.

A bathinette is a useful piece of equipment – there is a top stand for a bath and underneath are shelves for towels, nappies, and so on. Or it isn't difficult to adapt an existing piece of furniture to meet the same purpose.

Shopping may prove a major expedition – consider shopping in bulk say, once a month, for the basics, or it may be best to have a baby-sitter so that you can shop in comparative peace. There is nothing like a fractious baby in a pram for ensuring that you come home with half what you wanted, unless of course it is two fractious babies . . . When you choose a pram get all the catalogues and ask advice from any parent you know who has already had twins. Some side-by-side pushchairs, for instance, won't go through supermarket doors, but the Twins Club (page 230) will give excellent and practical advice on all these aspects. A mother of twins has written about two other aspects of having two babies at once.

'There is a strong temptation to give the babies 'matching' names – Ronald and Donald, or Jane and Joan – but our advice is "don't". There is nothing more personal than having one's own name – twins have to share their lives: don't ask them to share their names as well. Also, during the first few weeks, everyone wants to come and see the babies – if you don't establish "visiting hours" you'll never get any rest. Grandparents can be invaluable if they will take over certain

When one egg is fertilized by one sperm and then divides, the result will be identical twins with the same characteristics, usually sharing the placenta but each with its own cord.

If two eggs are released and then fertilized by two sperms the result will be fraternal or non-identical twins, each with its own placenta, bag of liquid and umbilical cord.

Twins mean a lot more work, particularly in the early days when father's help is doubly valuable.

jobs and be prepared to help. Don't treat your visiting family as guests – if anyone offers help, accept it!'

Insuring against having twins is possible although companies will raise the odds if there is a history of twins in the family. Obviously you will have to insure before you know you are going to have twins – so most companies won't take the risk after twenty-two weeks of pregnancy – and then only if the ultrasonic scan has shown one baby. If you suspect the likelihood get quotations in good time!

Fostering and adopting

Fostering children demands a very special kind of commitment. By its very nature you know that you will not be keeping the child or children indefinitely – you are not the parents although you are being asked to supply a parent's commitment and continuity of affection. If you wish to foster a child or children then you should apply to your local authority or Social Services department who will discuss your wishes, and assess your suitability and the quality of care you are likely to provide. They will also want to see your home and will probably make enquiries about your previous lifestyle.

If you are accepted for fostering then the natural parents will probably be given rights of access to visit their child. This could be an opportunity to provide great support to the natural parent – particularly if he or she is anxious to take the child back when circumstances permit. Many foster parents have become valued friends on whose experience the natural parents have relied and from which they have benefited. It is not easy to reconcile children to this divided care, particularly if they are toddlers, and it needs cooperation between the two sets of 'parents' so that one does not usurp or undermine the other's place in the child's affection. Social workers will provide assistance and information, and fostering often proves an invaluable temporary solution to a difficult situation.

Giving a child for fostering is a less irrevocable act than giving him for adoption and it could be a solution for the single parent. It could be a better choice than the child having to be cared for in a home, but it is a decision which will have to be discussed at length with a social worker. Foster parents are always in demand and social workers will need to be sure that the action of putting a child into a foster home is in the best interest of both natural parent and child. They are unlikely to countenance it if it is felt that it is a means of merely freeing the parent from responsibilities.

Adoption is less easy nowadays in an atmosphere where single parents (usually mothers) decide to keep their babies and bring them up alone. Even couples who appear to have everything in their favour may have to wait three years before they are given a chance to adopt. But such delay will probably not exist with the so-called 'difficult to place' children – in other words, children with special needs, older children, children of mixed race, children with handicaps. Adoption agencies exist for such specific adoptions (see page 230) but adopting such a child calls – again – for a very special kind of person. On the other hand the success rate of such adoptions is extremely high, though couples contemplating such a course will need professional counselling.

If a child is placed for potential adoption the natural parents have three months in which to change their minds and take their child back. They may do so at the last minute and the three-month waiting period is very hard for the adoptive parents since during that time they will have become attached to the child yet all the while fearing that they may have to relinquish him at the last moment. The whole area of adoption needs great thought and discussion and is never a situation to be entered into without preparation. The subject is explored at length in several books (see page 229), and discussion can also be arranged with adoption agencies (see page 230).

Children who are adopted now have the right to seek out their natural parents after the age of eighteen. They are given counselling before they are put in touch with their parents, and in some instances contact is not advised. It is worth remembering that parents who allow their children to be adopted no longer have the guarantee that the existence of the child will not be made known later in their lives. This could lead to difficulties in their current relationship (see page 229 for titles of books on the subject).

A CHILD'S HEALTH A-Z

Few children escape the early years without the occasional setback in health – from the bumps and bruises of everyday mishaps to the minor ailments of childhood. But however slight the illness it may still cause distress to the child and concern to the parents, especially if they are not sure what action to take.

This section details the ailments and conditions you are likely to meet most frequently during the years of caring for a young family. Of course you will only encounter a few of them, but to help you find quickly the entry you are looking for we have listed them alphabetically with cross references to other sections where necessary. As far as is practicable we have first described the illness or condition, then its cause, next its symptoms and finally its treatment.

Emergencies and accidents invariably demand calmness and speed – two essentials difficult to achieve when you are yourself upset and perhaps distracted by a tearful, frightened or injured child. So to help in these emergencies, situations needing immediate action are indicated with a telephone symbol. Make time to read through these entries *before* the emergencies arise. Hopefully they never will but if they do – and even if you don't remember the exact treatment – knowing where to find the directions will help you to keep control.

The following situations are the most likely to occur in ordinary families and so advance knowledge of what to do is essential: why not glance at the advice offered for these entries now?

- burns
- bites and stings
- choking
- concussion
- cuts and scrapes
- fits
- fractures
- kiss of life (see drawing)

Also in this section you will find listed conditions which you are most unlikely to meet in your own family – autism, dyslexia – but they are terms you may well come across in a wider context, and knowing more about such conditions adds much to our understanding of the problems.

Good health is a matter of prevention as much as cure and knowledge aids prevention. Understanding how digestion works (see page 100) helps us to keep it working, just as understanding the structure of different parts of the body – ears, throat, eyes – helps us realize how vulnerable they can be to infection or injury, and what we can do to prevent these.

The human body is a complicated and marvellous structure: understanding even some small part of its functions and abilities is a rewarding and fascinating achievement.

THE RECOVERY POSITION

This recovery position should be used in an emergency if your child is unconscious but still breathing.

Turn him over on to his stomach with limbs arranged as shown and head turned to one side while you go for immediate help.

Abrasions

If there is bleeding, wash well with water to which an antiseptic has been added, cleaning from the wound outwards. Pat dry and put on sterile dressing. If the bleeding has stopped and a scab is forming don't wash the scab as this encourages infection. Clean area round the scab. A plaster is not necessary.

Accidents to the teeth

These may be common as the one to two year old learns to walk and generally propel himself about. Teeth most often injured are the upper central incisors – as they are most prominent if the child loses his balance and falls against a hard object. The most common damage is small chips on the tooth which may be unnoticed. If haemorrhage occurs within the tooth, blood will become trapped and the tooth turn black; usually this will be left untreated unless an abscess forms which must be treated as the infection can damage the permanent tooth.

If the accident is more severe – if the tooth is knocked into the gum or the fracture is larger so that nerves and blood vessels are exposed, dental treatment is required immediately. If a tooth is knocked out, wash it under cold running water and push it back immediately into the socket. If you don't feel able to do this yourself, wash the tooth, wrap it in a clean damp cloth and take your child immediately to the dentist. Minutes count if the tooth is to be successfully replanted.

Adenoids

Two small collections of lymphatic tissues lying at the back of the nose. Up to the age of about fifteen they enlarge, after which they shrink. Adenoids in young children therefore seem large in proportion to the child's size.

Upper respiratory tract infections may affect the ears, causing deafness and earache and the adenoids to enlarge. When ear symptoms are troublesome it may be advised that the adenoids should be removed, but the value of the operation is disputed.

Allergies

An over-reaction of the body to something which in other individuals produces no symptoms. This reaction may be caused by eating, inhaling or touching. Likely to run in families but it may take different forms. Hay fever and nettle rash (hives) are also allergies. Symptoms are likely to improve as the child gets older. Allergies cannot be cured but symptoms can be reduced by the use of anti-allergic drugs such as antihistamines and cortisones. Your doctor may be able to determine which substance (allergen) is causing the disease and eliminate it from your child's surroundings. If the allergen is identi-

fied, small amounts of the substance may be injected until the child becomes immune. Such methods are not usually employed for young children, and the effects will not last for life. Tracking down the cause of an allergy may be a lengthy business: it could be easy – cats may bring on asthma, pollen result in hay fever – but a prolonged series of tests could cause the child more worry than the allergy itself. Nettle rash is usually caused by a food, so gradually eliminating different foods from the child's diet may identify the culprit: asthma and allergic rhinitis (itchy runny nose) are likely to be something in the air – hair, feathers, house dust mites. Additives in food may also cause allergies. Some washing powders may also provoke an allergy.

Ammonia Dermatitis

See NAPPY RASH

Anaemia

Condition in which there is insufficient number of red blood cells, or insufficient iron-containing pigment that carries oxygen and makes the cells red. May be caused by acute blood loss, lowered production of the cells, or excessive breakdown of the cells.

Anaemia should be distinguished from pallor (a pale complexion). Anaemia has many causes and must be properly investigated. If it should be due to iron deficiency this may be easily treated with iron medicines or altering the diet.

APPENDICITIS

Inflammation due to infection of the appendix (which leads off the lower intestine). The pain may be on the right side of the abdomen or around the navel: there may be diarrhoea, vomiting and fever. If the pain goes away in a few hours (say three or four) without treatment then it is not appendicitis, but a doctor should be called to diagnose as a burst appendix (which can happen in twenty-four hours) can cause peritonitis, which spreads infection through the abdomen. Treatment is by surgical removal of the appendix.

Artificial Respiration see DROWNING

Asthma

Spasms of the bronchi (air tubes) caused by over-sensitive lining of the membranes. Breathing is difficult and the asthmatic attacks are frightening. Sometimes difficult to distinguish from wheezy bronchitis but the treatment for both is the same. Asthma may be exacerbated by excitement or stress

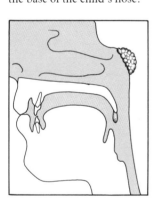

A cross-section of the head and neck to show the position of enlarged adenoids on either side of the base of the child's nose.

so it is possible to lessen the attacks if the cause of stress can be identified and removed. Asthma often improves in a dust-free climate or in a house where house dust mites have been eliminated as much as possible. Treatment is by anti-spasmodic drugs or inhalation. Physiotherapy is also of benefit and your doctor could arrange for attendance at a clinic. Asthma should be taken seriously and treated as an illness. If, in spite of medicine, attacks are severe and frequent, admission to hospital may be indicated.

Known causes of asthma include feather bedding, down, hair, pet fur, house dust mites.

See also ALLERGIES.

Autism
Autism is an extremely rare condition. The child does not respond to affection and seems indifferent to surroundings and people, as though he lives in a dream world. Often the condition is only noticed when he fails to respond to his mother at the time when a baby normally begins to react. Unable to communicate, the child seldom learns to speak or may repeat one or two words over and over again. He adopts obsessive patterns of behaviour – liking to do the same thing over and over again. The cause is not yet understood although there are thought to be several which contribute. Autistic children sometimes have a special gift – for drawing, mathematics, music. They learn to walk and care for themselves although slowly. For advice and guidance from specialist sources ask your doctor.

Bites
The most common bites from which your child is likely to suffer in the United Kingdom are from dogs, cats, domestic pets and – more rarely – from snakes. (Rabies from dog bites in this country is not at present a risk.) If your child's tetanus injections are up to date (see page 66) all that is usually needed with bites is to wash them clean and then apply a sterile dressing. If the wound is jagged then it may need stitching. Cleaning is all that is normally needed for dog and cat scratches. If they turn yellow or will not heal, consult your doctor. In Britain the only venomous snake is the adder – with a pronounced diamond pattern down the back and a V or X mark on the head – the bite from which causes pain and swelling. Wash, if possible; do *not* suck out the poison but take the child to the nearest emergency hospital department. Do not let him walk (this causes the poison to circulate), but carry him. A child bitten or stung may be shocked (see SHOCK for symptoms and treatment). For insect bites see STINGS.

Black eye
A bruise and possibly swelling of the tissues surrounding the eye. Could be caused by a blow or by a fracture at the base of the skull, so always keep careful check on injuries to the head and if in doubt, consult your doctor. Cold water compresses will help ease discomfort: the swelling will subside and the bruise disappear in a few days.

BLEEDING

Ordinary bleeding from a cut or scrape is usually controlled by pressure from a dressing or fingers. If an artery is damaged the blood will spurt dramatically and must be stopped at once. Forget about tourniquets but put your fingers on the spot from where the blood is coming and press hard. If this doesn't stop it, press just above the spot. If it stops put a firm dressing on, and if this does not work keep your fingers on the spot while you get him to hospital by ambulance.

Body lice
Body lice live in clothing and feed on the body, leaving small marks which are very irritating and easily become infected. Treatment is by cream or powder which can be bought without prescription.

Boil
A small red spot which feels tender, comes to a head and then bursts, discharging yellow pus. It may be necessary for the boil to be lanced if it does not burst of its own accord. A boil may form on the outer part of the ear and is very painful. Your doctor should be consulted, when antibiotics by mouth may be prescribed. Bathing in hot water or a hot pad will help healing after the boil has burst. Red streaks running under the skin from the boil mean that the infection is spreading.

Breathholding
The child may begin to cry out or take a deep breath as if about to let out a yell, but no sound comes. He turns red or purple – if he holds his breath so long that he deprives himself of oxygen he may have a convulsion. The cause is usually frustration, anger or sheer depth of feeling which the child cannot yet control. He is unlikely to have an attack when he's alone as the performance needs an audience – but it is nevertheless a genuine reaction. Slapping or throwing cold water over him won't help. The attacks are alarming but without danger.

Bronchitis
Inflammation of the lining of the air tubes

It is important that in the case of severe bleeding from a large wound, blood flow is restricted to encourage clotting. Give continual reassurance as you attend to the bleeding. A lot of blood can be frightening to a young child.

1. Squeeze the sides together gently but firmly for about ten minutes.

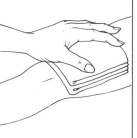

2. Once bleeding has ceased, apply a sterile dressing and press it down.

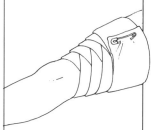

3. Secure with a bandage applied firmly and pinned. If bleeding recommences, apply a further dressing and bandage on top of the first.

(the bronchi) which lead into the lungs. 'Wheezy' bronchitis is most common in children – there is a characteristic wheezing noise as they breathe through the narrowed air passages. Nurse as for viral pneumonia (see page 222) – your doctor may prescribe drugs to clear the tubes of mucus or you may be taught exercises which will help the child to breathe properly.

Bruises
A blue-black mark on the skin caused when blood is released into the tissues. The colour changes as the blood is absorbed by the tissues and carried away. Caused by an injury to the tissues below the skin. Usually the bruise clears up within a week or so, but if the knock has been severe there may be a suspicion that the bone underneath is broken and an x-ray should be taken (see FRAC-TURE). A pad of wet cotton wool will help ease the discomfort. If your child bruises without obvious cause tell your doctor as it could suggest an underlying illness.

BURNS ☎

The larger the area of skin burnt the more serious the injury. If more than half the skin area is burnt death is probable.
Trivial burns: (that is, less than 2cm (1in) in diameter) can be treated at home. Do not touch the burn but immediately immerse in cold water. This cools and cleans the skin and reduces pain. Leave the burn open to the air unless a blister forms.
If a blister forms: do not prick, but apply a medicated plaster dressing. Keep the dressing dry and give junior aspirin to help pain.
Larger burns: cool immediately in water, cover with a clean cloth – sheet, linen handkerchief – fix the dressing in place and take the child to hospital.
Clothes on fire: roll the child in rug or blanket, do not remove clothes, cover with a clean sheet and take to hospital.
Clothes in scalding water: remove the clothes – cut them off if necessary – cover the child in a sheet and take to hospital.

Burns from acids and alkalis: wash the liquid off the skin immediately with plenty of cold water, then deal with the burnt skin as above. If possible, remember which liquid has caused the burn, or take the container to the hospital with you.
Burns from electricity: such burns may be deep although small. If they persist and seem slow to heal, take your child to the doctor.

HOW TO AVOID BURNS
DO NOT leave matches out.

For both minor and severe burns, quickly cool the burn in cold water. This gives instant relief and prevents further damage to underlying tissues.

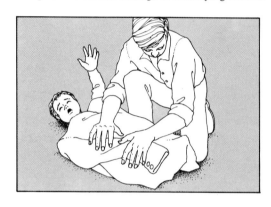

If your child's clothing is alight roll him in a rug, blanket or, failing these, smother the flames with your own body.

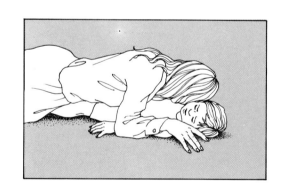

Wear pyjamas NOT nightdresses (use Flameproofed materials).
GUARD fires, hot water pipes, radiators. COVER electrical sockets, REMOVE cooking utensils to safe height, GUARD cookers, NEVER leave a child with hot kettles, bath water, steaming pots, etc. REMOVE acids and alkalis out of reach.

DO NOT put a dressing on serious burns since this will need to be removed at the hospital. Get to the hospital by the quickest

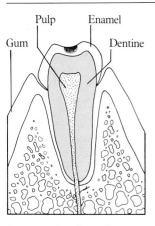

Pulp   Enamel

Gum   Dentine

Cross-section through a secondary tooth to show how a cavity forms.

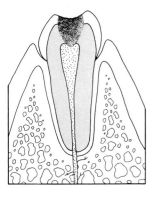

The enamel is eroded until the decay reaches the dentine where it can spread rapidly, eventually reaching the pulp.

route possible. Do you have the telephone number of your nearest hospital? There is a space on page 232 for you to put it in.

Burns cause more emotional upset than many other accidents so it is important that you keep calm through the emergency and comfort your child.

Candida Albicans see THRUSH

Cardiac Massage see DROWNING

Caries (Dental Decay)

Decay of enamel, resulting from plaque – a film of bacteria – on the teeth. Acid is formed which eats into the enamel and exposes the interior to infection. Sticky sweets, over-sweet drinks, puddings and sweet cakes can leave a harmful residue in which decay is encouraged. Leaving a child with a bottle of sweetened drink to suck during his nap results in pools of liquid forming and resting on the upper teeth, causing 'nursing caries'. Regular and efficient brushing and cleaning the teeth to remove plaque together with a sensible diet are the best ways of keeping healthy teeth. Most children like sweets, but it is best to keep them as part of a meal. In between meals encourage fruit, or, for instance, carrot sticks instead of haphazard sweet snacks (see page 88). It is better – if you must – to have one long session of eating sweets and then clean your teeth rather than eat them one at a time all day long. Encourage chewing of hard and tough foods which massage and exercise the gums and membranes. Fluoride added to the water in districts where there is insufficient natural fluoride gives protection by protecting enamel against attack. Fluoride tablets, crushed for babies, give protection if the water supply is not so treated. Toothpaste containing fluoride is also beneficial. Controversy surrounds the addition of fluoride to water supplies as some consider this should be a matter of choice but minority groups that oppose the proper fluoridation of water do not understand the problem. Fluoride is not a 'poison' but a substance present in small quantities in all water. Studies show that when the water supply contains less than a certain amount caries is more common.

Dental cavities are not inevitable if diet is controlled, plaque removed and efficient hygiene observed. You can begin to clean your baby's teeth as soon as they appear by wiping over the teeth and gums with a piece of gauze with toothpaste on. By eighteen months to two years the child can begin to wield his own toothbrush although you will have to supervise the up and down movements, going round corners and at the back (see page 87).

Cataracts

Opaque patches that form on the lens of the eye. If small they cause little problem but larger cataracts can impair vision. If hereditary they appear at birth, usually in both eyes. Prenatal infections can also cause them – previously they were common from rubella in the mother before immunization was offered. Cure is by surgery when the cataracts are removed and special glasses or contact lenses which replace the natural lens, can be worn. Cataract in one eye in a child can result in the eye becoming 'lazy' which can lead to blindness, and for this reason it will probably be operated on in the first few months of life (see also STRABISMUS).

Congenital cataracts can be operated upon in the first few weeks of life and babies can wear contact lenses.

Cerebral Palsy

Damage to the part of the brain controlling movement and muscle, caused either at birth, through lack of oxygen, or during early pregnancy by an infection (such as rubella) in the mother. In later pregnancy severe malnutrition may be a cause either in the mother or the fetus because of inefficient placenta. Severe jaundice may also be a cause. The child has little or no control over movement (either being 'floppy' or too stiff). The largest single group suffering from cerebral palsy is the spastic group. The condition may also affect mental development, hearing or sight depending on how near the damage is to the parts of the brain controlling these functions. A child suffering from cerebral palsy, or spasticity, may be of normal or high intelligence although in the past the uncontrolled movements led to the belief that there was also inevitable mental damage. The help available for spastics is widespread and efficient and enormous progress has been made in research and resources. See page 230 for the addresses of specialist agencies.

Chicken-pox

Spots are usually the first sign. These come out in crops – first as red pimples, then forming blisters and finally scabs which drop off after about ten days. The pink scars disappear in time. The spots may be intensely irritating but scratching must be discouraged or permanent scarring may result. Infection is for the most part by droplets, but spots are theoretically also infectious until covered by the scabs. (An adult with shingles can give chicken-pox to a child.) Spots can be dabbed with calamine to ease irritation or a cup of bicarbonate of soda in the bathwater will be soothing. If your child is in nappies, an ointment may be prescribed to apply to the spots in that area. If possible leave the nappy off so that the skin is exposed to the air.

Chilblains
Painful red swellings on fingers and toes, though they can also appear on the nose and ears. Intensely irritating, they are caused by poor circulation. Stop the child scratching as the chilblain may then burst and become infected: make sure hands and feet are kept warm in cold weather, that shoes or boots are not impairing circulation. Your doctor or chemist can prescribe ointment to help the itching.

Choking
Try to hook the object out with your finger but if this is not possible, turn the child upside down and slap him on the back. This should dislodge the object and make him cough it out. When a child begins mixed feeding, avoid giving small hard pieces of food. Never give a child peanuts: the oil in them is irritating if inhaled into the lungs – and never leave a baby to feed from a propped bottle which could make the milk go down the wrong way and cause choking and vomiting.

Circumcision
The surgical removal of the skin which covers the tip of the penis (glans). Believed at one time to be necessary to keep the area between foreskin and glans clear of secretions, this operation is no longer routinely performed in Britain. It is now known that at birth the foreskin and glans are joined as a natural protection for a sensitive area, and will therefore reduce the irritation from wet nappies. The two separate naturally about the age of three to four when your child can be taught to gently ease the foreskin back, and keep the area clean as part of the bathing and hygiene routine. If circumcision is necessary on advice from a doctor, the operation will be covered with a dressing and you will be shown how to care for the area.

Cleft lip
Condition at birth in which the lip is slit. Surgically corrected within two or three days of birth, the condition is sometimes referred to as Hare Lip, referring to the rabbit or hare with a similar split lip. If cleft lip is coupled with a cleft palate there may be difficulties in feeding and special techniques may be necessary which will be taught in hospital. Usually this involves holding the baby in a sitting position.

Cleft palate
The slit of a cleft lip extends to the palate or

During the development of the fetus the two sides of the face develop separately and then join along the lines shown (1). Sometimes fusion is incomplete on one side (2), sometimes both (3).

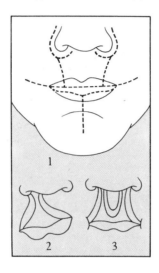

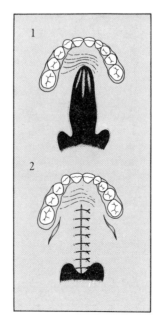

The slit of a cleft lip can extend to the palate (1) and is repaired as shown (2).

roof of the mouth. The condition originates between sixth and tenth week of pregnancy. Cause may be genetic or influenced by drugs, illness in the mother or exposure to radiation.

Cleft palates are usually repaired at about two years of age as this will allow for growth of the mouth to have taken place. (However the exact timing will depend on the plastic surgeons, whose advice should be sought.) The aim is to close the hole while allowing the soft palate to close off the passage between throat and nose so that air doesn't escape into the nose during speech. A child with a cleft palate is given special speech-training to prevent distortion of the voice, and also to maintain suitable dental and facial growth. Ear infections are a possibility and these could result in hearing loss, but will be monitored by specialists to whom the child will be referred.

Club foot (talipes)
Usually caused by the position of the feet before birth. One foot (or both) is mis-shapen, often being turned in at the ankle. It may be mild or severe. If mild, the foot can be manipulated into a normal position – all that is required is to put the foot straight several times a day. If severe, a normal position cannot be achieved without causing pain or requiring an anaesthetic. In this case splints and perhaps also operations may be required.

Coeliac disease
An inability to digest gluten, the protein in wheat flour. It will not be noticeable until the baby begins to be given cereal when the stools will be bulky, pale and offensive. Treatment will be by prescribing a gluten-free diet which has to continue for life. It is a relatively rare disease.

Colds
A cold is a layman's term and is often used to describe upper respiratory tract symptoms which are relatively mild and unimportant. Upper respiratory tract symptoms vary depending upon which group of viruses or bacteria is responsible. Conjunctivitis and fever and runny nose suggests one of the adenoviruses: aching with fever an influenza infection: a sore throat a streptococcal or EB virus infection (the virus of glandular fever). Treatment is directed at the symptoms – if appetite is poor, give liquids rather than solids: fluids are necessary to prevent dehydration. Nasal discharge is usually clear and watery: yellow or greenish pus may indicate sinus infection. At present there is no specific treatment for virus infections, so treatment is symptomatic – a little of what

you fancy. If the child does not improve in a few days or if after some improvement there is deterioration, complications such as an ear infection may have occurred and antibiotics may be advisable.

Colour blindness

More usual in boys than in girls (eight per cent to 0.4 per cent), the handicap may not be noticed at first because under three a child may not be distinguishing colours verbally with accuracy. A mild colour blindness might make it seem that the child is backward or being awkward. Problems may arise when the child begins school if he is expected to use colour-coded equipment, but he will learn to adjust. Red and green are the colours most frequently muddled. Tests have been devised to determine colour blindness in young children and your doctor will arrange for these if you suspect the condition.

CONCUSSION

Loss of consciousness which may follow a fall or bang on the head. A doctor should be called immediately: in the meantime, lay the child on the floor on one side with the upper leg drawn up so that he does not roll over. This is necessary so that if the child is sick, vomit is not inhaled. Check for breathing and heart beat (see DROWNING). Do not give anything to drink.

Congenital dislocation of the hip

A routine examination is carried out on every newborn baby to make sure there is no dislocation of the hips. Early diagnosis and treatment results in complete cures – the baby will be put into a splint for some months which will correct the position.

Conjunctivitis

Red, inflamed watering eyes or eye. Small amount of pus may be produced, usually noticeable after sleeping. Conjunctivitis often affects one eye for a day or two and then the other. Virtually always caused by a virus and may occur in epidemics – in a playgroup for instance.

Gently clean away dried discharge with moistened lint or soft cloth. Improvement is usual in two to three days. Eye drops or ointment (prescribed by chemist or doctor) may be necessary to treat. If there is pain, difficulty in seeing, pronounced swelling, fever, discharge or inflammation, consult your doctor, as MENINGITIS (qv) could be a complication. A baby under three months with red and discharging eyes should be seen promptly by a doctor as less common infections and conditions can occur at this age.

Constipation

The infrequent passing of hard stools (see page 100). What is infrequent to one is not to another. Some may move everyday, others twice a day or even every three or four days. Normally bowels move when the rectum is full and obsessive worrying about what is 'normal' will soon result in abnormality if you keep on giving fruit, laxatives, extra drinks and attention to the subject. If the movement causes pain then you may have to give milk of magnesia or more fruit or fruit juice. Don't keep asking your child if he has 'been yet' – you will make him worried about the whole business and this in itself can lead to constipation.

CONVULSIONS

The child twitches, his body shakes and he becomes unconscious. He breathes heavily, eyes roll up, teeth are clenched. He may wet himself. The attack may last a few seconds or a few minutes. The child then passes into sleep or regains consciousness and falls into sleep. If he breathes heavily or snores then this is not sleep but unconsciousness.

It is essential not to panic: stay with the child because although the convulsion is never fatal in itself, the child may be sick and inhale the vomit into his lungs which then could be fatal. If he comes round while you are away, he would be terrified. Lay the child on his stomach, head to one side so that vomit can trickle out of his mouth. Do not try to 'bring him round' – nor to still his limbs, but keep him out of the way of furniture, fires or anything else on which he might hurt himself. When the child comes round contact your doctor at once.

Most causes of febrile (fever) convulsions are 'idiopathic' that is they have no known cause, but they may be 'symptomatic' – the first sign of another illness. It is the doctor's job to think of all the possible causes among which may be head injuries, falls, breath-holding. The tendency that some children have to convulsions in association with fever is inherited. It is limited to the age of one to four years. They are not harmful unless they continue for a long time (half an hour or more). There is some evidence that a prolonged convulsion may lead to a temporal lobe epilepsy. Because of this many doctors give the parents of children with febrile convulsions an anti-convulsant to administer rectally to make sure the convulsion is brief.

A child who has had convulsions should not be vaccinated against whooping cough, nor if there is a history of convulsions in the family. The subject should be discussed with your doctor.

Cot Death (sudden infant death)

Cot death or the sudden infant death syndrome is the term given to the sudden unexplained death of an apparently healthy baby. It is most common between the ages of two and six months and although research continues into its cause no one factor has been isolated. It occurs more frequently in winter, in babies who are bottle-fed, in poorer families, and in districts where there are reports of chest infections. It has occurred in hospitals to otherwise apparently healthy babies. Among the contributory factors put forward are allergies, suffocation, overheating, or that the baby quite literally 'forgets to breathe'.

Because the tragedy is so devasting and so mysterious, a cot death usually attracts publicity so that it may seem these are more common than they really are.

Suffocation has largely been discounted as responsible since even a young baby can wriggle his face free if he feels uncomfortable. However, a baby can't lift a hand to pull a plastic covering or tight blanket away (see page 26). Chest infections can kill a baby with overwhelming suddenness even before parents or doctor have had the opportunity to realize the baby is not well.

Parents who have suffered such a sorrow must be helped not only by the support of friends and relations, but always by expert counselling. To the parents' overwhelming distress is added the trauma of the legal process because it is necessary to establish that the baby died from natural causes. Happily a more enlightened and sympathetic attitude is now usual from those responsible for administering the law as knowledge of the disease becomes more widespread, but great suffering has been caused by the occasional suggestion that the parents were in some way to blame for the death. 'Could I have prevented this?' must always be in the parents' minds without the inference of others, and so guilt and responsibility are often added to sorrow.

If you know anyone who has suffered such a loss it is natural that you may feel great reluctance to mention the subject to them, but parents of such babies invariably say that they have longed for their acquaintances to acknowledge their loss. Instead they have behaved as though the child has never existed. Parents and families have suffered a dreadful bereavement and a few words to recognize this – which can be prolonged into talk if the parents want it – is important. (See page 230.)

It is not only the parents who have suffered: other children, grandparents and relations are also afflicted. Older children in the family may also need extra love and comfort just at the time when the parents need it most themselves, and may find it difficult to give. It is important for parents not to shut themselves away at such times, either mentally, emotionally or physically. Mutual support and understanding between the parents can hope to deepen the ties between them.

Such counselling and advice is available through professionals – doctors, priests, counsellors – and support groups (see page 230 for addresses). Your health visitor may also know of parents or organizations in the locality who can help. A period of grieving is essential: the sorrow should not lead to the birth of a second child as a 'replacement' before the first has been fully mourned. Nor should fear of another such catastrophe dissuade parents from having another child.

Cradle cap see SEBORRHOEA

Croup

Inflammation around the vocal chords due to a viral or bacterial infection. Breathing is difficult because the inflammation causes obstruction to the passage of air. The illness may begin with a mild cold, but there is a characteristic high-pitched 'croaking' sound accompanying each breath when croup develops. Often an attack develops at night when the child wakes, unable to breathe: the chest may heave rapidly and the lower ribs be drawn in. Tension makes the breathing worse so it is imperative for you to keep calm and help the child not to panic. Croup should not be lightly dismissed and you should call the doctor immediately if there is a real difficulty in breathing. In the meantime, prop the child up, stay with him to relieve his distress and – if the room is centrally heated – open the windows. A steamy atmosphere will help breathing so you could take the child to the bathroom and turn on the hot taps or keep a steaming kettle going in the room he is in. (Don't leave the child alone with the kettle.) Croup tends to recur and is frequent in children from about two to four: your doctor will prescribe treatment and will also show you how to manage any other attacks that may occur. Admission to hospital may be considered advisable.

Cuts

If a cut is deep and happens out of doors a tetanus injection may be necessary if your child's immunizations are not up to date. Take him to your doctor or hospital without delay.

If the cut bleeds, applying pressure to the wound with a clean lint pad will help to stop it. Treatment can then be as page 207 unless the cut is deep, extensive or has edges that don't meet, in which case take to your doctor or hospital as stitches may be necessary.

When applying plasters to a cut do so across the wound, that is, draw the edges of the cut together. If a cut is surrounded by reddened skin and is painful there may be infection, so consult your doctor.

Cystic fibrosis
Cystic fibrosis is an inherited disease through abnormal genes from both parents. In a baby the symptoms are repeated lung infections, failure to thrive and digestive upsets. There is no cure but it can be treated with antibiotics and pancreatic extracts.

See also GENETIC COUNSELLING.

Deafness
In babies and children deafness is easily unrecognized. A deaf baby will begin to make sounds at the same age as a baby with normal hearing, but because he can't hear his own voice or those of others he receives no stimulus or encouragement and his speech fails to develop. He may watch your lips or facial expressions as you speak to him and will respond to those instead of your voice, without your recognizing his deafness. At about six months, it can be noticed that, because his babbling does not have all the variety of sounds a child with normal hearing would make, there may be a suspicion of partial deafness. Since listening is the beginning of speaking, the deaf child could become dumb – as used to happen in the past, before the two conditions were associated.

Checks for hearing should be made at the baby clinic or by your own doctor. A baby can wear a hearing aid from about six months old and speech therapists and special teachers will come to the home to help both parents and child to cope with the condition. In the past deaf children, while learning to speak, often did so with distorted sounds since they had no means of hearing correct pronunciation, but recently the development of ultra-sensitive equipment has achieved so much that children who had never even heard their parents' voices can now do so.

See GLUE EAR.

Dehydration
A drying out of the body caused by excessive diarrhoea or vomiting, which causes chemistry changes. Eyes look sunken, there is listlessness, weight loss, dry lips and mouth and a decreased urine output. A doctor must be consulted without delay. Treatment will be by giving the correct liquids after analysis of blood and urine. If there is vomiting, the liquid may be given into a vein. Dehydration can be avoided by giving fluids and keeping fever down since the sweating which accompanies fever can contribute to water loss. See SWEATING.

Dental decay see CARIES

Diabetes
A failure of part of the pancreas causes a lack of insulin needed to break up sugar in the blood. Sugar builds up in the blood and passes out in the urine. Comparatively rare in children, the disease comes on suddenly and without warning. Symptoms are intense thirst and increased output of pale urine. There may be abdominal pain and sickness. Some adults can be given drugs to control their diabetes by mouth but treatment by insulin injections is always necessary in children. They can be taught to do this for themselves while still very young. Diet may be controlled. Diabetes can't be cured, but it can be kept under control so that a normal life is possible. (See page 231 for support group.)

Diarrhoea
Loose and more frequent motions caused by infection or, in older children, emotional stress. In babies the motions may be green caused by the shorter time that the matter has remained in the intestines. Diarrhoea accompanied by vomiting must be taken seriously as this can rapidly lead to dehydration. In diarrhoea without vomiting there is a disproportionate loss of potassium. Weak salt water drinks (sodium chloride) may be helpful when there is vomiting but can lead to too much sodium in the blood stream (hypernatraemia) if given for diarrhoea. If the child with diarrhoea is not ill, the symptoms need not cause undue alarm. Give plenty of drinks, milk, water, fruit juice. Diarrhoea can also be caused by antibiotics and by milk intolerance. Kaolin medicines may be prescribed or other medicines to ease stomachache. Antibiotics may be prescribed if the diarrhoea is caused by bacteria (which can only be discovered by laboratory tests). See COELIAC DISEASE and CYSTIC FIBROSIS.

Diphtheria
Immunization has practically eliminated this illness in the West. When immunized the child is fully protected. Diphtheria is a killing disease and it is therefore of the utmost importance that your child should be protected through the programme of immunization (see page 66).

Down's Syndrome (Mongolism)
Down's Syndrome is caused by abnormal chromosomes. Normal cells each have forty-

six chromosomes which carry inherited characteristics: in Down's Syndrome babies, each cell has an extra chromosome. The chances of this condition increase with the mother's age. The eyes of these babies slant in the oriental fashion and they often suffer from colds and chest infections. They are affectionate and active and, although they are mentally slow, they are able to achieve certain skills, depending on the degree of their affliction. The condition can be determined before birth by amniocentesis (see page 21) when an abortion may be considered.

DROWNING

A baby can drown in a few centimetres of water and so can a toddler if he is unable to scramble out – for instance – from a garden pond. A pond is a dangerous thing with a toddler around but, if you must have one in the garden, then fence it in, or at least make sure the sides are straight and not sloping – that way the child at least has a chance of climbing out on his knees. His feet may slip on sloping sides and the panic make him fall backwards.

A baby should never be left in the bath alone, nor with a toddler who may turn on the taps or push the baby under. Near drowning will provoke coughing and perhaps vomiting. If the child is not breathing then begin artificial respiration at once (see below). The brain and heart can only survive a few minutes without oxygen. While you are doing this, think how you will get help – perhaps by calling or getting to the telephone. If you can't leave the child, drag him towards the telephone or open window or door so that you can call out. Artificial respiration is very tiring and you may have to continue it for a long time until the child begins breathing for himself. You could take turns with anyone else who is near. Every second counts, so begin right away.

ARTIFICIAL RESPIRATION (KISS OF LIFE)
Place child on back and pull chin forward. Clear mouth of obstruction. Close nostrils. Take a deep breath and seal the child's mouth completely by putting your own mouth over it. If patient is small enough you can seal both mouth and nose with your own mouth.

Blow gently and if abdomen rises the air is not getting to the lungs so arch the neck still further. A hand on the abdomen helps get air to lungs.

Take your mouth off to allow his chest to contract. Breathe in yourself, then repeat blowing.

Blow for the first few times in quick succession, then at about 15 blows a minute.

Continue until the child breathes for himself. Watch the child after he has begun to breathe and keep him warm. Send for your doctor or an ambulance.

While you are waiting for his breathing to resume, feel for the carotid pulse in the neck – this is to the side of the windpipe (practise finding it on yourself now). If you find the pulse and the child is beginning to breathe you can stop the kiss of life, but stay watching him.

If you can feel the pulse but he is not breathing, then continue with kiss of life. If you do not feel a pulse and he is not breathing, start cardiac massage (see below).

CARDIAC MASSAGE
If the child is under one year of age place two or three fingers over the lower half of the breastbone and depress about 1.5cm (.75in). If you depress too deeply you may cause

Artificial respiration for a young child should be administered quickly but gently.

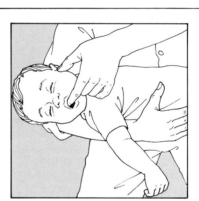

1. If the child is very young cradle him, tilt head and clear mouth.

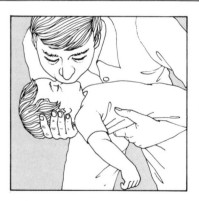

2. Place your mouth over the child's mouth and nose and breathe out gently, watch for chest to rise.

3. If chest fails to rise, turn child over, pat between shoulder blades try again.

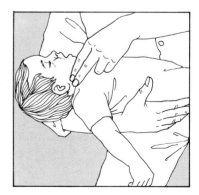

4. Check for carotid pulse in neck. If present, continue with respiration; if not apply cardiac massage.

internal injuries: if you don't press deeply enough the blood will not circulate into the heart, which is what you are trying to achieve. You must continue this pumping action at the rate of about forty to fifty times a minute, at the same time continuing with the kiss of life resuscitation. If the child is over one year you will probably need to use the heel of one hand to compress the chest and will need to depress about 2cm (1in). Don't stop until help arrives or your child begins to breathe. As soon as normal breathing is restored, place the casualty in the recovery position (page 204).

It is difficult for one person to maintain both cardiac massage and mouth-to-mouth resuscitation: it is also very tiring. The Red Cross and St John's Ambulance service run courses to teach resuscitation and you are strongly advised to learn the method through them. It may be that your local hospital will also give suitable demonstrations – ask your health visitor for information. In the meantime you could practise following the instructions on your own.

Dyslexia
The inability to sort out the order of words or letters. It is unlikely to be recognized, and will not become a problem, until the child reaches the age of reading. It is important not to see the condition before it exists: when the child begins school at five could be the time when the difficulty becomes apparent. It may be difficult to sort out children with this specific disadvantage from the slow-to-read child, or indeed from a child thought to be lazy and uncooperative. Dyslexic children are of normal intelligence, with normal sight: for reasons not yet completely understood, letters and words appear as a jumble to them and they are unable to translate sound into correct spelling.

Treatment consisting of individual lessons from a remedial teacher – available through the school – can help a great deal. (See page 231 for support groups.)

Earache, Otitis Media
Infection of the middle ear which may cause inflammation. Caused by bacteria from throat or nose, which is more common in children since the EUSTACHIAN TUBES (qv) are shorter, straighter and wider than an adult's. The infection can follow on from another infection – for instance, colds, measles. If your child seems deaf when he has a cold ask your doctor to check for inflammation. Treatment is by antibiotic and probably nose drops which will keep the tubes open. See also RUNNY EAR.

Children often complain of earache when in fact they have sore throats or mumps.

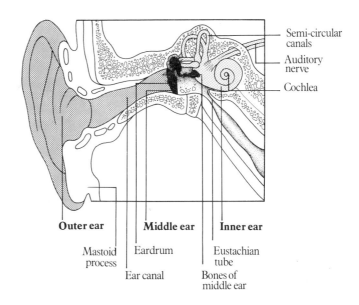

A cross-section to show the major divisions of the ear and the position of the sensitive parts within the skull.

Semi-circular canals
Auditory nerve
Cochlea

Outer ear   **Middle ear**   **Inner ear**

Mastoid process   Eardrum   Eustachian tube

Ear canal   Bones of middle ear

Warmed cotton wool pads help to soothe.

Earache, Otitis Externa
Inflammation of the outer ear, sometimes caused by poking things into the ears. Moving the ear will be painful and there may be a discharge. Consult your doctor without delay and don't let your child swim.

Ears
See DEAFNESS, EARACHE, WAX IN THE EAR, WATER IN THE EAR, BOIL, GLUE EAR, RUNNY EAR.

Eczema
More common in boys than girls, infantile eczema begins as red patches on cheeks and forehead then becomes moist and may spread all over the body. Scratching leads to infection and the baby is miserable and fractious. It is slightly less common in babies who are breast-fed exclusively. If the eczema begins when the baby's changed from breast to cow's milk, consult your doctor as to whether you should change to soya-based milk. Some foods seem to make the condition worse, so can soap and water (clean with oil instead), and woolly materials (though cotton garments don't aggravate the condition). Eczema leaves no scars and most children grow out of the tendency in two to three years. Ointments can be prescribed to keep down the inflammation and a sedative may be prescribed in the early stages to help with the irritation.

Eczema is not catching, but an allergic condition that tends to run in families – or if a relative has associated allergies – asthma, hay fever. It is worsened if the child becomes upset. The discomfort can be enormous and one of the more wearying aspects is that the child must be kept from scratching. Keep fingernails short. There is no cure for eczema but ointments and treatment as detailed can help reduce the trouble.

EEG
An electroencephalogram test to record the brain-waves, it may be done to help diagnose the cause of fits or seizures. The test takes one or two hours, but does not involve the child staying in hospital. Electrical wires are stuck to the scalp with a special glue, and the brain-waves – which with epilepsy are different from normal brain waves – are recorded. The test is painless, although the wires and equipment may look frightening. If your child needs an EEG test and is old enough to cooperate, prepare him by explaining what is to be done and let him practise on teddy at home.

ELECTRIC SHOCK

If the shock is so severe that the child can't move his hand away or if he has lost consciousness, don't touch him or you too will get the shock. First, switch off wall plug and if this is not possible, move the child away, either by dragging at his clothes, or pushing with broom or other non-metal object. If necessary give artificial respiration (page 214), or if there are burns, treat as for BURNS from electricity (page 208).

Epicanthic Folds see STRABISMUS

Epilepsy
Recurring fits as for convulsions. In what is called Petit mal, the child may look vacant for a second or two, may momentarily lose consciousness, then continue with what he was doing – taking up the conversation or resuming an activity as though nothing had happened. Not to be confused with daydreaming when the child can be brought back to his surroundings quite easily. Grand mal looks like a febrile convulsion but is not brought on by fever, although it may cause a rise in temperature. Immediate treatment is as for convulsions but the condition will need to be controlled by drugs. Much of the fear of epilepsy has been caused by society's attitudes – it is somehow thought of as a disgrace and parents sometimes wrongly feared they had caused the condition by mismanage-

If you can't find the power supply switch, push the child away from the cable with anything that will not conduct electricity. In this case the broom end is preferable to the handle.

ment. Children with epilepsy can be treated as any other children, although they will need to be supervised for certain activities – swimming and cycling for instance. They can be encouraged to play games and enter into ordinary activities but should not be left alone in the bath in case of a fit. Treat the episodes as matter-of-factly as you can while taking precautions as detailed above. Long-term treatment with drugs often eliminates the tendency to epileptic fits.

Eustachian tubes
The two small tubes, one on each side, which lead from the back of the throat to the middle ear, and which equalize pressure on either side of the eardrum. Because in a baby the tubes are short, and because a baby spends a lot of his time lying down it is easier for bacteria to travel along to the middle ear.

Eyes
See STRABISMUS (SQUINT or LAZY EYE), CONJUNCTIVITIS, STYES, COLOUR BLINDNESS, STICKY EYE, FOREIGN BODY IN THE EYE, BLACK EYE, CATARACTS, GLAUCOMA.

Fainting
Caused by insufficient blood reaching the brain. It is rare in children under three. May be caused by a hot, stuffy atmosphere or when a child has to stand for long periods. There may be a preliminary warning of a feeling of dizziness or sickness. Treatment is to make the child sit down with his head between his knees. The feeling will soon pass.

Fever
A fever is one of the body's defence mechanisms and is not always dangerous in its own

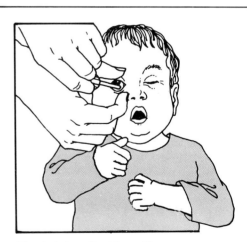

To administer liquid paraffin or castor oil, lay the child down, gently pull apart the lids, and let the drops fall between the eye and the eyelid.

right. In febrile convulsions nursing should be directed to lowering the temperature (see CONVULSIONS) but in other fevers the aim should be to find out the possible cause of the raised temperature. Collect and save a specimen of urine in the fridge, keep a record of symptoms, and where pain seems to be. If there is any cough, vomiting or diarrhoea, when were the bowels last open? The question should always be 'is this something serious? Is the child more ill than one would expect with the recorded temperature?' Nursing care should be directed to comforting the patient: wiping the forehead with a damp flannel is soothing.

Children vary in the body temperature they can tolerate without being ill. In some this is 38-39.5°C (101-103°F); others show symptoms of delirium, sleepiness and vomiting at a lower reading. The causes vary; they can be:

Infections: the commonest cause, with respiratory infections the most frequent.

Dehydration: usually from vomiting and/or diarrhoea but sometimes from drinking too little or voiding too much.

Environment: caused by over-dressing, over-heating from activity, over-heating from atmosphere.

Immunizations: occasionally produce a slight fever. The triple vaccine may cause restlessness on the day it is given. The measles vaccine reaction would be from seven to ten days after the injection.

Medications: occasionally cause fever – but these would be monitored by your doctor who is treating the primary illness.

Variations in temperature: normal temperature fluctuates between 36-37.5°C (97-99.5°F) by mouth. It is one degree higher when taken by rectum and one degree lower if taken under the arm. Temperature will vary if the child has been very active, excited or crying.

If bringing the temperature down is recommended by your doctor, these are the ways:

Discourage activity (to a baby, crying is activity), encourage sweating by letting the child wear loose clothing, keep the room at about 20-21.1°C (68-70°F), give plenty of fluids.

If the temperature is very high (over 39.5°C (103°F)), more immediate methods may be necessary. Cooling the skin will help. There is a tendency to wrap up a child who is feverish too much – make sure that there are not too many clothes or bedclothes. It may be soothing to tepid sponge him as though he were subject to febrile convulsions.

Give aspirin or baby aspirin following the labelled recommended dose.

Tepid sponging for a child subject to febrile convulsions is also a way of bringing a child's temperature down. Undress the child and either put him on a waterproof sheet or, if he's small enough, hold him on your lap in a towel. Wring out a flannel or sponge with tepid water and pass over his face, neck, inside of arms and legs, and all over the body. Take his temperature every ten minutes or so to check if it's falling and stop when it gets down to 38.5°C (101-102°F). Cover him lightly and if the temperature rises repeat the process.

Cooling a child in this way and bringing down his fever lessens the chance of convulsions.

First Aid box
Keep your first aid box in a place where the child can't reach it or in a child-proof, locked

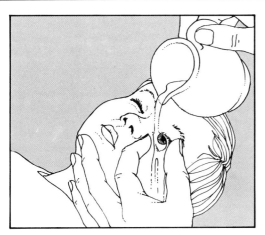

You should wash the eye in water if you can see the foreign body, or if the child has been splashed with corrosive fluid.

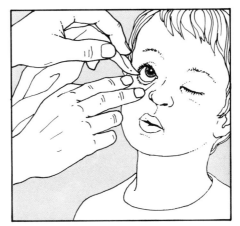

Wait until the foreign body has moved to outer edge of eye, then lift off with the corner of a handkerchief while holding lower lid.

box. If the latter, don't let the child see where you keep the key.

The box should contain: the telephone numbers of your doctor, hospital, chemist, health visitor, poison centre. Adhesive and non-adhesive bandages of assorted sizes, safety pins, crepe bandage, cotton wool and paper tissues, tweezers, two triangular bandages (scarf would do as well). Small scissors, baby aspirin, calamine lotion, castor oil to soothe eyes if object gets in. Antihistamine cream, disinfectant to add to water to clean wounds, thermometer. See also page 34.

Foreign body in the eye
A small speck of dust or other foreign body in the eye will cause watering and the offender may float out. Rubbing the eye will probably make the object embed itself more firmly so encourage blinking rather than rubbing – or rub the other eye to encourage both to water. If the offending object stays in, use an eyebath and if this doesn't work, gently lift it off with the edge of a handkerchief, waiting until it has moved to the outer edge of the eye. Don't press against the eyeball. If this proves difficult a chemist will take the intruder out for you: if the eye is still sore, two or three drops of liquid paraffin or castor oil dropped into the eye and covered with a pad, will be soothing.

If the object in the eye is causing real injury then your child should, of course, be taken to a hospital at once. Cover the eye lightly with a pad first. If a corrosive liquid has splashed into the eye, dilute it immediately by pouring water over the eye. Don't mind about the objection or the mess, and ring your doctor as soon as possible for further advice, telling him which liquid it was. (See drawings on page 216-7.)

FRACTURE ☎

A broken bone. It may be obvious with the bones out of alignment, or may not be easily diagnosed unless under an x-ray. Children's bones are supple and heal quickly and greenstick fractures are more common than in adults. This is when the bone bends but doesn't break. A simple fracture is when the bone breaks cleanly: compound is when the bone pierces the skin, and comminuted when the bone is shattered. The bones must be set in hospital and fixed in place with a plaster cast which supports the fracture as it heals – six to ten weeks may be needed. It may be difficult to distinguish between a fracture and a bad sprain since both are painful and

Bones can fracture in a variety of ways. Children tend to suffer partial or greenstick fractures (1). In a simple fracture (2) the break is clean; in a compound fracture (3) the skin is punctured; and in a comminuted fracture (4) the bone is broken in several places.

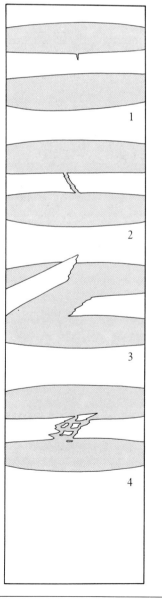

cause swelling, but usually it's possible to put some weight on a sprain, but not with a fracture. If you suspect a fracture, don't give food or drink. If a general anaesthetic is necessary it can't be given on a full stomach.

Skull fractures must be taken seriously and need immediate attention. If a child hits his head and loses consciousness, take him to an emergency unit of your hospital. If, after a fall, he is drowsy, sick or loses fluid from nose or ears, get medical help at once.

Frostbite
The blood vessels under the skin contract and cut off the blood supply to the surface. The skin turns hard and pale and if not treated, permanent damage can set in. Caused by prolonged exposure to intense cold, the symptoms are intense pain in the first-to-be-affected areas – usually hands, feet, nose and ears. Treated promptly there is unlikely to be permanent damage. Immerse gently in warm water.

Gastroenteritis
An infection of stomach and bowels caused by virus or bacteria. The symptoms are sickness and diarrhoea and the germs are spread through faeces to food. Highly infectious, so it is essential that hands should be washed after dealing with the patient or the disease can spread throughout the family. In a young baby DEHYDRATION is a danger so your doctor should be called at once. Water or fruit juice should be given. Sickness and diarrhoea need not necessarily mean gastroenteritis: they could be symptoms of another hazard, so don't try to diagnose the illness yourself, but consult your doctor.

Genetic counselling
Advice from professionals on the likelihood of risk to your children of inherited diseases. Certain illnesses are inherited from parents, either one or both, or can be passed down in families. Genetic counsellors will discuss with parents the possibility of their children suffering from such diseases, some of which are passed through the male line and some from the female. Your doctor will arrange for you to be seen by such professionals if there is need.

German measles see MEASLES

Glaucoma
Condition of the eye in which the pressure of the fluid inside the eye is raised, causing blocking of the channel between the front and back of the lens. Fluid builds up in the anterior compartment of the eye and results in a hard, painful eyeball. Vision may be disturbed with tunnel vision and 'haloes'

around objects. If not treated, glaucoma can lead to blindness. The condition runs in families though why is not known. Treatment is with eyedrops, drugs or surgery when part of the iris is removed so that it no longer interferes with fluid drainage.

Glue Ear

Often there is no complaint or sign of earache, but the child may seem deaf. Examination shows that a sticky glue-like substance has formed in the middle ear which prevents the ear drum moving in the usual way. If decongestant medicines don't clear the trouble, a grommet may be inserted into the ear drum under general anaesthetic with a one night stay in hospital. This is a small plastic tube which acts as an air passage to equalize pressure on either side of the drum. It is a simple and widely practised operation but long-term benefits are uncertain and like all operations there may be complications.

After a few months the grommet usually drops out of its own accord. Ask your doctor whether he will allow your child to swim or bath.

Haemophilia

The inability of the blood to clot caused by the absence of a blood-clotting protein. Almost all sufferers are male, but the disease is inherited and passed on by the mother. Even small injuries – cuts, scratches, etc. – can provoke prolonged bleeding, but spontaneous bleeding may also occur.

Bleeding after specific injuries – dental extraction, for instance – may occur in some individuals.

Sufferers from the disease usually carry an identification in case they are involved in an accident; hospital treatment would be necessary in most cases to stem the bleeding and takes the form of injections of the missing protein or transfusion of plasma.

Hare Lip see CLEFT LIP

Hay Fever see ALLERGIES

Herpetic Gingivostomatitis see STOMATITIS

Hives see NETTLE RASH

Hydrocephalus (water on the brain)

Cerebrospinal fluid accumulating in the brain stretches the skull out of proportion to the face. The fluid presses on the brain and pushes the skull bones outward. Often associated with spina bifida, hydrocephalus can be treated by the insertion of a shunt which relieves the pressure of fluid on the brain.

Hyperactivity

Term used to describe behaviour of over-active children. Some experts believe such children are 'normal' but of such intelligence that they are not being fully occupied and stimulated by their environment. The Feingold diet – pioneered in America – is additive-free and is claimed to be effective in helping such children, although opinions vary greatly among professionals as to its efficacy. Details from Hyperactive Children's Support Group (page 231) who will also advise about daily management, safe food and current research into the condition.

HYPOTHERMIA

Lower than normal body temperature. Body temperature is usually constant but what is 'normal' varies in different individuals, ranging from 36° to 37.5°C (97° and 99.5°F). If measured in the armpit it will be 1°F lower, if in the rectum 1°F higher. On average the temperature taken in the mouth from a child at rest is around 37°C (98.4°F). A newborn baby can't shiver, which is the body's way of keeping warm, and for this reason a baby should be kept in a constantly warm temperature of about 30°C (68°F). Premature babies can lose heat easily because their heat-regulating system is immature. For this reason they are usually kept in an incubator where the temperature is at a constant – usually between 21.1°C and 26.7°C (70° and 80°F). If babies become too chilled, hypothermia may set in. The skin turns a pale blue although the face and extremities may still look pink. The body feels cold and the baby becomes listless and loses his appetite. He will become quiet because he has not the energy to cry. A doctor is needed at once but in the meantime warm the baby with your own body heat. Don't put on extra wrapping as this will trap the cold inside. Medical treatment will be directed at carefully controlled raising of the temperature, probably by immersion in warm water and injections. With an older child, warm gently in a bath and give a warm, sweet drink.

Provided the baby is well wrapped up, a short outing in cold weather (down to 10°C (50°F)) won't harm him, but don't leave him outside for hours in a pram when a well ventilated room inside gives him enough 'fresh air', while still providing warmth.

Impetigo

Small red spots turning into watery blisters and then into yellow crusts. Mostly found on face, hands and scalp, impetigo is contagious so the child and his clothes should be washed separately from the family and theirs. Consult your doctor as antibiotic ointment will be necessary to clear it up. Impetigo can be a complication of another condition or may occur on its own.

Influenza
Cold, feverishness and pains in the legs, arms and abdomen. There may be sickness and nosebleeds. Children are less likely to get influenza than adults. Antibiotics may be prescribed – otherwise treatment is as for colds (qv).

Jaundice in the newborn
A yellow colour due to the accumulation of bilirubin (a yellow pigment) in the newborn is usually due to one of two causes and rarely due to abnormality of the liver. When red blood cells are broken down haemoglobin is converted into bilirubin. If red cells are for some reason broken down too quickly there is said to be haemolysis. Excessive red cell destruction leads to the excessive production of bilirubin and so jaundice. Any jaundice which develops in the first twenty-four hours of life should be suspected of being haemolytic and a precise laboratory diagnosis must be made. When it is first produced, bilirubin is insoluble and so can't be excreted. In newborn babies the enzymes which are necessary to render it soluble are often inactive for a few days so that jaundice results. This is known as physiological jaundice and there is no disease process. Jaundice is more usual in preterm babies.
See also CEREBRAL PALSY

Kiss of Life see DROWNING

Lazy Eye see STRABISMUS

Lisps
Imperfect speech before the child has learned to cope with adult speech. Loss of front teeth causes a temporary lisp or it may be prolonged beyond the baby stage from habit. It may be due to slight deafness, which should be watched for. If the cause is a faulty action of the tongue your doctor will refer you to a speech therapist.

Lumbar Puncture see MENINGITIS

Measles
First symptoms are cold, cough and red eyes. The child may be feverish, sick or have diarrhoea before the rash of small red spots comes out about the third or fourth day. When the rash appears the child will feel better. Previously the fever may be so high he may be delirious. The illness can be confirmed by the appearance of small white spots (Koplik's spots) on the inside of the cheeks. Spread by droplet infection, the disease is highly infectious and should be taken seriously, as complications can develop. The child can stay up if he wishes, bathing the eyes with plain water will help soreness, and he will probably need liquids more than food. Possible complications are bronchitis, earache, coughs and, very rarely, encephalitis. Incubation period is ten to fourteen days and isolation is ten days from the beginning of the rash. Immunization against measles is now routine (see page 66).

German measles (rubella) is a milder complaint than measles. A rash begins behind the ears and spreads on to the forehead and over the body. Lasting only one or two days. There may be a mild fever and swollen glands at the back of the neck. Spread by droplet infection: incubation of fourteen to twenty-one days. Isolation seven days after the rash has appeared. Complications are rare but the danger of the illness is the damage it can cause to the unborn baby if an expectant mother catches the illness in the first four months of pregnancy. If an expectant mother, who has not been immunized, is in contact with the illness she should tell her doctor immediately. He can arrange for appropriate antibody tests to be done. If she has antibodies at the time of exposure either from immunization or previous infection her baby will not be affected. An injection of gammaglobulin may be recommended by your doctor to give a degree of protection to the baby. Immunization is available (see page 66) and all should take advantage of it.

No special nursing is needed, other than keeping the child isolated to prevent the infection spreading, and the normal precautions of rest, warmth and plenty of liquids.
See ROSEOLA INFANTUM.

Meatal Ulcer
This is a small ulcer which forms at the tip of a circumcised penis. Caused by the rubbing of wet nappies it can be very painful and cause the baby to scream when urine passes over it. An ointment, prescribed by your doctor, can form a barrier between the urine and the ulcer until the latter has healed. In uncircumcised babies the foreskin protects against this irritation.

Meningitis
Inflammation of the meninges – linings that surround the brain and spinal cord. Caused by infection by virus or bacteria. Symptoms in adults are stiff neck, headache, dislike of light, but these may not occur in young children when the symptoms may be loss of appetite, sickness, convulsions and an abrupt

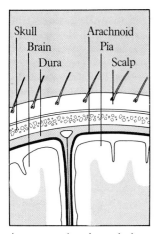

A cross-section through the skull to show the dura, arachnoid and pia – the three meninges that protect the brain and spinal cord.

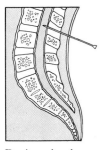

During a lumbar puncture, fluid is drawn from the space in the spinal column and used to test for meningitis.

change of behaviour when the child becomes suddenly drastically irritable. In the early stages this serious infection may be mistaken for a trivial upper respiratory infection. Bacterial meningitis requires urgent and intensive treatment with the appropriate antibiotics. Meningitis can result as a complication of another infection so if your child is already ill and there are changes in this way, recall your doctor. A lumbar puncture will confirm the illness. With this test the child lies on one side and, after a local anaesthetic is given, a needle is inserted between two of the bones of the spine and a sample of cerebrospinal fluid is drawn off for tests. Bacterial meningitis is treated with antibiotics and the results are good if the illness is diagnosed early enough. The illness can impair hearing, so check this afterwards.

Migraine

A severe recurring headache, often confined to one side of the head. There may be a feeling of nausea and distortion of sight – spots and shapes before the eyes or the feeling that the room is going round before the headache worsens. The condition tends to be hereditary and attacks may be as frequent as once or twice a week or as infrequent as once or twice a year. The attacks are caused by narrowing of the blood vessels in the head which then widen and cause pain as the nerve endings are stretched. Migraine can be triggered by several factors or a combination of them: food (cheese, chocolate, dairy products, concentrated yeast extracts, fried and fatty food have all been found to be responsible in different cases); overexertion; intense noise and bright sunlight or glare are some of the known factors. A doctor should be consulted at the first attack and pain-killers will then be prescribed: keep the child in a darkened room and give sips of sweetened drink. Sleep will usually follow an attack and between attacks there will be no symptoms. It is sometimes possible to foresee an attack and give the child medicine to ward off the migraine. Keeping records of meals, situations or conditions which precede the attack often make it possible to identify contributory causes and avoid them.

Mongolism see DOWN'S SYNDROME

Mumps

Swollen and tender parotid gland which runs from behind the ear to beneath the jaw. Dry mouth and pain on opening mouth and swallowing. Only one side of the face may be affected or the other side may swell when the first has subsided. Incubation period is up to twenty-eight days and isolation is seven days

from the disappearance of the swelling. Rare in children under five, it's not highly infectious so your child may not catch it even though he has been in contact with the disease.

A doctor should confirm the diagnosis. Paracetamol can be given if the child is in pain and since swallowing is difficult, milky drinks, soups etc. will provide nourishment. A woolly scarf wrapped round the neck is a comfort.

Complications can be mumps meningitis – fever, stiff neck and sore throat – but recovery is complete: or deafness. In adults, mumps is more painful and may result in swelling of the testicles: although sterility is rare, it is wise for men to avoid contact if they have not already had the disease.

Nappy Rash

A nappy rash may be due to:
1 Ammonia dermatitis
2 Irritation from detergent or washing powder
3 Thrush

Even when nappies are changed frequently it's not possible to keep your baby's bottom completely dry and unsoiled all the time. The skin becomes red and spotty and may then wrinkle and look thick. Breast-fed babies suffer less than those fed on cow's milk as their stools don't cause as much irritation. Nappies must be washed in a pure soap product and rinsed well – or use disposables. Leave them off altogether in warm weather. Applying zinc and castor oil ointment, petroleum jelly or similar ointment will form a barrier between the skin and the nappy.

Ammonia dermatitis begins round the genitals and there is strong smell of ammonia when you change the nappy – this is because bacteria in the stool interact with urea in the urine to produce ammonia. The rash can spread all round the tops of the legs and lower abdomen. Rinsing the nappies in a final solution of 25 ml vinegar to 4.5 litres of water (1 fluid ounce to one gallon) will help to reduce the likelihood of ammonia being produced. Special ointments are also available.

If the baby has thrush (qv) in his mouth the fungus will also be present in his stools and this will cause a rash, usually on the buttocks only. Nystatin by mouth or applied locally is effective.

See SEBORRHOEIC DERMATITIS

Nettle Rash, Urticaria or Hives

Small white spots and reddened skin which causes intense itching. Possible causes are allergies to drugs, foods, or insect bites. Emotional stress can also produce the symptoms. Calamine lotion dabbed on the spots soothes the itching and add two tablespoons-ful of sodium bicarbonate to the bath water. Not a dangerous complaint; the weals disappear in a few hours although others may appear which means the condition could continue for several weeks.

See ALLERGIES.

Nightmares
Your child may wake up crying and afraid but realizes he has been dreaming, and once you have settled and comforted him he'll go off to sleep again. He may have such nightmares because of overexcitement just before bedtime or during the day. If they are frequent there may be something worrying him, and you need to try to find the cause by gentle questioning. Children who have nightmares are often more intelligent than average and have active imaginations.

Night Terrors
A child who wakes up screaming and refuses to be comforted because he doesn't seem to be aware of you, has probably had a night terror. He won't be able to tell you what has frightened him, and all you can do is cuddle and comfort him until he slowly 'comes to' and goes to sleep again. Night terrors usually happen shortly after going off to sleep.

Nits
Nits are the grey-white eggs of the head louse which are firmly attached to the hair and are just visible. They can be killed with special shampoo prescribed by your chemist. The dead nits should then be removed with a fine comb. The irritation they cause can lead to IMPETIGO (qv) if the child scratches them so much that infection results. Most parents are horrified if their child has nits, but it's no

reflection on their hygiene: the condition can run through a playgroup, for instance, within a matter of days. It may be necessary for all members of the family to use the special shampoo prescribed.

Nosebleed
Not usually as serious as it looks. Make the child sit still with head bent forward so that he doesn't swallow the blood. Breathe through the mouth if necessary, press with a finger on the side of the nose from which the blood is coming.

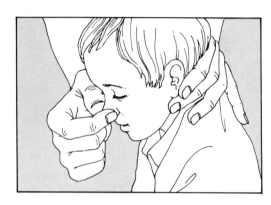

For nosebleed, lean the child forward and pinch his nose gently to stem the flow.

Pneumonia
An infection of the lung, caused by virus or bacteria, the second being more common. Pneumonia is a medical diagnosis usually made by a doctor with the help of an x-ray. A shadow interpreted as 'consolidation' is required for the diagnosis. If there's no such shadow, there's no 'pneumonia' though the child may be very ill with a respiratory infection (for instance bronchiolitis). Pneumonia is often *not* serious, and is one of the most satisfactory conditions to treat. It is a common misconception dating from the pre-antibiotic era that pneumonia is still serious, but with present-day antibiotics, it is not always necessary for the child to enter hospital. Influenza can cause pneumonia and when this is present the illness is more severe with a higher fever. Pneumonia may complicate upper respiratory infections but more importantly, it may present itself as a feverish illness which does not obviously involve the respiratory tract. A child with pneumonia (as opposed to bronchitis) is ill, listless and unresponsive as well as feverish. Propping the child up in bed may help with breathing. Decongestants may be prescribed or medicines for wheezing. The appetite is poor but liquids with vitamin supplements should be given. If pneumonia is suspected, a doctor should be consulted.

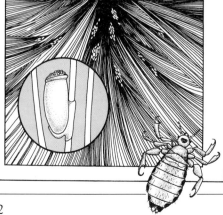

Nits are tiny, cylindrical eggs of the louse, cemented to hairs in clumps near the scalp. The inset left shows a magnified egg; the inset right shows an adult louse.

POISONING

Try to identify what poison your child has taken. If the substance is caustic (see below) making him sick will damage his lungs, by being inhaled. The lining of his throat can also be burned as the poison comes up. You could give a drink of milk or water.

Poisons where vomiting should not be induced include:

Strong acids such as garden weedkillers, creosote and nitric acid, sulphuric acid, carbolic. Petrol-based products such as paraffin, polishes, turps, dry-cleaning fluids, lighter fuel. Alkalis such as bleach, washing soda.

If the child has taken pills, give him a drink then make him sick by putting him face down over your lap and putting your fingers near the back of his throat, or the handle of a spoon down – take care not to injure his throat. If this doesn't work, give him a tablespoon of salt in warm water to drink. Give twice to make him sick twice. Take the child to hospital by quickest route possible. Take the container with you to hospital and a sample of the vomit if possible and remember how many pills the child took and when.

HOW TO AVOID POISONING
Keep pills, household cleaners out of reach. DO NOT let the child play in places where there are do-it-yourself or gardening liquids and substances. NEVER, NEVER put acids, cleaners or any liquid into a lemonade or fruit juice bottle so that the child mistakes the contents and takes a drink.

Poliomyelitis (Polio)
Immunization in the western world has largely eliminated this though it is still prevalent in the tropics. Poliomyelitis is highly infectious so anyone who has been in contact with the illness should be isolated for three weeks: infection is spread by droplets or through the stools. Symptoms in children are influenza-type illnesses. If there is polio in the area a watch should be kept if your child has not been immunized. MENINGITIS (qv) or paralysis may develop. (See also page 66).

Projectile Vomiting see PYLORIC STENOSIS

Pyloric Stenosis
More common among boys, the baby at about two or three weeks old vomits with such force that a whole feed can be shot across the room, though the baby continues to have a good appetite. The condition is caused by the thickening of the pyloric muscle at the end of the stomach which narrows the exit channel to the duodenum. Treatment is by surgery when cure is complete. Although the condition will have been present from birth, symptoms may be mild and not obvious until after six weeks. Symptoms in older children can be treated without operation but they do not persist after four months of age.

Ringworm
Fungus infection of the skin. The ring grows from the inside in a circular rash with small bumps at the outer edges. Ringworm on the scalp produces bald patches covered with scales. Consult your doctor at once as ringworm is highly infectious and brushes, towels and combs must be kept separately from those of other members of the family. Antibiotics will be prescribed and as the ringworm disappears, new hair will grow. Ask your doctor if your child should be kept away from other children, or may mix with sensible precautions. Ringworm may cause soft and cracked skin between the toes when it is called athlete's foot. Do not let your child go barefoot until it is cleared up.

Roseola Infantum
Easily confused with German measles (see page 220) this begins with raised temperature which, as it falls, is followed by a rash of small pink spots. It is so mild that it is often unrecognized. It is a virus infection and it may be associated with a convulsion. This will not be a 'febrile' convulsion, but a 'symptomatic' one.

Rubella see MEASLES, GERMAN

Runny Ear
A discharging ear should always be taken seriously since delaying treatment can lead to deafness. Pus from the ear drum may point to a middle ear infection.
See EARACHE, OTITIS MEDIA.

Scabies
Infectious skin disease caused by a mite which burrows into the skin and lays eggs: the mites then return to the surface, mate and begin the cycle again. There is intense itching, especially at night and mainly between the fingers, armpits, round the waist, and a rash made up of little blisters appears. Extremely infectious, it can be transmitted through person-to-person contact of bedding, clothing, towels, linen. Treatment is by applying benzyl benzoate solution once a day for three days. Infected bedding and clothing must be thoroughly washed.

Children are easily attracted to the bright berries and leaves of many poisonous plants. Be aware of those potentially dangerous plants in your home and garden. Three common species are shown here; others are laburnum seeds, deadly nightshade, yew, privet and laurel berries.

Holly

Poinsettia

Lily-of-the-valley

Scarlet Fever

Loss of appetite, sickness, fever, possibly with sore throat and stomach-ache (caused by swollen glands). On the second day a rash of small red spots covers neck, chest and body. The area around the mouth remains free of spots. Caused by a streptococcus infection. The rash lasts for about a week then flakes off. Treatment is by penicillin, unless the patient is known to be sensitive to this, in which case erythromycin should be given. Home nursing as for sore throat. Possible complications could be inflammation of the kidneys, rheumatic fever or middle ear infections, but these are now rare.

See ABRASIONS

Seborrhoea (Cradle Cap)

Layer of brown or yellowish crusts on the scalp, caused by greasy skin or too gentle washing of the baby's head. If the trouble spreads it can cause a red scaly inflammation with cracks above the ears. In its early stages cradle cap can be washed away with a solution of 5 ml (one teaspoon) of sodium bicarbonate to half a litre (one pint) water, or by soaking it with olive oil and leaving to soften when the crusts can be lifted off gently with a comb. If the skin underneath is red ask your health visitor for advice. Medicated shampoos for baby are available.

See below and NAPPY RASH.

Seborrhoeic Dermatitis

Caused by SEBORRHOEA (qv), the brownish 'cradle cap' from which flakes may fall and spread the trouble to other areas – in the armpits, in groin and genitals and also around the ears. It is brownish red in colour and your doctor will probably prescribe a medicated shampoo to clear up the scalp and an ointment for the nappy rash.

See NAPPY RASH

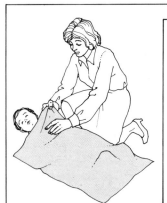

Lay a child in shock down and keep him warm.

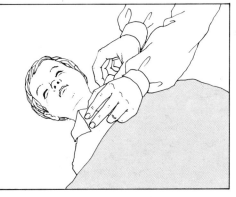

To help circulation and assist his breathing loosen any tight clothing around the neck.

Seizures – see CONVULSIONS

SHOCK

A child in shock may show many symptoms – paleness, rapid breathing, sweating, sickness and even unconsciousness. The state could follow an accident or severe emotional upset. Deal first with the cause – an injury – then with the condition. Keep calm yourself, lay the child down, loosen his clothing and cover him with a blanket. Don't give drinks if you think an anaesthetic will be needed to treat any injury. Don't apply hot-water bottles to warm him – these may cause sweating which will make him even colder, and this may also reduce circulation. If the state is severe the child should be taken to the hospital.

Skin Infections

See CHICKEN POX, IMPETIGO, THRUSH, SCABIES, ECZEMA, RINGWORM.

Smallpox

Smallpox is believed to have been eliminated from the world. If there should be an outbreak – which is unlikely – a vaccination programme would be set up. Vaccination gives immediate protection.

Sore Throat

Uncommon in a child under three, although tonsillitis can occur before this age. May be accompanied by fever, poor appetite and listlessness. Improvement is usual in two to five days. May be caused by virus or bacteria; in the latter case antibiotics will be prescribed. Give liquids and 'easy' foods – ice cream, yoghurt, jelly, blancmange, stewed or puréed fruit, or other favourite foods.

A high fever accompanying a sore throat can last as long as seven days; mouth sprays may be necessary to counteract pain so that the child can drink adequately. Discuss their use with your doctor.

Complications can be ear infection, swollen glands or SCARLET FEVER (qv) and, very rarely, a throat abcess.

See TONSILLITIS, SCARLET FEVER.

Spina Bifida

Spina bifida is the malformation of the spine when vertebrae are split into two. When the skin also is split, the spinal cord is left unprotected and often malformed. Hydrocephalus is a frequent complication. Paralysis of the legs, and bladder and rectum valves results in incontinence. Surgery can close the skin, but can't correct the damaged spinal cord, and the paralysis cannot be cured though much can be achieved through orthopaedic care. The condition can be discovered before birth (see page 21).

Splinter
Provided it causes no discomfort a small splinter can safely be left to work its way out. A larger splinter can be removed with tweezers (previously sterilized by passing several times through a flame). Deeply embedded splinters or those which have become infected should be seen by a doctor – as also should those of metal and glass. Check that tetanus injections are up to date.

Squint see STRABISMUS

Sticky Eye
New babies frequently have a sticky eye caused by substances getting into the eye during birth. The eye should be bathed with a wet cotton wool swab, always wiping outwards from inside corner of the eye to avoid the infection passing to the other eye. Always put the baby into his crib with the infected eye nearest the mattress so that the infection or substance can't flow from one eye down to the other. If the condition persists antibiotic ointment may be prescribed.

Stings
Most stings from insects in this country need only be treated by washing with cool water and soothing with calamine lotion. If the sting is visible, try to tease it out gently with your finger nail. Using tweezers can compress the sting and cause more poison to be released. Spraying the area with one of the proprietary prescriptions on the market gives instant relief – your chemist will stock these. If the child is stung on or inside the mouth, swelling may hinder breathing so give the child an ice cube or lolly to suck and take him to the hospital, or your doctor. Occasionally a wasp or bee sting can cause allergic reaction – paleness, severe pain and inflammation – in which case, consult your doctor who will also arrange for your child to be desensitized after recovery.

Stomatitis
Primary herpes simplex stomatitis infection may cause blisters on the lips and in the mouth which may become very painful. At the same time there is fever and misery and swelling of lymph glands in the neck. The first (primary) infection with herpes simplex virus may take the form of stomatitis. The inside of the mouth is covered with painful blisters which burst to become ulcers and the child is feverish and miserable. Most adults and older children are immune having had

Six muscles control the movement of each eyeball and a squint (1) occurs if on one side they are not strong enough to hold the eye in alignment. Some apparent squints, however, are caused by wide folds of skin – epicanthic folds – over the corner of the eye (2).

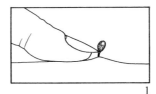

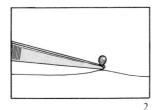

Try to tease out an insect sting with your fingernail (1). If this fails grip the sting below the poison sac with a pair of tweezers (2) and remove.

an unrecognized infection in childhood. Care must be taken to protect infants or children with eczema from herpes simplex virus infection as it may produce a severe generalized eruption.

Strabismus (Squint or Lazy eye)
The new baby may look cross-eyed since he has not yet achieved the muscle power to enable both eyes to work together. If a baby over three months always looks cross-eyed, he should be seen by a doctor who may refer him to an eye specialist. Early treatment is essential because the brain can suppress one of the two images of double vision, which may be resulting from the squint, and one eye may go blind. Treatment may be by exercise (if the child is old enough to cooperate), by blanking off an eye by an eye patch, or a blacked-out lens of spectacles, or by surgery. A squint may develop after an illness. Occasionally a child may look as if he is squinting because wide vertical folds of skin (known as epicanthic folds) overlie the inner corners of the eye. This usually runs in families and causes no problem.

Styes
Infection of the hair follicle in an eyelash causing small boil on eyelid. By applying heat to the swelling the infection is helped to clear more quickly. Soak a small pad of lint in hot salt water and hold against the stye. The lash may also be removed by tweezers which will let the pus drain away. Styes can be transferred from one eye to the other so make sure your child does not rub his eyes. Keep face flannel and towels separate from other members of the family.

Sudden Infant Death see COT DEATH

Sunburn
Painful reddening and scorching of the skin caused by the sun. Blisters may form. Fair and red-haired children burn more easily than dark skinned, but don't let your child play outside in steady sun for longer than half an hour for the first two or three days. Sun by the sea can be deceptive: a breeze may make the atmosphere cooler, but the sun is still strong. The burns won't be painful until some time after the child has been burned. Creams help but don't give complete protection so let the child wear a loose shirt over a bathing suit. Shoulders, back of the neck and legs are particularly vulnerable if the child is squatting to play or dig in the sand, so keep these covered. Calamine lotion will soothe the skin and paracetamol helps the pain. The burns will probably blister, and will gradually fade and peel.

Sweating

Sweating is the body's way of bringing down temperature. Sweat evaporating from the body surface causes heat loss. If the air is hot and too humid the temperature isn't lowered. When they get too hot – by running around, for instance – most children will stop of their own accord: if they get too excited they may have to be made to do so. Overdressing your baby or toddler, or being in an overheated room or atmosphere can make it impossible for the child to sweat properly. Provided sweating is normal it is possible to tolerate a temperature of 100°C (212°F). If the air is humid there will be less evaporative heat loss, if it is fully saturated there will be none.

See SHOCK.

Talipes see CLUB FOOT

Teeth see ACCIDENTS TO THE TEETH, CARIES (DENTAL DECAY)

Thermometer see page 108

Thrush (Candida Albicans)

White patches on the inside of cheeks and possibly on tongue and palate. They make feeding painful so that the baby will stop sucking to cry. Cause is a fungus infection, possibly contracted at birth through the birth canal if the mother has vaginal thrush, or through an incompletely sterilized teat. It is also a common complication of antibiotic treatment. Treatment is by Nystatin which can be given as drops.

See NAPPY RASH.

Tonsillitis

A red or sore throat in a child who has intact tonsils is often called tonsillitis. This is unfortunate because it implies that the tonsils are responsible for the symptoms. Upper respiratory tract infection with virus or bacteria leads to a response by the tonsils and adenoids which help the body to produce antibodies for the body's defence. Upper respiratory tract infections are no less common or less severe after tonsillectomy - there is some evidence that they are more common and complications more frequent. Tonsils in a young baby are quite small but grow larger after the first year: their job is to trap harmful germs and prevent them taking a hold.

Toxocara Canis

The roundworm of the dog. The dog passes stools which contain the eggs of the worm. If a child's hands become contaminated and he then puts his hands to his mouth the eggs hatch in the intestine and larvae may be widely distributed. They have been found in almost every organ of the body. They may be responsible for a wide variety of symptoms including very occasionally blindness in an eye. It is unlikely that the contamination will arise from the family dog, if it is kept free from worms, but the soil of public parks has been shown to be contaminated with eggs which may remain viable for years. Toddlers not infrequently eat soil and may become infected in this way. Puppies should be wormed at six weeks of age.

Travel Sickness

Some children are upset by the motion of a car or bus – and more rarely by aeroplanes or trains. Some of this may be caused by excitement and anticipation of an outing or holiday. Give a light meal without too much to drink an hour or so before setting out: glucose sweets and dry biscuits can be eaten on the journey. Don't anticipate that your child will be sick and keep asking him – he probably then will be. Take a plastic bag in case, but keep it out of sight otherwise it might actually provoke the sickness. Anti-sickness pills are available either on prescription or from your chemist.

Umbilical Hernia

Common in babies, when the gap in the navel through which the umbilical cord has passed does not immediately close so that a small piece of intestine shows through in a lump. Left untreated it will almost always disappear and is not painful.

Urinary Infections

These are uncommon in young children and there may be few indications that this is a problem until some of the symptoms – poor appetite, fever, sickness, failure to thrive – lead your doctor to test urine when he has eliminated other explanations. If your child has difficulty or pain when passing urine, does so very frequently, has bloodstained urine, or – with a boy – if he does not pass a steady stream but 'dribbles' (which may indicate an obstruction) he should be seen by your doctor. He will test a sterile specimen (he will tell you how to obtain this) and once the infection is diagnosed antibiotics usually clear the trouble very rapidly.

A baby's urine is usually clear, becoming pale yellow as he gets older. After sleep when the urine is more concentrated, it may be darker in colour – this is normal: it will also be darker if your child has a fever or in hot weather, which is an indication that he needs more fluids. If left standing, urine may become cloudy or form a white deposit, but this again is normal and so also is a pink spot on the nappy – which is caused by uric acid. Urine which is cloudy when passed is abnormal and you should see your doctor if this happens. A smell of ammonia when changing a nappy is caused by the breakdown of the urine and is nothing to worry about, but if there is a fishy smell, consult your doctor. If your baby cries with pain when passing urine this could be caused by a MEATAL ULCER on the penis (qv), or by stinging of the urine on NAPPY RASH (qv).

Urticaria see NETTLE RASH

Verrucae (Warts)
Painless and harmless skin growths caused by a virus, mostly appearing on hands and feet although, being infectious, they can spread to other parts of the body or to other people with whom the child has been in contact. Verrucae on the feet may be painful as the child is walking on them, in which case ask your doctor for treatment – usually by ointment, soaking in formalin, or cutting out. If your toddler has plantar warts he should not walk about barefoot and should wear protective socks if he goes swimming. Warts usually disappear without treatment but ointments are available without prescriptions from a doctor.

Warts see VERRUCAE

Water in the Ear
It seldom causes problems if water gets in the ears during bathing or swimming, unless the child already has an ear infection. The water won't go beyond the ear drum and will drain out again. But there's no need to try to clean inside the ears.

Water on the Brain see HYDROCEPHALUS

Wax in the Ear
Wax is a natural protective and cleaning secretion. It protects the ear from dust and should naturally reach the outer edge where it can be wiped away. Don't prod about in your child's ears, especially with cotton buds – it is unnecessary and may cause damage.

Whooping Cough
First symptom is usually a runny nose with a cough which, after a few days, develops into paroxysms, when the child coughs several times in succession. The cough takes the child by surprise and the air rushing back into the lungs causes the 'whoop'. There is sometimes sickness. Incubation is from seven to ten days and the child is infectious for twenty-eight days from the onset of the symptoms. It is the most dangerous of all the infectious fevers and especially so in babies under a year; the immunity does not pass over from the mother to the baby so im-

munization is necessary as soon as possible (see page 66). Children who have been immunized may sometimes catch the illness, although it will then be milder. Complications are middle-ear infections and bronchopneumonia: partial collapse of the lungs is also possible and this may be suspected if the child goes on coughing for more than four or five weeks. Treatment is by antibiotics but the cough will continue. Feeding may be a problem if the child is frequently sick, so 'small and often' rather than large meals, will reduce the chance of vomiting. The attacks are very frightening so the child needs to be held and comforted calmly. Fresh air is good so don't hesitate to take him out of doors in suitable weather.

FURTHER READING

BECOMING A PARENT
General interest
The Child, the Family and the Outside World, D.W. Winnicott, Pelican
Marriage, Maureen Green, Fontana Paperback, 1984
Babyshock, A Mother's First Five Years, Dr John Cobb, Arrow Books, 1984
To Have and to Hold: Marriage and the First Baby, Christopher Clulow, University of Aberdeen Press, 1982
Fatherhood, Brian Jackson, Allen and Unwin, 1984
Women as Mothers, Sheila Kitzinger, Fontana, 1978

Nutrition
Eating Well for a Healthy Pregnancy, Dr Barbara M. Pickard, Sheldon, 1984
Nutrition in Pregnancy, British Medical Association Booklet
Leaflets also available from British Nutrition Foundation, 15 Belgrave Square, London SW1X 8PS

Pregnancy and Birth
Pregnancy Book, Health Education Council, 1984 (free from HEC, PO Box 416, London SE99 6YE; they also issue leaflets on smoking, breast-feeding, bottle-feeding and many other subjects: ring your local Health Education Unit for a list)
Maternity Care in Action, Part II, DHSS Care during Childbirth, DHSS, PO Box 21, Cannons Park, Government Buildings, Honeypot Lane, Stanmore, Middlesex HA7 1AY
The Psychology of Childbirth, Aidan Macfarlane, Fontana, 1978
Pregnancy, Dr Gordon Bourne, Pan 1984
Childbirth Without Fear, Dr Grantly Dick Read, Pan
Birth Without Violence, Frederic Leboyer, Fontana, 1984
Entering the World, Michel Odent, Marion Boyars, 1984
Birth Reborn, Michel Odent, Souvenir, 1984
The Experience of Childbirth, Sheila Kitzinger, Pelican, 1984
The New Good Birth Guide, Sheila Kitzinger, Penguin, 1982 (lists hospitals where Leboyer deliveries are encouraged)
Active Birth, Janet Balaskas, with foreword by Michel Odent
Choices in Childbirth, Penny and Andrew Stanway, Pan, 1984

Miscarriage, Ann Oakley, Dr Ann McPherson and Helen Roberts, Fontana Paperbacks, 1984
Birthrights, Sally Inch, Hutchinson, 1982
Getting Ready for Pregnancy and *Understanding Pregnancy and Birth*, two Open University courses, containing guides, cassettes, booklets etc. Details available from the Community Education Officer, Open University, Walton Hall, Milton Keynes MK7 6AA

DAILY CARE
My Child Won't Sleep, Jo Douglas and Naomi Richman, Penguin, 1984
Coping with Young Children, Jo Douglas and Naomi Richman, Penguin, 1984
Sleepless Children, Dr David Haslam, Piatkus, 1984
Supertot: a Parent's Guide to Toddlers, J. Marzollo, Allen and Unwin
Fathers, Mothers and Others, Rapoport and Strelitz, Kegan Paul, 1981
Running a Mother and Toddler Club, Joyce Donoghue, Unwin Paperbacks, 1984
Play in Hospital, Susan Harvey and Ann Hales-Took, Faber, 1972
Young Children in Hospital and *A Two Year Old Goes to Hospital*, James Robertson. Two films made by Tavistock Child Development Unit and available from Concord Films Council, Ipswich, Suffolk

Books for children
All About Me Books: Zebra Books, Walker Books
Dinosaur Books by Althea include:
Visiting the Dentist, I have Asthma, Having an Eye Test, I have Diabetes, My Childminder, No more Nappies, Having a Hearing Test, I can't Talk Like You, Going to the Doctor

YOUR GROWING CHILD
Babies need Books, Cushla and Her Books, Dorothy Butler, Pelican, 1982
Living with a Gifted Child, Frieda Painter, Human Horizons Series, Souvenir, 1984
Living with a Gifted Child, Miriam Wood, Souvenir, 1984
Gifted Children, Dr Joan Freeman, MTP Press
Clever Children, Dr Joan Freeman, Hamlyn
Your Exceptional Child, Brian Jackson, Fontana, 1982
Living with a Hyperactive Child, Miriam Wood, Souvenir, 1984
The Hyperactive Child, Belinda Barnes and Irene Colquhoun, Thorsons

Children's Minds, Margaret Donaldson, Fontana, 1982
A to Z of Children's Emotional Problems, Tom Crabtree, Unwin, 1984
The Wheelchair Child, Philippa Russell, Souvenir, 1984
Susan's Story, Susan Hampshire, Sidgwick and Jackson, 1983 (the story of how the actress author overcame dyslexia)
The Good Toy Guide available from the Toy Libraries Association, Seabrook House, Darkes Lane, Potters Bar, Herts EN6 2AB
Toys and Playthings, Professors John and Elizabeth Newson, Allen and Unwin/ Penguin
Play is a Feeling, Brenda Crowe, Allen and Unwin, 1983
The Magic Years, Selma Fraiberg, Methuen
Play, Dreams and Imitation in Childhood, J. Pigget, Routledge
Playing and Reality, D.W. Winnicott, Pelican
The Playgroup Movement, Brenda Crowe, Allen and Unwin, 1982
Working with Under Fives, Under Fives in Britain, Childwatching at Playgroup and Nursery School, Children and Minders, Children and Day Nurseries, all published by Grant McIntyre (1980) are the result of a project – the Oxford Preschool Research Project – which looked into the care provided for the under fives in Britain.
Common Sense About Babies and Children, Dr Hugh Jolly, Unwin, 1983
Where's Spot? Eric Hill, Puffin, 1983

FAMILY MATTERS
All about Twins, a handbook for parents, Gillian Leigh, Routledge Kegan Paul, 1983
Adopting the Older Child, Claudia Jewett, Harvard Common Press, 1978
Yours by Choice, a Guide for Adoptive Parents, Jane Rowe, Routledge, 1982
Adopting a Child, British Agencies for Adoption and Fostering (11 Southwark Street, London SE1 1RQ)
How to Survive as a Working Mother, Lesley Garner
Working Mothers Handbook, Clapham NCT Working Mothers Group (advice about resources, day nurseries, etc; 80p from 167 Fentiman Road, London SW8 1JY)
Childminding, Brian Jackson and Sonia Jackson, Routledge, 1981
How to Survive as a Childminder, National Childminding Association (covers health, money, registration, play, diets, etc; from 204 High Street, Bromley, Kent BR1 1PP)

Maternal Deprivation Reassessed, Michael Rutter, Penguin, 1981
Children Under Stress, Sula Wolff, Pelican
Surviving the Breakup, Judith Wallerstein and Joan Barlin Kelly, Grant McIntyre

Books for Children
Jane is Adopted, Althea, Dinosaur Books
David and his Sister, Carol, Althea, Dinosaur Books
Mr Fairweather and his family, Kornitzer, Bodley Head
Why was I adopted? Carole Livingstone, Angus and Robertson

A CHILD'S HEALTH A-Z
All About Children, Oxford University Press
Encyclopaedia of Child Health, Andrew and Penny Stanway, Sphere
Good Housekeeping Encyclopaedia of Family Health, Ebury Press
First Aid Manual, St John Ambulance, Red Cross and St Andrew Ambulance, Dorling Kindersley, 1983
What Can I Give Him Today? from 19a Parton Road, Churchdown, Gloucester GL3 2AB (written by the mother of a son with milk and dairy allergies; recipes for children with the same problem)

Other dietary advice can be obtained from particular societies and support groups

ASSOCIATIONS AND SOCIETIES

BECOMING A PARENT

National Childbirth Trust, 9 Queensborough Terrace, London W2 3TB (run antenatal classes, give breast-feeding advice and practical support; ring 01-221 3833 for details of your nearest branch)

British Acupuncture Association, 34 Alderney Street, London SW1V 4EU and *British Society of Hypnotherapists*, 51 Queen Anne Street, London W1M 9FA: details of anaesthetists in childbirth

Society to support Home Confinements, 17 Laburnam Avenue, Durham DHy 4HA (support and information for women who want to give birth at home)

La Leche League (Great Britain), BM 3434, London WC1V 6XX (help and information on breast-feeding; send an sae for nearest counsellor)

Association of Breast-feeding Mothers, 131 Mayow Road, Sydenham, London SE26 4HZ (advice service to breast-feeding mothers)

The Birth Centre, 101 Tufnell Park Road, London N7 (information on natural childbirth)

Maternity Alliance, 309 Kentish Town Road, London NW5 2TJ (information on maternity rights and services)

Association for Improvements in the Maternity Services (AIMS), 163 Liverpool Road, London N1 0RF (aims for improvements in maternity services and offers advice about rights and choice of maternity care)

Caesarean Support Groups, 9 Nightingale Grove, London SE13 6EY (support and advice for mothers who have had or will have Caesarean delivery)

Stillbirth and Neonatal Death Society, 9 Argyle House, 29-31 Euston Road, London NW1 2SD (national network of support groups for parents)

The Miscarriage Association, Dolphin Cottage, 4 Ashfield Terrace, Thorpe, Wakefield, West Yorks (support for women who are having or have had a miscarriage)

Compassionate Friends, 5 Lower Clifton Hill, Clifton, Bristol BF8 1BT (support and friendship for bereaved parents)

Health Education Council, 78 New Oxford Street, London WC1A 1AA

DAILY CARE

OPUS (Organization for Parents Under Stress), 26 Manor Drive, Pickering, North Yorks YO18 8DD. Believing that isolation causes stress and may lead to child abuse, these self-help groups keep in touch with newsletters, a telephone service and drop-in centres. Different branches may go under different names so look in your local telephone directory under Parents Lifeline, Parents Anonymous, Parents Helpline, Parents Help Centre, Tell a Friend.

Network, Chris Savage, 2 Tavistock Road, North Watford, Herts (started in Watford, is now spreading nationally; members offer support, baby-sitting, a 'listening ear' in emergencies)

Meet a Mum Association (MAMA), 26a Cumnor Hill, Cumnor, Oxford OX2 9HA (for isolated mothers or those suffering from postnatal depression)

Parents Anonymous, 6 Manor Gardens, London N7 6LA; tel 01-263 8918 (a twenty-four telephone service for parents who can't cope and fear they may abuse their children)

Register of Parents' Helplines, National Children's Centre, Longroyd Bridge, Huddersfield, West Yorks (a list of resources available)

National Society for Prevention of Cruelty to Children (NSPCC), 67 Saffron Hill, London EC1N 8RF (the Society will give support and advice: their role today is preventative and not punitive. They will advise and help families who are under stress and fear they may abuse their children.

National Children's Bureau, 8 Wakley Street, London EC1V 7QE

National Association for the Welfare of Children in Hospital, Argyle House, 29-31 Euston Road, London NW1 2SD

YOUR GROWING CHILD

National Association for Gifted Children, 1 South Audley Street, London W1

Play Matters (Toy Libraries Association), Seabrook House, Wyllotts Manor, Darkes Lane, Potters Bar, Herts

Amateur Swimming Association, Derby Square, Loughborough, Leics

Pre-School Playgroups Association, Alford House, Aveline Street, London SE11 5DM

FAMILY MATTERS

Twins Clubs Association, Pooh Corner, 54 Broad Lane, Hampton, Middlesex

British Agencies for Adoption and Fostering, 11 Southwark Street, London SE1 1RQ

National Step Family Association, Maris House, Trumpington, Cambridge CB2 2LB

Adoption Resource Exchange, 40 Brunswick Square, London WC1 1AZ

Independent Adoption Society, 160 Peckham Rye, London SE22

National Association for the Childless, 318 Summer Lane, Birmingham B19 3RL
National Foster Care Association, Francis House, Francis Street, London SW1P 1DE
National Childminders Association, 13a London Road, Bromley, Kent BR1 1DE
Universal Aunts, 250 Kings Road, London
Norland Nursery Training College, Denford Park, Hungerford, Berks (residential nursery for emergencies)
Nanny Share Register, 42 Park Road, East Molesey, Surrey (arranges nanny sharing for families living near each other)
Nannies Galore, 44 Foresters Drive, Wallington, Surrey
Minders, The Old Rectory, Marsh Baldon, Oxon OX9 9LS
Consultus, 17 London Rd, Tonbridge, Kent
Baxter's Agency, PO Box 12, Peterborough, Cambs PE3 6JN
Guardian Angels Bureau, 29 Stymperlowe View, Sheffield S19 3QU
(Advertisements also appear in *Nursery World* and *The Lady*)
Gingerbread, 35 Wellington Street, London WC2 7BN (self-help association for one-parent families. Organizes local groups for friendship, support and advice)
National Council for One-Parent Families, 255 Kentish Town Road, London NW5 2LX (advice on pregnancy, maternity benefits, housing, etc)
Cruse, 126 Sheen Road, Richmond, Surrey (for widows and widowers)
National Association of Widows, c/o Stafford District Voluntary Service Centre, Chell Road, Stafford ST16 2QA (advice and help on widows' rights)
National Council for the Divorced and Separated, 13 High Street, Little Shelford, Cambridge
Families Need Fathers, 97a Shakespeare Walk, London N16 6LA (for fathers separated from their children)
KIDS (National Society for Handicapped Children), 16 Strutton Ground, London SW1P 2HP (charity to help the parents of children with special needs: professional staff work with children from birth to school leaving age – either in play centres or in their homes)

A CHILD'S HEALTH A-Z
Addresses of organizations for specific conditions
Association for All Speech-Impaired Children, 347 Central Markets, Smithfields, London EC1

Asthma Society, St Thomas's Hospital, Lambeth Palace Road, London SE1 7EH
Coeliac Society, PO Box No 181, London NW2 2QY
Contact a Family, 16 Strutton Ground, London SW1P 2HP (for parents of handicapped children)
National Deaf Children's Association, 45 Hereford Road, London W2 5AH
British Diabetic Association, 3-6 Alfred Place, London WC1E 7EE
Central Council for the Disabled, 34 Eccleston Square, London SW1V 1PE
Down's Children's Association, 3rd floor, 4 Oxford Street, London W1N 9FL
Scottish Down's Syndrome Association, 48 Govan Road, Glasgow G51 1JL
Dyslexia Institute, 133 Gresham Road, Staines, Middlesex
British Dyslexia Association, 4 Hobart Place, London SW1W 0HU
Disabled Living Foundation, 346 Kensington High Street, London W14
British Epilepsy Association, Crowthorne House, Bigshotte, New Wokingham Road, Wokingham, Berks RG11 3AY
Eczema Society, Tavistock Square, London WC1H 9SR
Hyperactive Children's Support Group, 59 Meadowside, Angmering, Sussex BN16 4BW
Invalid Children's Aid Association, 126 Buckingham Palace Road, London SW1W 9SB
Royal Society for Mentally Handicapped Children (MENCAP), 123 Golden Lane, London EC1Y 0RT
Migraine Trust, 45 Great Ormond Street, London WC1
British Migraine Association, 178a High Road, Byfleet, Weybridge, Surrey KT14 7ED
British Polio Fellowship, Bell Close, West End Road, Ruislip, Middlesex HA4 6LP
Spastics Society, 12 Park Crescent, London W1N 4EQ
Association for Spina Bifida and Hydrocephalus, 30 Devonshire Street, London W1N 2BE
Voluntary Council for Handicapped Children, 8 Wakley Street, London WC1V 7QE
Association of Parents of Vaccine Damaged Children, 2 Church Street, Shipton on Stour, Warks CC36 4AP
The Sunday Times Self-Help Directory, Granada, 1982, is a mine of information and addresses on all groups and associations which cater for special needs

BABY RECORDS PAGE

Use this page to plot your baby's weight and height, list those important telephone numbers, and record the dates your baby was immunized.
The tinted areas on the graphs show the range between 'heavy' and 'light' babies. Don't expect your baby to follow the curves exactly.

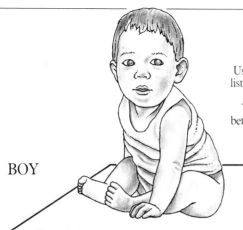

BOY

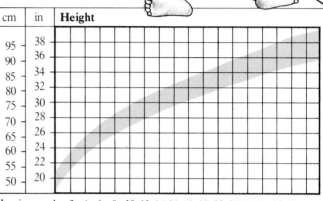

GIRL

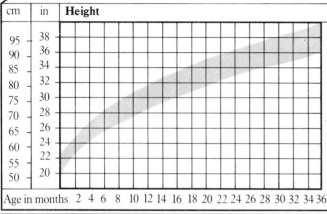

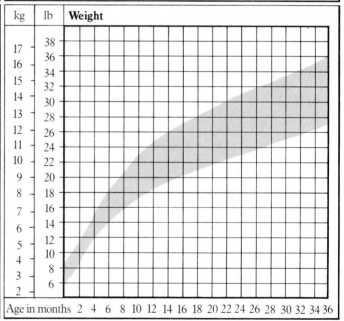

cm	in	**Height**
95	38	
90	36	
85	34	
80	32	
75	30	
70	28	
65	26	
60	24	
55	22	
50	20	

Age in months 2 4 6 8 10 12 14 16 18 20 22 24 26 28 30 32 34 36

cm	in	**Height**
95	38	
90	36	
85	34	
80	32	
75	30	
70	28	
65	26	
60	24	
55	22	
50	20	

Age in months 2 4 6 8 10 12 14 16 18 20 22 24 26 28 30 32 34 36

kg	lb	**Weight**
17	38	
16	36	
15	34	
14	32	
13	30	
12	28	
11	26	
10	24	
9	22	
8	20	
7	18	
6	16	
5	14	
4	12	
3	10	
2	8	
	6	

Age in months 2 4 6 8 10 12 14 16 18 20 22 24 26 28 30 32 34 36

kg	lb	**Weight**
17	38	
16	36	
15	34	
14	32	
13	30	
12	28	
11	26	
10	24	
9	22	
8	20	
7	18	
6	16	
5	14	
4	12	
3	10	
2	8	
	6	

Age in months 2 4 6 8 10 12 14 16 18 20 22 24 26 28 30 32 34 36

Important telephone numbers

Health Centre _____
Health visitor _____
Doctor _____
Hospital _____
Chemist _____
Poison Centre _____
Dentist _____

Immunization dates

	First baby		Second baby	
	date	age	date	age
Diptheria, whooping cough, tetanus, polio				
Booster for above				
Second booster for above				
Measles				

See page 66 for recommended timing for innoculations beyond three years of age.

INDEX

Page numbers in *italics* refer to illustrations, captions to illustrations and to illustrative materials such as tables.

C

D

E

F

G

H

I

J

K

L

M

N

O

P

R

S

T

U

V

W

X

HOUSE ACKNOWLEDGEMENTS

Editorial Director   Ian Jackson
Art Director   Nick Eddison

Designer   Wendy Bann
Design Assistant   Amanda Barlow
Picture Researcher   Liz Eddison
Indexer   Jackie Pinhey
Production   Bob Towell

Eddison Sadd Editions wish to extend special thanks to the following friends for their endless patience and assistance with photographs: Sally Connelly, Adam and Charlotte; Maud da Rocha and Rowena; Sue and Bruce Degnam, Josie and Oliver; Siobhan Haley and Vivienne; Julia Nicholson, Becky and Hannah; the Pinner Parkside Playgroup; Georgina Steeds and Tony Armolea; Clare Walker; and especially to Sam and Edward Eddison

ARTISTS

T = Top B = Bottom M = Middle L = Left R = Right

David Ashby 14T, 14B, 29TL, 29LM, 58BL, 60L, 60T, 60B, 64-5, 76T, 78, 82, 117, 118, 126-7B, 130, 139, 165, 173, 232T; Brian Bull (retouching) 23B, 56-7M, 115, 188, 197; Chris Chapman (Spectron Artists) 13, 27, 28, 126T, 160-1, 162-3, 182-3; Claire Davies 32-3B; Anthony Duke 232; Andrew Farmer 17, 52-3, 83B, 103, 120, 131, 136-7, 147, 166-7, 185; Industrial Art Studio (David Lewis Artists) 29TR, 29MR, 29BR, 30-1, 32TL, 33TR, 34-5T, 34B, 36, 38, 55, 62-3; Dee McLean and Clive Spong (Linden Artists) 21, 39, 42, 43, 56B, 57TL, TR, BL, BR, 58BR, 86L, 86B, 87B, 100B, 108, 201, 204-225

PHOTOGRAPHIC CREDITS

T = Top B = Bottom M = Middle L = Left R = Right

Malcolm Aird prelims and section openers, 138, 177, 196, 200; Art Directors Photo Library 92, 119, 145, 176, 199; Daily Telegraph Colour Library: Shaun Skelly 24, Audrey Stirling 128, William Strode 20T; Nick Eddison 187; Mary Evans Picture Library 23T, 182T; D. Garrow 25T, 44; Sally and Richard Greenhill Photo Library 39, 50, 54, 67, 71 (SENSE), 73, 96, 122B, 125, 163, 164R, 174T, 186, 188, 198; Susan Griggs Agency Ltd: Sandra Lousada 130, 133T, 202, Dick Rowan 193, Patrick Ward 140; Jessop Acoustics 150; King's College Hospital 20B; Pictorial Press Photo Library 109; Trannies: Liz Eddison 23B, 81, 87, 88, 97, 101, 105, 112, 114, 115, 116, 118, 120, 121T, 121B, 124T, 124B, 127, 133B, 134B, 135T, 143B, 146, 148T, 148B, 151, 154, 156, 157T, 157B, 158, 159, 160, 170, 173L, 173R, 174B, 180, 191, 195; Vision International 142: S. Cunningham 168, Anthea Sieveking 10, 19, 21, 25B, 37, 40T, 40B, 41TR, 41TL, 42, 45, 48, 56, 58, 59, 60, 69, 72, 75, 76, 77, 80, 84, 89, 91, 94, 98, 102, 107, 122T, 132, 133ML, 133MR, 134T, 135B, 137, 143T, 153, 164L, 171L, 171R